Genders and Sexualities in the Social Sciences

Series Editors: **Victoria Robinson**, University of Sheffield, UK and **Diane Richardson**, University of Newcastle, UK

Editorial Board: **Raewyn Connell**, University of Sydney, Australia, **Kathy Davis**, Utrecht University, The Netherlands, **Stevi Jackson**, University of York, UK, **Michael Kimmel**, State University of New York, Stony Brook, USA, **Kimiko Kimoto**, Hitotsubashi University, Japan, **Jasbir Puar**, Rutgers University, USA, **Steven Seidman**, State University of New York, Albany, USA, **Carol Smart**, University of Manchester, UK, **Liz Stanley**, University of Edinburgh, UK, **Gill Valentine**, University of Leeds, UK, **Jeffrey Weeks**, South Bank University, UK, **Kath Woodward**, The Open University, UK

Titles include:

Niall Hanlon
MASCULINITIES, CARE AND EQUALITY
Identity and Nurture in Men's Lives

Sally Hines and Yvette Taylor (*editors*)
SEXUALITIES
Past Reflections, Future Directions

Victoria Robinson and Jenny Hockey
MASCULINITIES IN TRANSITION

Yvette Taylor, Sally Hines and Mark E. Casey (*editors*)
THEORIZING INTERSECTIONALITY AND SEXUALITY

Kath Woodward
SEX POWER AND THE GAMES

Genders and Sexualities in the Social Sciences
Series Standing Order ISBN   978–0–230–27254–5 hardback
978–0–230–27255–2 paperback
(outside North America only)

You can receive future titles in this series as they are published by placing a standing order. Please contact your bookseller or, in case of difficulty, write to us at the address below with your name and address, the title of the series and one of the ISBNs quoted above.

Customer Services Department, Macmillan Distribution Ltd, Houndmills, Basingstoke, Hampshire RG21 6XS, England

Sex Power and the Games

Kath Woodward
Open University, UK

First published 2012 by
PALGRAVE MACMILLAN

Palgrave Macmillan in the UK is an imprint of Macmillan Publishers Limited, registered in England, company number 785998, of Houndmills, Basingstoke, Hampshire RG21 6XS.

Palgrave Macmillan in the US is a division of St Martin's Press LLC, 175 Fifth Avenue, New York, NY 10010.

Palgrave Macmillan is the global academic imprint of the above companies and has companies and representatives throughout the world.

Palgrave® and Macmillan® are registered trademarks in the United States, the United Kingdom, Europe and other countries

ISBN: 978–0–230–28319–0

This book is printed on paper suitable for recycling and made from fully managed and sustained forest sources. Logging, pulping and manufacturing processes are expected to conform to the environmental regulations of the country of origin.

A catalogue record for this book is available from the British Library.

A catalog record for this book is available from the Library of Congress.

10 9 8 7 6 5 4 3 2 1
21 20 19 18 17 16 15 14 13 12

Transferred to Digital Printing in 2013

To Steve
and this book is for Eppy.

Contents

Figures

Acknowledgements

I would like to thank everyone who has supported me in writing this book: Ann Aldridge at Lloyds TSB, Art of Sport project, and the local heroes and artists who talked to me about their work, especially Will Rochford and Jeremy Houghton, who each let me include paintings in the book. I am grateful to the British Library UK Archive project for their help in putting together the web archive of material cited in this book.

I am very grateful to Philippa Grand at Palgrave Macmillan for her patience as well as for her enthusiasm and to Andrew James who works with Philippa. I also wish to acknowledge the team at Newgen Knowledge Works in the production of my work.

Thanks to Steve Woodward for all his scholarly advice on the Games in the Ancient World and for undertaking the task of compiling the index.

1
Introduction: Putting Sex Gender on the Agenda

This is a book about how power operates in the Olympic Games: the systems and processes through which social relations are forged and generated in what is one of the biggest shows on earth – probably the biggest show on earth – involving more nations, more spectators and more sports than any other competition and seemingly one of the most democratic and inclusive of sporting events. *Sex Power and the Games* explores how power operates to instate social inclusion and exclusion and in particular reinforce inequalities. The book considers whether an interrogation of the systems and processes through which power operates is sufficient to explain the endurance of inequalities, notably those which are based on the binary logic of sex gender. A focus on sex gender is offered as a means of making material the enfleshed exclusion of categories of person. Sport, however, especially the Olympic Games, offers possibilities for democratic engagement and widening participation, so it is not surprising that discussion of the games includes its possibilities and promises as well as the excitement and passion sport evokes.

It may not have been all about sport, but in her traditional Christmas broadcast to the people of Britain and the Commonwealth in 2010, Queen Elizabeth II took advantage of the proximity of the 2012 London Olympics to extol the values of sport (Royalty, 2010). Her speech focused upon the synergies between religion and politics in the context of the promotion of social inclusion and everyday community participation. It may not be surprising that the head of a state with an established church should do so, but the monarch's approach is illustrative of the reconfiguration of sport within the language of governance in its alliances with discourses of community and widening participation. This is a language which resonates with the spirit of the Olympic Movement.

The speech, delivered at Hampton Court in London, also celebrated 400 years of the King James Bible in the English translation and brought together the unifying elements of religion and sport. The Queen argued that the production of the King James Bible was an enterprise driven by an interest in reaching agreement for the wider benefit of the community and for bringing harmony to the kingdoms of England and Scotland. She then went on to suggest that in the twenty-first century sport could play a similar role in bringing people together that had been undertaken through the translation of a religious text at the start of the seventeenth century. This could be seen as a contentious statement especially by many believers, although the claims the Queen made as head of an established church are more likely to be read as innocuous. The comparison between sport and religion is not without precedent. Sport, especially football, has been compared to religion in the passionate commitment it invokes and the scale on which it recruits followers.

It is likely that the 2012 Olympics, the second of the modern Games to be held in London and both within the present Queen's lifetime, were the trigger for the choice of sport as the main subject of the speech. The version of sport expressed in the broadcast was as an everyday, an ordinary and a community activity, both through active embodied participation and through the encouragement of others within an altruistic paradigm of shared endeavour. The discourses of sport invoked in this speech were both local and global and transnational, in fact global/local in distinctive ways which appertain to sport. Whilst the advantages of representing one's country were celebrated, however, one site at which international competition was enacted, the Commonwealth Games, was described as the 'Friendly Games' within the context of a family atmosphere where the loudest support came from the smallest nations rather than those with massive resources that dominate international sport. The cosy intimacy of 'friendly' Commonwealth Games masks the legacy of empire and the inequalities and exploitation of colonialism, but the main thrust of the argument in the Christmas broadcast is to emphasise the positive community aspects of sport and of its democratising possibilities. The Queen stressed the importance of sport in bringing people together from all backgrounds, from all walks of life and across generations, invoking the kinship networks that underpin some fan bases and traditional supporter networks. Sport is competitive but it brings people together. Indeed, it is the case that for the duration of the Games, the athletes live together in the Olympic Village, which suggests an, albeit transitory, experience of traditional rural community.

This rhetoric resonates with the ideals of the Olympic Movement. At Beijing in 2008 Jacques Rogge, the International Olympic Committee (IOC) President, invoked this language in his speech at the Opening Ceremony on 4 August 2008, by referring to the 'Olympic family' (Rogge, 2011).

There is some slippage between friendly and family; neither sounds threatening and family has particularly gendered associations. In traditional sociological and social policy research in the 1950s and 1960s women were not only always subsumed under the heading of 'family', based on the assumption that family is of particular importance to women and is their domain, but also women were rarely named as such. Women's lives were assumed to be domestic and hence embraced by the intimate relations of the familial.

Sport, in the Queen's speech, was construed as both familial and supportive and as providing the experience of other cultures, ways of living and value systems (albeit within the rules of organised sport). Sport permits a healthy lifestyle through its embodied practices and through the social, interpersonal values that taking part in sport requires; a very familiar discourse in the promotion of sport as in the Latin prescription *mens sana in corpore sano*.

Sport and politics clearly do mix. Politics embraces assemblages of systems, from those of the state, governance and religion to the politics of the personal, and different social and cultural relations in a multiplicity of manifestations. Although women are an empirical category in sport, the power relations of sexual politics have often been unremarked. The message of the Queen's broadcast acknowledges and reinstates the cultural and political importance of sport and especially the unifying properties of the Olympics.

The Olympics: power and sex

The Olympics are particular and distinctive as sporting events in that they are both democratic, imbued with the ideals of amateurism, diversity and full participation, and elite, highly competitive and increasingly professional. This professionalism is, however, re-created through the affects of contemporary commercialised, globalised sport along with those of the amateur principles of widening participation and equal opportunities. The Paralympics were born of the struggle for inclusion. The Games have also frequently been the site of political protest in the history of the modern Olympics (Miah, 2011a), which have demonstrated the contradictions of political resistance and attempts to redress matters of social inequalities in sport (Lenskyj, 2000, 2002, 2008). Such mega sporting events, which in the language of hyperbole but with substance in the case of the Games can be described as the greatest show on earth, attract massive attention and are thus useful sites at which to stage protests and to voice political dissent. The main purpose of such sporting spectacles is, nonetheless, elite competition and celebration of athletic success and achievement. The opportunities offered by such mega events include those to make profit, as is evident in the role of global capital and commercial interests in the bidding process and role of host cities (Preuss, 2008). The Games also offer a wide range of sports, including non-mainstream sports, team and individual games as well as major world sports. Not only do athletes from all parts of the globe compete, but the mega event is itself staged at increasingly diverse locations. For example, Beijing in 2008 demonstrated the possibilities of new transnational conversations as well as a diversity of sports.

The Games invoke diverse affects. There is a routine repetition and predictability of the four-yearly cycle of mega sporting events, the Summer and Winter games and the Paralympics, which now means that the Games happen every two years. The rituals of the Games encompass the whole panoply of sporting practices from the training ground, gym, pool, ring and track to those of the public global arena of the stadium, including the opening and closing ceremonies that are transmitted by satellite across the globe. The mega events of the games may seem distant from the cosy intimacy of the rhetoric of community and the 'family games', but they are interconnected in diverse ways. The period of intensive and routine preparations between the events generates expectations of the gargantuan spectacles of the Games themselves at which global stars and local heroes perform and are viewed and celebrated, their achievements recorded in the maelstrom of personal, collective and national investments. One of the concerns of this book is with everyday participation in sport and the local heroes, who always carry the possibility of metamorphosis into global, public stars, who are the focus of much of the activity in the preparatory periods between Games, for example, as is evident in the example of the Lloyds TSB sponsorship of London 2012, which is discussed in Chapter 6. This sponsorship project , like the Queen's speech, is framed by charitable discourses of patronage which, it is suggested, widen participation rather than any engagement with power structures which underpin inequalities to which redress might be more effectively translated into human rights issues.

The run-up to 2012 and the London Olympics (Lee, 2006) also demonstrated some of the contradictions that beset the Games, especially between the opportunities offered and the costs and constraints that have been central to policies, both of nation states and of the regulatory bodies of sport including international bodies like the IOC, practices and media coverage. This book focuses on the ambivalences of social inclusion policies and the democratic possibilities of the Games and brings together critical theories of sport as a site for the promotion of cohesion and diversity in light of the Olympic Movement and the politics of the Games. Different power axes intersect in the assemblages of events and the processes that make up the sporting practices and performances of the games. Sex gender is a particular aspect through which to explore inequalities, contradictions, social cohesion and exclusion in sport and, in particular, the politics of the Olympics and a broader dimension of the social, cultural and political worlds in which sport is situated. Sex gender has the particular advantage of addressing the absent presences – inequalities that persist but that not only are not explored but also remain unstated.

The Games have been the site of controversy and corruption, as in the case of Salt Lake City in 2002, of political exploitation as in 'Hitler's Games' in 1936 and political protest in 1968 and in 2008 at Beijing, to name but a few examples. Gender has not been as visible as other dimensions of the power axes of the Games. The Olympics are mega sporting events but they also offer a site at which to explore more routine practices of social inclusion; the possibilities and opportunities afforded by sport in a changing world as is currently recognised in a number of initiatives that have taken place in the responses and engagement of existing international organisations, including the United Nations as demonstrated by groups like UN Habitat with its focus on youth and sustainable urban development (UN Habitat, 2011). There has also been a proliferation of new agencies in the lead-up to 2012, such as Beyond Sport, the online global organisation (Beyond Sport, 2011a, 2011b) that promoted, developed and supported the use of sport to create positive social change through global networks, in partnership with Barclays, Time media and United Nations Children's Fund (UNICEF), providing social entrepreneurship and advice. All have been dedicated to using sport to enhance life experience in the contemporary world and most, like Beyond Sport, draw upon commercial partnerships and sponsorship. In this book some of the processes are explored using both global sponsorship and some more local projects, for example, as linked to the Cultural Olympiad.

This book includes a discussion of the regulatory practices of the IOC and the Olympic Movement, the wider political and social terrain and the embodied practices of participants in the run-up to 2012, especially in the relationship between Olympic ideals, some of which underpin the Queen's message, and the highly competitive, profit-led field of contemporary elite sport.

The book explores the interconnected themes which are framed by the twin issues of the gendered sexed body in politics and the body politic. Sex gender as explanatory categories and conceptualisations offers a useful focus on material, enfleshed differences and the centrality of corporeality which is so much part of sport. It focuses upon the dual processes of classification and regulation, including categorisation of embodied selves as athletes and the spatial and temporal processes through which athletes and the categories that define them, for example, as women or men are made and remade, in order to reflect upon the democratising and constraining dimensions of the Olympics.

The focus is on the dynamics of regulation and creativity in the material transformation of territories and of bodies. This book develops an analysis of social cohesion, social exclusion and fragmentation by focusing on issues of how class, ethnicity, gender, sexuality, dis/ability and age are mobilised and transformed in large-scale mega sporting events like the Olympics by deploying feminist critiques of sex and gender (Butler, 1990, 1993, 2009, Braidotti, 1994, 2002, Delphy, 1993, Grosz, 1994, Irigaray, 1984, 1991) as a prime site for critical analyses of inequality and diversity in such a way as to get beyond a focus on the elective dynamics of participation. This involves looking at the limits of intersectionality as well as its strengths (Taylor, 2011) and suggesting ways in which it can be developed to include both critical analyses and recognition of the materialities of sexual politics. Sex gender is seen as implicated with other areas of inequality that intersect in the field of sport and as a useful way of explaining the inequities of embodied performance. The book explores the potential of new technologies and interventions in bodies and body practices, their transformative promise and the dangers of their disturbing, threatening, destabilising or their excessive effects. Sex and gender and the combination of the two in sex gender are deployed as categories and materialities which constitute a lens through which to explore the technologies of social inclusion and exclusion and the political possibilities of sport and, in particular, the Olympic Games. Sex gender provides the conceptual basis of the book which is concerned with all aspects of inequality and is not confined to empirical categories of sex which, in sport, are based on a binary logic which divides enfleshed participation in sporting activities and competitions. Sex gender intersects with the other social and cultural forces in complex ways, especially in the politics of widening participation and social inclusion, and power is always implicated in these processes.

The approach taken is interdisciplinary and draws strongly on feminist materialist critiques of regulatory practices and of the reconfiguration of citizenship through sport. Gendered bodies are discursive (Markula, 2009) and can be deconstructed (Cole, 1998, 2002) but in sport are engaged in a particular set of competitive practices that engage corporeality and where inequalities are enfleshed as well as discursive. Enfleshed bodies also have different capacities, the material differences of which have to be acknowledged.

The Olympics also offer a particular site for discussion of the politics of social inclusion because of their history of amateurism and genealogies of participation. Sport presents particular dilemmas for the promotion of social inclusion because sport is based on embodied practices that are largely measured by competitive success in outcomes (Tomlinson and Sugden, 2002, Wagg, 2004). Representation is also central to sport (Markula, 2009) but intersects with other forces and is implicated in diverse networks. The Games offer a particular mix of materialities and technologies; histories, enfleshed actualities, classificatory systems including those of gender verification, economic and political power geometries, all configured around a set of both competitive and egalitarian practices and ideas. Sometimes they connect, frequently they do not and often sex gender is a force of disruption and a source of inequality. Policies to promote social inclusion and cohesion through sport have been framed within a number of different discourses, notably those of charity, of utilitarian functionalism and lastly and most radically of human rights (Woodward, 2008). The friendly Commonwealth Games, or at least their promotion, would be most likely located within a charitable discourse, which rewards effort and values joining in. One of my key questions concerns where sex gender inequalities and attempts to redress them are located within charitable discourses which classify the recipients of, for example, diversity policies as victims. The Olympics offer a particular blend of global widening participation, national identification and embodied sporting achievement, all of which are located within a changing global landscape of economic and political transformation and enmeshed with financial forces and flows of capital investment.

It is my concern not only to use feminist critiques, as part of the theoretical framework of the book, but also to use the example of sport and, in particular the Games, to develop ways of thinking about the operation of power relations. How power underpins ex and gender has, of course, been central to feminist debate, but much less to the sociology of sport, and sport has not been a prime empirical concern of feminist theories. This book aims to bring them together using the conceptualization of sex gender. The impact of changes arising from feminist theoretical contributions and political activism and from gender studies has led to a shifting language within sport, for example, from sex to gender in order to embrace the power and possibilities of change of cultural forces and avoid the dangers of biological reductionism. Sport, however, remains pretty firmly entrenched in the female/male gender binary. The troubling problems of gender verification and the centrality of enfleshed bodies in sport combine to make it a very useful field in which to explore the connections between sex and gender, which have relevance to the wider social terrain. This book traces some of the debates from the separation of sex and gender and some of the biologist assumptions about sex, through an increased emphasis on gender and a preference for its social construction and capacities for transformation, to a reappraisal of sex and the implications of sex rather than gender for a politics of difference that identifies and locates the operations and intersections of different power axes.

Methodologies and methods

The methodological approaches adopted in this book are diverse and eclectic but are all focused on issues of sex and power and upon accessing and giving voice to the Olympic stories, which are largely not central or immediately visible, and to making connections between different strands in these Olympic stories. Making visible has involved textual analyses and deconstruction of different materials, some of which are publicly available, albeit often in the apparently ephemeral cyberspaces. Other sources are located within more official documentation, for example, of the governance of sport and the Olympic charter. I have also drawn upon fieldwork, which includes my engagement with the media and sponsorship projects in the run-up to 2012. My main concern has been with in/visibility and with what is said and not said.

Demonstrating the invisibility of women in the public arena of representation has a long history in feminist critiques. Women have been 'hidden from history' to quote the title of Sheila Rowbotham's famous 1975 book, or they have been an 'absent presence', as claimed in the work of French psychoanalytic feminists (Irigaray, 1984,1991, Cixous, 1980). History and none more so than the history of sport has often been written as if only white men from the middle and upper classes were agents and protagonists who matter. We know the stories which feature men, because they are recorded, but women, if mentioned at all, are frequently relegated to the domestic sphere of familial and intimate relationships, where they are assumed to be present even though they are absent from what is made visible, for example, as mothers, who often do not even need to be named (Kaplan, 1992, Woodward, 1997). Women 'just are'; the umbrella category of 'family' and, more recently, 'parents' subsumes women. Women have been absent and invisible and yet they are also present because what women do is taken for granted. My questions include those concerned with where women are in the Olympic family and in the communities of the Games and what a theoretical conceptualisation of sex gender can contribute to an understanding of social inequalities and divisions and how they might be understood and addressed.

The slippery nature of in/visible women presents problems for the researcher. Now you see them and now you don't and where are they? Often they are not where you expect them. In researching women in sport, for *Sex Power and the Games*, it seems that women are increasingly visible; they belong to an empirical category of persons defined by sex. There are women and men and the gender binary is embedded in the rules of the game. Sex gender, however, emerges as a problem because sometimes classifying sex is problematic as is evident in the coverage of gender verification testing, which is the subject of Chapter 3. The female/male dualism may not be as clear as the regulators of sport might hope. Women in the field of sport are certainly not as visible as women increasingly are in other sexualised spaces of the mass media but they do constitute an empirical, marked category. Men are not usually marked in sport, however, except in athletics. The World Cup in football means the men's competition; women's events say so. This does present problems for the researcher. Websites are classified by sport, for example, football, tennis or athletics (the most gender egalitarian of embodied sporting practices) with subdivisions for women's activities. Women are always a subcategory of the mainstream, male stream web pages. Home pages of sports have links and although increasingly women are mentioned as a subgroup, sometimes they have to be extracted from classifications such as 'community' or 'diversity' and 'social inclusion' policies. Anti-racist sites often encompass gender, dis/ability, sexuality and myriad aspects of social exclusion and marginalisation.

If women are invisible on the sports web pages, sport may similarly be absent from – or at least not central to – feminist and women's education websites. For the purposes of this book I have sought to draw upon some of the websites which might be categorised as ephemeral, including feminist websites where they do engage with matters related to sport and provide feminist critiques of emerging issues and current events as they happen. I am grateful to the British Library in London (British Library Archive, 2011) for securing some of these sites in their archive collection so that interested readers can follow up a reference with the assurance that they will be able to access the site.

The Women's Library (Women's Library, 2011) does, however, classify sport within its extensive collections, but although sport is visible, the archive can only include what has previously been made visible, which means that the focus is more on the margins of sporting activities than on the centre. Making women visible within a field in which they have been largely invisible is difficult, especially at a historical moment when the public sphere is saturated with sexualised, gendered discourses, in an endeavour which is more than just capturing the ephemeral. Nonetheless, accessing what may not otherwise last is a good starting point.

Outline of the book

Chapter 2 (*Regulating Frameworks: Playing by the Rules*) starts with regulatory systems and explores genealogies and histories of the Olympics and Paralympics, for example, the development of the IOC and National Olympic Committees (NOCs), and a historical analysis of the changing regulatory practices of the Games from the Ancient Games through to the 'founding fathers' (sic) of the modern Games to later developments (IOC Women, 2011, IOC Women and Sport, 2011). The modern Games still resonate with some of the ideals and principles of the Ancient Games which are not infrequently invoked although reworked into more contemporary language. Olympian ideals were not only rediscovered but also reconfigured within nineteenth-century patriarchal discourses. The Olympics offer particular genealogies that can be traced through the development of the modern games. The rules have been transformed through political activism (Hill, 1996, Lenskyj, 2000, 2002, 2008) and through widening participation, including most notably the Paralympics (Paralympics, 2011) and more recently the Special Olympics (Special Olympics, 2011). A major aspect of regulatory practices and source of monitoring is the sexual division of sport into women's and men's competitions. This chapter uses the particular instance of gender binaries and empirically the discursive regimes which frame sex gender categories. The chapter maps out the debates and then uses the case study of women's boxing, which, although there was a demonstration of the sport in 1904, was banned throughout the remainder of the twentieth century, but included in 2012. Boxing as a sport so powerfully imbricated in hegemonic masculinity (Woodward, 2007, 2008, 2011b, 2011c) highlights the intersection of diverse forces in the constitution of gender categories.

Chapter 3 (*Finding the Truth: Hoping for Certainty*) builds on and develops Chapter 2's examination of the importance of the discursive regimes of sex gender to demonstrate some of the problems with an overemphasis upon social construction and discursive apparatuses. This chapter uses the example of gender verification testing as a case study of the processes and intersections of power axes which meet in the materiality of enfleshed selves, corporeal systems and genetic make-up; bone structure as well as comportment and body practices and other classificatory systems, such as psychological testing, are invoked. The concept of the enfleshed self permits an understanding of collective selves and thus collective action and responsibilities which retain the materiality of the flesh. Flesh is central to sport and its practices and the culture and politics of sport.

The chapter makes the case for the conceptualisation of sex as well as gender as an explanatory tool in making sense of difference and in configuring a politics of difference that can engage with the materialities of enfleshed inequalities in sport. Chapter 2 uses the example of the athlete Caster Semenya, who was subjected to extensive media coverage in 2009, more due to having to undergo gender verification tests than for her considerable athletic achievement in the 800 metres at the European championships. This chapter draws upon my own experience of broadcasting and blogging on the case in the summer of 2009. Sex connects to other materialities such as wealth and poverty, race and place (Taylor et al., 2011). The processes and points of connection and disconnection are spatially located, which is further explored in relation to nation, diaspora and transnational identifications in the next chapter.

Chapter 4 (*Nation, Host Cities and Opportunities*) explores some of the more directly visible inequalities within the politics of sport between nations that are manifest in the systems of engagement in the Olympics and in sporting outcomes – success or failure in the binary language of sporting competition. These inequities are also evident in competing arguments about the processes of bidding for the Games and the politics and economics of the city (Gold and Gold, 2007, Preuss, 2004, 2008) and at the diverse ways in which hosting a mega sporting event can mobilise space. Hosting the Games provides employment opportunities and the potential for a vastly enhanced infrastructure, as well as creates enormous debts through the expanding demands for finance. The history of host cities also raises questions of corruption in the history of the Games (Jennings, 1992, 1996, 2000, Guttmann, 1984, 2002) and this chapter presents an evaluation of these contradictions and tensions within the context of debates about social inclusion.

The Olympics are closely tied to national identifications (Hill, 1996, Guttmann, 2005) through the processes of inclusion in the Games through national teams and through the kudos that can go with hosting the Games. Spatial identifications are central to the Games but these operate in complex ways at the Olympics; medals are awarded to individuals as representatives of nations, but early versions of amateurism and national identities have long been abandoned in the Olympics as in the rest of global and national sport. This chapter maps some of the historical changes that have taken place in the Games in modern times against a background of reframing the nation at other sporting sites. The chapter uses the case study of football (soccer), a sport which is not as central to the Games as athletics, to explore how national identifications are changing and how the Games can accommodate these changes in a sport that is increasingly popular among women, but dominated in the public arena by the male game (Caudwell, 2007, Hargreaves, 2007, 1994). There are also significant synergies between the regulatory bodies of the Olympics and football through the personnel, many of whom have membership of the IOC and FIFA, for example, as well as the histories of the apparatuses of regulation and bureaucracy.

Chapter 5 (*Spectacles and Spectators*) develops the debates set up in earlier chapters about the measures and mechanisms of representation and symbolic systems and focuses on the nature of the media spectacle and the mega event – in the case of the games the rituals, pageants and opening and closing ceremonies in particular, including the politics of spectacle and spectatorship (Horne, 2007, Houlihan, 2008, Miller and et al., 2001, Scambler, 2005, Tomlinson, 1996, 2011). Gender has played a key part in analyses of the coverage of such sporting spectacles (Daddario, 1998, Markula, 2009) and this chapter critiques the spectacle and its visibility in promoting possibilities of inclusion. Sensation, visibility and sound are central to the making of the Games and of who is in and who is out, who speaks and how silence is configured. This chapter offers a critique of spectacle and sensation as well as an analysis of how the spectacles, the ceremonies and media coverage throughout of the Games are contingent and temporally and spatially located as well as governed by commercial, economic and political factors.

Chapter 6 (*The Art of Sport*) focuses on another set of processes which bring together art and sport. These processes draw upon Deleuzian notions of affect and sensation including art as a less explicitly and overtly gendered field than sport. The particular context is an aspect of diversity and widening participation programmes which links art and sport and the developments of the Cultural Olympia. What happens when art and sport are brought together in programmes which aim to promote diversity? Each field is one where passions are evoked and each is heavily dependent upon representation and symbolic systems. The chapter looks at representation through an alternative conceptualisation of the materialities of art through different genres, interpretations and images of sport, including posters. The Cultural Olympiad is becoming more important in the Games with 2012 having the most ambitious cultural projects to date. There are synergies between art and sport and points of connection in the intensities and expressions of each field: each has popularising possibilities if not traditions and this provides opportunities for the inclusion of underrepresented and marginalised people. Both art and sport generate affects of emotion, passion and unmediated sensation.

The chapter retains the book's concerns with equalities and inequalities and the governance of diversity and social cohesion through a deconstruction of a 2012 project, The Art of Sport, sponsored by Lloyds TSB bank, which was one of the first sponsors of the London Games. This project brought together young artists and young athletes in a promotional fundraising venture. Art is understood as affect (Clough, 2007, Deleuze, 2005, Gregg and Seigworth, 2010), where art objects themselves generate affects and are affected by spectators and instigators of such projects. The participation of a big bank in a role that draws on a legacy of patronage, reconfigured in a particular economic climate of recession, demonstrates some of the points of connection and disconnection between a wealthy charitable benefactor and the recipients of charity and patronage using the combination of art and sport. This example demonstrates the affects of art and of sport and the need to go beyond discursive regimes and argue for the materiality of power in the mix of forces which intersect in the creation and maintenance of inequalities as well as presenting challenges and promoting social inclusion.

Chapter 7 (*Contradictions, Controversies and Disruptions*) engages with questions about challenges and disruptions both to the democratic ideals of the Olympic Movement and to the trajectory of progress in relation to social inclusion; it explores the extent to which and how the Games are the site of public protest and in particular at how resistance at such sites might be gendered. Sport at the Olympics is a field where opportunities are created, as Chapter 4 demonstrates in its coverage of the bidding process; but the games are also implicated in exploitation and the creation of inequalities. This chapter looks at how inequalities are played out locally in host cities and globally through the structural inequalities of the wider social field of the globalised economy, which also generate resistance. The Olympics offer a site for political resistance (Lenskjy, 2008), as has been evident on many occasions including at Beijing in 2008 where the focus was upon human rights, and the making of political statements, the most famous and iconic of which is probably Tommie Smith and John Carlos in 1968 (Smith and Steele, 2007), although the Games have presented opportunities for the making of public political statements at a variety of sites. Sex gender is implicated in expressions of protest as well as in the inequalities that give rise to protest, and the concept of sex gender can be invoked to make sense of the inequalities which permeate the Olympics. This chapter brings in some of the points of connection between sex and sexuality and the need to explore some of the advantages of the idea of the collective action of material, enfleshed selves. This chapter explores the ways in which political activism is specific to the Games through their topographies and topologies and argues that the Olympics offer particularities within sport because of their history and constitution. The Games also offer less dramatic and more routine opportunities for disruption, for example, in relation to less mainstream sports, whereby an Olympic presence can make visible a more marginal sport as well as otherwise underrepresented athletes.

Chapter 8 (*Sex Power and the Games: The Conclusion*) sums up some of the issues that have been highlighted in this discussion of the Games and the contribution which the intellectual understanding of sex gender as well as the empirical consideration of gender issues can make to making sense of the games. Sex gender has a wider remit than explaining the empirical presence or absence of women. Sex gender is deeply imbricated with the operations of power and the making and remaking of contradictions and inequalities and provides a means of going beyond internal, discursive processes. This focus has facilitated an understanding that extends beyond the Olympic Games, yet is also specific to it. The conclusion returns to the centrality of sex and power. Gender and categorisation of sex gender have been used to demonstrate some of the systems through which exclusion operates, through enmeshed discursive and material regimes, and to put the materialities of collective enfleshed selves into the discussion.

The Olympics are a site of social transformation and are affected by and affect the wider social, political and cultural world which the games inhabit. There is a trajectory of change but there are also powerful endurances and the reiteration of inequalities, although the games offer a particularly important site for challenges to the persistence of the assemblage of inequities in which race, sex gender, ethnicity, disability and location intersect. Sport has the advantage of encompassing so many different elements of social life and of having the creative capacities to generate passion and intensity which can be productive of change and progress.

The book makes a case for a revaluation of sex gender in understanding the intersections of different power axes in order to maintain a focus upon enfleshed differences as well as phenomenological experiences of inequality. The Games are about individuals, communities and nations as well as transnational governance and economic and financial systems. Sex gender as a marker of difference operates unevenly at times, such as in the politics of diversity, and by promoting social inclusion, gender is characterised by victimhood and justified by biological difference read as inferiority in sporting practices. At other times the gender of women and of men is largely unmarked, for example, in the Art of Sport project, and class differences are more centrally in play. Thus the Games present particularly good examples of the ways in which different dimensions of power, inclusion and exclusion are caught up in events that are both everyday and spectacular and that encompass structural social, cultural, economic and political constraints and reworkings of intentionality on the part of the enfleshed selves who participate.

Change has been rhizomic and disjointed rather than following a single or linear trajectory but examination of the plane of equality offers useful insights into the assemblages that make up the intersections of different power axes in sport. Policies and practices change across time and space and are materially as well as spatially located. The Games have particular histories that can be read through the stated policies of the Olympic Movement as well as through the enfleshed sporting practices the Games encompass and the media and wider public interest they generate. Because the Olympics have so explicit a set of democratic principles they offer a useful and interesting focus for exploring the possibilities of sport for promoting social inclusion as well as the impossibilities in an increasingly commercial world in which the sports media–commerce nexus, framed by patriarchy, can be seen to dominate. Discursive critiques of the representations through which meanings are transmitted and reproduced do not tell the whole story. Arguments based entirely on a critique of the operation of regulatory practices and symbolic systems cannot accommodate the specificities of space which the Olympics present, nor how to conceptualise the engaged action of participants and the affects of sport, its spaces and technologies. This book argues for a materialist understanding of the practices of inclusion and exclusion that also permit political activism and change and puts sex back on to the agenda.

2
Regulatory Frameworks: Playing by the Rules

This chapter is concerned with the operations of rules and regulations in instating and reinstating normalising assumptions about the Games and indeed, by implication, sport in the wider social context. Rules matter in sport, but regulatory practices go beyond what is and what is not permitted on the pitch, track or field, in the ring or the pool. Regulatory practices in sport are constitutive of the wider cultural terrain of social and political relations besides being shaped by those social forces (Woodward, 2009).

The Olympics have social and cultural significance in relation to their histories and the interrelationships between national, local, global and transnational economic and political axes of power. Much of the debate about the status and importance of the modern Olympics has been framed by the extent to which they have become so deeply embedded in global capital (Guttmann, 2002, Horne, 2007, Houlihan, 2008, Sugden and Tomlinson, 2011, Tomlinson, 1996, 2008) and what Richard Giulianotti calls *hyper commodification* (Giulianotti, 1999) especially in the late twentieth century, through the media–commerce nexus that could be seen to be in contradiction to the founding ideals of the games, ideals, nonetheless, which require some deconstruction in relation to the extent of the equity and democratic principles by which they were informed. De Coubertin's aspirations and idealism did not include any possibilities for women athletes. The amateurism on which the modern Games were based assumed personal wealth that made financial remuneration unnecessary; the amateur was a gentleman who did not need to compete for money. The gendered assumption about who might fit into the category of independent gentlemen of means is clearly an example of the intersection of gender, class and ethnicity (Taylor et al., 2011). Women as an empirical category of participants were explicitly banned by de Coubertin, but independent means assumes that it is men who have the means.

An exploration of the regulatory frameworks of the Games has to be located within the shifting relationships between politics, culture and economics which have become imbricated with the media in the commercialisation of the spectacle (Sugden and Tomlinson, 2011, Tomlinson, 2011). This is a set of phenomena and a series of events which has increasingly come to be seen as in conflict with the idealisation of the Olympic Movement and its founding principles of equity and opportunity.

The modern Games have moved from being a grand socio-political project with a limited economic profile to a period, from the early 1930s to the early 1980s, to an intensely politicised event. More recently the Games have developed into a site for transnational capital investment. Gender politics are largely absent from this chronology, as they were from the equity of the founding principles, but the point about the shifts in relation to the economy and to a particular view of politics is well made.

The modern Games have been subject to massive transformation over the last 100 years or so, none more so than in relation to gender even if sexual politics remain unchronicled (Guttmann, 2002). This is in contrast to the continuities in the lifespan of the Ancient Games, the principles of which still retain traces of influence, albeit most powerfully through their nineteenth-century reiterations. The rules of the Ancient Games, according to admittedly much more limited evidence than there is of modern times, remained more or less constant over 1,200 years (Spivey, 2004). The evidence does, however, demonstrate the importance of the Olympics to cultural, social and political life and routine of the Games every four years regulated by established rules. As Nigel Spivey argues, whatever the purchase of the Ancient Greek philosopher Herakleitos' claims that 'all things are in flux' (2004: xx), when it came to the Games, the rules stayed the same for over a 1,000 years. Change may be more a characteristic of modernity and perhaps especially postmodernity, although the linear progression of change can be overstated. Change has, however, taken place within the bureaucratic regulatory systems of the games, which demonstrates the intersection of the different social and political forces in play.

This chapter explores some of the genealogies and histories of the Olympics and Paralympics, within a framework of what is normalised, through IOC and NOC rules and an historical analysis of the changing regulatory practices of the Games from its 'founding fathers' (sic) to later developments (IOC). The 'founding fathers' include the strati-fied deposits and evidential traces of the Ancient Games which were reconstituted in the nineteenth century within different versions of patriarchal systems. The rules have been transformed through political activism (Hill, 2002, Lenskyj, 2008) and through widening participa-tion, including most notably the Paralympics and more recently the Special Olympics. This chapter uses the particular instance of gender binaries and empirically the discursive regimes which frame sex/gender categories and the connections and disjunctions between the games and the wider social, political and cultural terrain. The chapter maps out the debates which are emerging from an expanding feminist litera-ture on sport and then uses the case study of women's boxing, which, although there was a demonstration of the sport in 1904, was banned throughout the twentieth century, but has been included in 2012. Boxing as a sport so powerfully imbricated in hegemonic masculinity (Woodward, 2007, 2008) highlights the intersection of diverse forces in the constitution of sex gender categories.

Framing the Modern Games: traces of the Ancient Games

The exclusion of women from the Ancient Games is well documented if not always fully explored, as Mary Lefkowitz and Maureen Fant demon-strate in their sourcebook on women's lives in Greece and Rome (2005). Assumptions about patriarchal practices in the ancient world have become reimagined at different historical moments, especially in the gendered ideological configurations of the modern Olympics. At some points it is difficult to ascertain the routes through which the connec-tions between ancient and modern are made and the claims of the nine-teenth-century 'founding fathers' can be very selective. The evidence of men's participation in the Ancient Games, whatever the limitations of time and reliable sources, is vastly more substantial than that which is available for women. Spivey suggests that the 'revival' of the Olympics in the late nineteenth century was not modelled on the ancient ideal but merely based on prevailing gender stereotypes including the exclu-sion of women from political, military and financial affairs (Spivey, 2004:117). Allen Guttmann too argues that de Coubertin shared 'fully the prejudices of his age [and] continued to oppose the participation of female athletes' (2002: 46).

Evidence from the ancient world may be relatively sparse and the games were clearly the men's games, but women did participate in sport. For example, Pausanias, the Greek traveller and writer of the second-century AD, in his guide to classical Greece describes the festival of Hera, which featured races for young girls (translated as virgins, Pausanias, 1971). These girls ran on an Olympic track minus about one-sixth; then too women ran shorter distances, but it was the same track. Pausanias notes that 'the servants who wait on the committee of 16 who hold the games are also women. They trace the girls' games to antiquity as well as the men's' (in Pausanias, 1971: 245, Book V 16.2–8). This demonstrates that women's, or at least girls', events had some status, for example, in their location and organisation through a formal committee, even if men's and boys' events predominated. Girls (translated as virgins) particularly connote a relationship to the repro-ductive process; these are girls who are not yet mothers. Maternity is a key component in the discourses of opposition to women's full partici-pation in competitive sport (Hargreaves, 1994). In modernity, even late modernity, medical and ethical factors combine and elide to exclude or pathologise mothers who are engaged in athletic endeavour and in exercise which might be seen to impair women's fertility. The concerns of the Ancient Games might be rearticulated and transformed by the discourses of science, but concerns about women and motherhood underpin much contemporary debate too.

There is also evidence of adult women's participation in the Ancient Games in a variety of ways. For example, Spivey cites the case of Kallipateira, a widow, who disguised herself as her son's trainer and brought him to the Games where he ultimately won the boys' boxing contest in 404 BCE. There is some irony in the practice of women having to pass as men to take part in the Ancient Games; in the modern Games, however, women who adopt what are perceived as masculine presenta-tion of the self and masculine comportment are treated as suspicious.

Married women were forbidden and barred from the games, but Kallipateira might have hoped that her disguise would work, as trainers could remain clothed at that time, unlike athletes (apart from chari-oteers) who were naked. Somewhat surprisingly, however, she exposed herself and broke her own cover. She was only let off the death penalty because she came from a family of victors, including her husband and brother: a case of feminist activism supported by class privilege which achieved results if not those that were intended. Her actions did, however, have significant outcomes in changing the rules, because trainers subse-quently had to appear naked too (Spivey, 2004: 153–4). Gender verifica-tion in the ancient world seems to have been clearly based on outward physical appearance, as it was well into the twentieth century. Body appearance and comportment remain particularly important in the twenty-first century however, when performing masculinity is still taken as a key signifier of gender, albeit one that is accompanied and endorsed by a battery of cultural, scientific and quasi-scientific evidence as Chapter 3 shows.

There is evidence of other cases of women participating in the Games in some form, for example, in the second-century BCE women participated in chariot races – Bilistiche, Aristoclea, Zeuxo and others along with women victors at Delphi (Lefkowitz and Fant, 2005: 161–2). Social class was then as now clearly relevant. In order to participate in a chariot race you had to have horses. Ownership of horses was indication of aristocratic status. This is supported by inscriptions, for example, of the royal status of the charioteer Cynisca whose inscription at Olympia records that 'I Cynisca, won a victory with my swift running horses and set up this statue. I claim that I am the only woman to have won this crown' (ibid: 162). Lefkowitz and Fant point out that the wording suggests that she owned the horses, which clearly signifies her aristocratic status.

Women are present, if only occasionally, and most of the evidence cited by Lefkowitz and Fant suggests that a great deal of effort went into keeping women in insubordinate positions. There are assumptions that oppressive exclusionary practices are necessary to control and constrain women. The formal exclusion of women is clearly a point of connection between the Ancient and the modern Games and one to which corporeality and the commonalities of flesh are central. This is, however, a much more complex mix than nineteenth-century patriarchal discourses admit.

There are differences in that women in Sparta seem to have been accorded greater freedom than those in Athens, and there are class differences, but there is limited evidence of much engagement in the Olympics for women. The anxiety about women encroaching into the arena of male power is further evidenced in later sources such as with the Roman writer Juvenal who mocks the idea of women's sporting activities. It is worth noting because of the use of satire, the assumptions about women's bodies as their husbands' property and the notes of deep misogyny which underpin the humour. Of the concept of women fencers, he says

> We've all seen them, stabbing the stump with a foil
> Shield well advanced, going through the proper motions:
> Just the right training needed to blow a matronly horn
> At the Floral festival – unless they have higher ambitions
> ... .

> Helmeted hoyden, a renegade from her sex,
> Who thrives on masculine violence...
> What a fine sight for some husband – *it might be you* – *his wife's*
> Equipment put up for auction...
>   (Juvenal, 1967: 136, 6: 246–67, italics in original translation)

The idea of women engaging in sporting activity is presented as absurd, contrary to appropriate feminine behaviour and implying inadequacy on the part of the man whose wife so acts. Women's embodied practices are sexualised in ways that men's are not, especially in the context of sport as part of the assemblage of sexualised identifications that are available. The ancient Western world that was so often invoked in its rediscovery and re-articulation in the nineteenth century is not quite as far removed and disassociated from the modern world as might at first appear to be the case. A contemporary case that has been made against women's boxing has some resonance with these ancient sexualised discourses, for example, as reflected in Joyce Carol Oates's assertion that women's boxing is a parody of the real thing, which is the men's sport (Oates, 1987).

Women can also be excluded through mockery and what routinely passes for jokes about women's alleged incompetence, within the networks of hegemonic masculinity even on the peripheries of sport in the twenty-first century. In 2011, women's participation, for example, as referees in football in the United Kingdom, was greeted with ribald and patronising mockery and derision, as in the case of Sian Massey, an assistant referee whose competent and accurate refereeing on the sideline and correct call on offside was mocked by commentators Andy Gray and Richard Keays with references to women's innate inabilities to grasp the off side rule (Woodward, 2011c). What is different in the twenty-first century is that this incident triggered a public furore in the media in which challenges to patriarchy were given voice. There was serious recognition of the inappropriateness of the commentators' remarks and of their attitudes. The commentators were dismissed, only to be reappointed to new highly paid posts on another channel within a couple of weeks. The media storm embraced different aspects of the debate, much of which centred on the sexualisation and marginalisation of women and was still framed by the idea that they were 'only joking' and holding on to hostile interpretations of what constitutes political correctness and accusations of missing the joke. Contemporary jokes made at women's expense do not, as Juvenal did, suggest their husbands should control them or present them as fearsome figures, but the very idea of women running the line in men's Premiership football is still seen as amusing and the aim remains to exclude women. What passes for humour is still a device for marginalising women, especially in sport, and makes up the informal mechanisms of regulation. Disciplinary techniques include these practices as well as the more formal apparatuses of governance.

The modern Olympics, like the Ancient Games, are political, not the least through the operation of sexual politics and a regulatory framework based upon gender. In contrast to the Ancient Games with their regulatory continuities, however, the modern Games manifest significant changes with sex gender as one of the axes of power and discursive frameworks which have been most transformative. Inequalities manifest in the informal and the formal aspects of governmentality (Rose, 1986) have been challenged.

From Ancient to Modern: governance of the Modern Games

Accounts of the development of the governance of the modern Games have been largely related as narratives of progress from simple to complex systems. Such narratives have also featured key protagonists who are construed as agents of governance and often as heroic figures. The modern Games are universally attributed to the efforts of Baron Pierre de Coubertin, although in the folk history of the modern Olympiad, he was not alone in the nineteenth century in seeking to reinterpret and revive the Ancient Games. Dr W. P. Brookes had been holding an Olympic festival in Much Wenlock in Shropshire in the United Kingdom from 1849 (Guttmann, 2002). These games featured Greek banners and laurels for the victors in games as diverse as mounted tilting at hoops, cricket and artistic competitions, although it is difficult to find evidence of the gender of the participants at these relatively local affairs. Explanations of the Olympics and their myths of origin most commonly take the form of a linear narrative with de Coubertin as the main protagonist inspiring the modern Games. Whilst de Coubertin himself was one element in the mix of events, there was a particular confluence of different dimensions of political power, institutions, social class, culture, embodied practices, gender politics and military history which created the possibility of the Olympic Movement and the modern Games.

What distinguished de Coubertin in this mix and ensured the success of the project as he articulated it was, firstly, his position in class-based patriarchal networks and, secondly, the generation of an Olympic ideology that was attractive and even inspirational to key constituencies.

Thirdly, the aspiration attributed to de Coubertin was of an international event which would require transnational, global governance structures. What is most commonly narrated as an individual story is a confluence of factors, many of which are embodied in this privileged Frenchman. Intentionality is caught up in this combination of social class and cultural influences and practices within particular historical circumstances. The spatial and temporal context included France's reaction to the country's cataclysmic defeat in the Franco-Prussian War of 1870 which generated explanations for the defeat in terms of connections between athleticism and military prowess. Prussia's athletic militarism and nationalist gymnastic movement suggested better preparation than what was construed as French indolence; indolent and effete were adjectives with all the connotations of feminisation that this implied at the time (Forth, 2008). This was a historical moment when the idea of linking sporting achievement and discipline to national pride and self-esteem had considerable purchase. Needless to say, the associations of disciplined sporting endeavour and military success were also inflected with dominant masculinities (Forth, 2008). At several points in this assemblage of systems, ethnicised masculinities intersect with processes of militarism, class and politics.

The sports militarism associated with the project of the modern Games attributed to de Coubertin was also transformed by encounters with the sporting elite cultures of Britain and the United States, where sport was part of a mix of imperialism and muscular Christianity allied to notions of personal and moral responsibility and development. This was also a vision of sport as a separate realm of values and ethics which could be disengaged from economic and political power. These were all components of the assemblage of elements which went into, firstly, de Coubertin's activities organising French sport and subsequently into the explicitly international project which included aspirations to place sport above nation in what became the Olympic Movement. This version of internationalism has resonance with the disavowal of politics and the claims well into the twentieth century that sport and politics do not and should not mix. Internationalism was central to the modern Olympics (whereas, perhaps ironically, the Ancient Games were configured around glorifying one state – Greece). As de Coubertin is reported to have said at the 1892 meeting celebrating the fifth anniversary of the French sports' federation, Union des Sociétés Francaises de Sports Athlétiques (USFAS), 'It is necessary to internationalize sport...it is necessary to organize anew the Olympic Games' (quoted in Guttmann, 2002:2). He overcame the puzzlement of his audience in 1892 and went on to establish connections in the United States and Britain, which led to the first modern Games in 1896.

The first members of the IOC were men from Germany, France, Czechoslovakia, Greece, Hungary, Russia and Sweden and the Athens games of 1896 featured 14 NOCs. By 1912, the number of NOCs had risen to 28. This was just the start of the growth of the organisational framework of the games. Growth has always been closely and inextricably enmeshed with all that is entailed in the mixing of sport, politics and culture of the Olympic Movement, which is explicitly described in the introduction to the governance of the games on the IOC website as 'the concerted, organized, universal and permanent action, carried out under the supreme authority of the IOC, of all individuals and entities who are inspired by the values of the movement' (IOC, 2011).

The modern Games also laid claim to reviving an ancient idealised set of sporting practices, albeit in many contradictory ways. There are also many assumptions about the modern Games and their connections to the Ancient Games. The Olympic Charter makes no reference to amateurism although Article 26 defines professionalism (IOC 2007: 81). Amateurism is strongly linked to democratic discourses of diversity and equal opportunities in the modern Olympic Movement and also underpins ideas about sport and well-being – the friendly Commonwealth Games of the Queen's speech discussed in Chapter 1.

Whist celebrating and insisting upon amateurism and rejecting any financial rewards for participating, that is, cash prizes for each competition, the nineteenth-century revivalists failed to acknowledge the very common practices, which are well supported by archaeological evidence (Spivey, 2004), of prizes in the form of land, services, gifts and slaves which victors of the Ancient Games received. It was a very upper-class, white masculine version of amateurism which was created in the setting up of the modern Games (Olympic Movement, 2011).

Getting it down on paper

The governance of the modern Games is embedded in the Olympic Charter which encompasses a vast range of articles setting out approved principles and practices. The Charter has expanded to accommodate change. Bureaucratic processes and the bureaucratic explosion in the governance of the games is thus located within a Weberian framework of rationality and efficiency. Allied to this is the idea that bureaucratic systems can secure equal opportunities and promote wider participation by under-represented groups which is also contested in sport (Wagg,

2004) as in sexual politics (Taylor et al., 2011). The Olympic Charter with its 5 chapters and 61 articles which come to 96 pages in the most recent version (at the time of writing) of February 2010, official pdf file on the IOC site, outlines the guidelines and rules of governance of the Olympic Games, the Olympic movement and its three main constituents, that is, the International Olympic Committee, the International Federations and the NOCs (Olympic Charter, 2010). This bureaucratic edifice is both generative and reflexive of contemporary social norms and organisation but resonates with the origins and founding principles of the modern Games and of the principles upon which they were based.

The Olympic system involves a complex set of processes that have been modified and transformed in light of social and cultural changes as well, most notably, in response to charges of corruption and deception. The Olympic system came late to ethical regulation with an Ethics Commission only being set up in 1999, the same year as the World Anti-Doping Agency (WADA) was established, in a climate of controversy and crisis for the IOC when there was not only media coverage of administrative corruption, but there were also revelations of drug abuse by athletes and coaches.

The modern Olympics incorporate a vast regulatory system which is a global institution, which can be seen as an 'informal civil institution' and one of the 'less visible aspects of global governance' as Jean-Loup Chappelat and Brenda Kubler Mabbott suggest in the introduction to their detailed discussion of the International Olympics Committee and the Olympic System, (2008: xiii).The governance of the Games includes a network of actors. These are the key players of the IOC itself, the organising committees of particular games, which are contingent about the host city of course and last only for the duration of the games, the International Sports Federations, the NOCs and National Sports Federations. The NOCs are responsible for governing the selection and development of the teams that represent their nation in the Olympic and Paralympic Games.

Paralympics: new sets of rules

The Paralympics were not developed until well after the establishment of the modern Games. Their origins too belong to a particular historical moment when a number of factors combined to create the possibility of such a sporting competition. Militarism, heroic masculinities and embodied sporting practices combine to generate new organisations and practices in the Paralympics too. The Paralympics have gender specific roots, having been set up for war veterans at the end of World War II to provide sport seen as appropriate therapy for men who had received injuries in the war.

The Paralympics were set up as parallel to the Olympics, that is, to operate alongside the Summer and Winter games, rather than to be alternate games. Categories of disability that were formulated as allowable disabilities can be broken down into six broad categories. The categories are amputee, cerebral palsy, intellectual disability, wheelchair, visually impaired and 'others', which includes conditions such as multiple sclerosis and congenital impairments which have different manifestations (IPC, 2011). These categories set the parameters of allowable disabilities which incorporate criteria of embodied capacities and incapacities and the technologies deployed to redress incapacities, such as wheelchair use. Some disabilities have different regulatory bodies, for example, the Deaflympics for deaf people (Deaflympics, 2011) and the Special Games (Special Olympics, 2011) for athletes with intellectual incapacities.

The International Paralympic Committee (IPC) is the global governing body of the Paralympic Movement. The IPC organises the Summer and Winter Paralympic Games, and serves as the International Federation for nine sports, for which it supervises and coordinates the World Championships and other competitions. 'The IPC is committed to enabling Paralympic athletes to achieve sporting excellence and to developing sport opportunities for all persons with a disability from the beginner to elite level. In addition, the IPC aims to promote the Paralympic values, which include courage, determination, inspiration and equality' (IPC, 2011).

The IPC was founded on 22 September 1989, as an international non-profit organisation formed and run by 170 National Paralympic Committees (NPCs) from five regions and four disability-specific International Sports Federations (IOSDs). The IPC headquarters and its management team which are located in Bonn, Germany, are described in the contemporary language of diversity politics and the management of social inclusion as having a democratic constitution and structure, made up of elected representatives (IPC, 2011).

Whereas other international sports organisations for athletes with a disability are limited either to one disability group or to one specific sport, the IPC is an umbrella organisation which represents several sports and disabilities. Social, cultural and medical changes have impacted upon the organisation of the Paralympics for example leading to classification of disability which have led to the creation of multi-disability competitions, which have become included in the Paralympic Games. The Paralympics have grown fast and become important international sport events. The need to govern the Games more efficiently and to speak with a single voice to the IOC resulted in the foundation of the ICC, the International Co-ordination Committee of World Sports Organizations for the Disabled in 1982. Ten years later, the ICC was replaced by the IPC. The Winter Paralympics in Lillehammer in 1994 were the first Paralympic Games under the management of IPC, which numbers about 165 member nations. More countries competed at the Beijing 2008 Paralympics (3,951 athletes, 146 countries) than in the Munich 1972 Olympic Games. In Beijing, the degree of media coverage was unprecedented in spite of anxieties about the status of the Paralympics and disabled athletes prior to the Beijing Games in 2008 that were given voice in the media. With interest in and acceptance for sport for persons with a disability growing, the expansion of the Paralympics is most likely to continue in the future. This is not without controversy and problems though and, as chapter 3 suggests some of the troubles of classifying sex gender also apply to the difficulties of categorising able-bodied and disabled.

Sex gender and disability

When Paralympic sport was introduced in England, in 1948, it was primarily geared towards ex-servicemen injured in the conflicts of World War II. The notable disparity in the balance of male and female athletes was attributed to the preponderance of male ex-servicemen. However, 60 years later, the 2008 Beijing Games still demonstrated a dominance of male athletic participation of almost 2:1, suggesting that gender inequality remains a significant issue. Some athletes dispute this. For example multi-Paralympic Winter Games gold medallist Verena Bentel argues that women's sport is growing at a faster rate then men's and becoming more competitive by the year. She does, however, acknowledge that it is not just about embodied competing, but also the governmentality in which sport is enmeshed, including coaching practices.

> Previously women in sport were often reduced to their looks and the focus was not on their sporting talent. There has definitely been a change and a very positive one at that…There is definitely a challenge that you have to stand your ground with male functionaries and coaches…Although more women are becoming coaches it is

still dominated by men. This means that women have a different standing and I have experienced it myself. It is a challenge to stand your grounds and ask for your rights. (Bentel, 2011)

The Games have been heavily weighted in favour of an assumed participant who is white male and able-bodied, whatever the extent of protestations about a meritocratic discourse of democratic inclusion. The mix includes assumptions about heterosexuality which are evident in some of the intersections between militarism and sporting masculinities which endure long after the heterosexist, patriarchal underpinnings of the establishment of the Paralympics in 1948. Heterosexism pervades the common sense of militarism within contemporary popular culture.

There is a popular UK television series in which an engaging, talented choir master, Gareth Malone, trains disparate often unexpected (especially in that they lack previous experience and confidence in their ability to sing) groups of people to form a choir which can deliver very acceptable performances. The 2011 target was army wives who came together to perform as a choir which ultimately sang at the prestigious venue of the Albert Hall in London, in a Remembrance Day concert to celebrate war heroes. The series generated emotive affects through the expressions of anxiety among the women that their men might not return. Women in the military or anyone with a same-sex partner make up the silences and invisibilities within this frame. The iterative discourse was of waiting wives and absent men and demonstrates how sexuality can be subsumed even when critical analysis recognises the combination of elements which come together in generating social relations and social divisions.

The modern Olympics present an event which is a particularly massive and large-scale version of the nexus of sociocultural forces of sport, which reflect and refract dominant discourses and practices, reiterated through regulatory frameworks and everyday practices. Sex gender is central to these discourses, which are both reinforced and challenged in the processes that are implicated in the making and transforming of the rules, regulations and disciplinary practices through which we make sense of sport.

Sex gender and the Modern Games

Gender politics at the Modern Games have been marked by the emphatic statements of Pierre de Coubertin, describing the spirit of the Olympic movement as 'the solemn and periodic exaltation of male athleticism, based on internationalism, by means of fairness, in an artistic setting, with the applause of women as the reward' (de Coubertin, 2000:713). Coubertin opposed the participation of women in the Games and argued, rather in the same way as currently it is argued in some conservative states, for example, in the case of women's football in Iran, that women's sports should have no spectators. The Modern Games were not so different from the Ancient Games in their patriarchal organisation. Women competitors were firmly excluded from the first modern Olympics of 1896 and only very gradually gained entry to track and field events at subsequent Olympiads. Sex gender as played out in the games has been measured by the particular embodied practices in which each sex engages in their gender-specific competitions. The classificatory processes deployed in the regulatory systems of the Modern Games resonate with iris Marion Young's discussion of gendered embodied dispositions and manners of comportment – of what it is in effect to 'throw like a girl' (Young, 205). Athletics had been central to the Ancient Games. Women were discouraged from participating in athletics and sports like tennis, archery and swimming were seen as more appropriate. Phokian Clias's book on women's sports and exercise, *Kalisthenie*, published in 1829 had emphasised graceful movement rather than robust and strenuous competitive activity. As Allen Guttmann notes, any suggestion that women might compete actively and engage in competitive embodied sporting practices was greeted with hysterical reactions expressed within a framework of masculinisation and cries of 'Amazons' (Guttmann, 2002: 45). Guttmann sees these fears as belonging to the anxieties and threats of the nineteenth and twentieth century but, as this book demonstrates, they are alive and well in the twenty-first century, when women athletes remain threatened by accusations that they are insufficiently feminine and are compelled to prove their authentic femininity through its acceptable and accepted performances. This is also a femininity that is strongly linked to reproductive capacities; too much athleticism might lead to infertility for women (Hargreaves, 1994). The relationship between motherhood and women's athleticism remains problematic, although it has been reconfigured. Whereas in its nineteenth- and earlier twentieth-century versions it was largely based upon a discourse of hygiene, a gendered aesthetic and, of course, reproductive health, none of these dimensions remains untainted by ethical discourses, where health and morality and imperceptibly and inextricably entwined.

In the 1900 Games a few women golfers and tennis players were allowed to participate, and in 1912 women divers and swimmers were included. Women's inclusion and exclusion is marked by social class but not in a clear-cut or simple way. Class mattered and enabled some upper-class women to engage in sports like tennis, but fencing was not permitted for women in spite of the fact that women in the aristocratic class that dominated the IOC in the early twentieth century did quite often engage in this sport. Sex gender, culture, ethnicity and class intersect in different ways in the make-up of the Games and in their histories. Athletics, the central pivot of the Ancient Games, was the main bar: track and field events are central to the Olympics and most of the resistance to women's participation was focused on the inclusion of these events. A separate women's Games were held in Paris in 1922 at which the Fédération Sportive Féminine Internationale (FSFI) sponsored track and field championships for women.

There was, however, some limited backing for women from the regulatory bodies of the Olympics. In 1924 the IOC responded to a resolution by the Frenchman Comte de Clary by stating that 'as far as the participation of women in the Olympic Games is concerned, the status quo ought to be maintained' (Guttmann, 2002: 46). Women in Europe, for example, in the international Jeux Féminins, however, sponsored by the principality of Monaco, organised their own events. There was little support from the United States, although the US team, which came second in track and field in 1922, had been sent by the Amateur Athletics Union, despite opposition from other women who allied with men in expressing their disapproval as educators of women's sporting activities, especially in the track and field events. In 1924 the International Association of Athletics federations (IAAF) voted to allow women's track and field but did not support a second woman's Olympics. It was agreed that FSFI-supported events would drop the term Olympics. Maybe it would be acceptable for women to engage in competitive athletics without the glory of being accredited with Olympic status, a practice which parallels women's admission to universities like Oxford and Cambridge to study, but without the possibility of being awarded the full degree of Bachelor of Arts, only a diploma in the first part of the twentieth century. These were troubling times and there was not a clear trajectory of progress; however, there were marginal, incremental changes.

At the 1928 Games in Amsterdam five women's athletic events were permitted, which resulted in British women boycotting the Games. Hostility to women was expressed through discourses of corporeality and characterised by reference to enfleshed inequalities. There was considerable concern about women's capabilities and especially their powers of endurance in longer races in the case of those women who did participate. For example, some women collapsed after the 800 metres, the longest race of the five women's events; even the winner, Lina Radke, was reported as looking exhausted (Guttmann, 2002). This led to the withdrawal of this event which was not reinstated until 1960. Guttmann describes the *New York Times* reporting of the event in 1928 as 'a macabre verbal picture on which the cinder track was strewn with damsels in agonised distress' (2002: 47), although the Canadian press was much more positive in its coverage of Ethel Catherwood's gold medal leading Canada's 4 × 100 m relay. If women collapse exhausted after extreme exertion it may be deemed unfeminine (as it was and still is in some situations) and the embodied practices which for a man signify manly, honourable endeavour for a woman convey a whole different set of meanings. If women sweat and collapse in a sporting competition this suggests dangers both physical and psychological. At this historical moment, of course, the women may simply have been unprepared and have had little if any experience of competitive sport at this level.

Changing the rules

Change has been slow and uneven, as some of the dates of changes to the rules in this chapter demonstrate, although there has been a vast proliferation of bureaucratic amendments and an expansion of the Olympic Charter. Through the twentieth century there was enormous progress made in the growth of women's participation in the games, in terms of the number of women who took part, the number of events in which they could compete and the policies which facilitate these opportunities. Participation as athletes, in terms of excluded groups, has been marked. The white, class-based, gendered ethnocentricity of the first five Modern Games, in which there were no black athletes until 1912 and disabled athletes did not appear and were not thought possible as competitors until the second half of the twentieth century, has been transformed and this is recognised in the governance of the games.

The IOC, as leader of the Olympic Movement, whose objectives are to promote Olympism and develop sport worldwide, has made some progress in establishing a positive trend to increase women's participation in sport at all levels, and especially over the latter part of the twentieth century. Although there is enormous global variation, access to sport has been included in international instruments and documents that the UN and other institutions approved and promoted in the 1970s and 1980s. Sport and physical activities have been recognised as having a positive impact on health and as being a tool to eliminate socially constructed gender stereotypes (Woodward, 2011a).

The Olympic Movement and the sports community have responded to this movement and progressively undertaken initiatives to allow broader participation by women in sport in general. More sports and disciplines have been opened up to women at all levels and in most countries of the world. In the last 20 years especially, the IOC has pressed for the women's programme at the Olympic Games to be enlarged, in cooperation with the respective International Sports Federations (IFs) and the Organising Committees for the Olympic Games (OCOGs). This development has been further reinforced by the IOC's decision that all sports seeking inclusion in the programme must include women's events. The IOC also started to work on women's involvement at the leadership level in sport in 1981, under the initiative of former President Juan Antonio Samaranch, who suggested having women co-opted as IOC members. As a result, 16 members out of 107 are women (IOC Women, 2011), which is billed as progress, which it is from a starting point of zero, but does also reflect the slow progress of organisational, bureaucratic change in the governance of the games. Change within patriarchal institutions like the IOC also tends to take form not only as marginal incrementalism, but it also remains dependent on paternalism. It was not until the twenty-first century that the charter was itself changed.

The Olympic Charter (2010) was amended to include, for the first time in history, but not until the twenty-first century, an explicit reference to the need for work in this area:

> The IOC encourages and supports the promotion of women in sport at all levels and in all structures, with a view to implementing the principle of equality of men and women. (Rule 2, paragraph 7, Olympic Charter in force as from 07.07.2007 (Olympic Charter, 2010)

The status of women in the Olympics presents a useful means of tracing the route through the structure and organisation of regulation in sport, in particular, in the case of the Olympics, in critiquing the IOC, NOCs and associated organising regulatory bodies. The IOC retains the pretext of gender neutrality as expressed in masculine pronouns, even in the twenty-first century.

> In the Olympic Charter, the masculine gender used in relation to any physical person (for example, names such as president,

vice-president, chairman, member, leader, official, chef de mission, participant, competitor, athlete, judge, referee, member of a jury, attaché, candidate or personnel, or pronouns such as he, they or them) shall, unless there is a specific provision to the contrary, be understood as including the feminine gender. (Olympic Charter, 2010: 9)

In a field which retains an insistence on the binary differentiation of two sexes in its competitions, this demonstrates how troubling the sex gender debate is in sport as in the wider political terrain of governance. Women's organisations or those developed to promote and monitor women's participation in the games are playing a part in advancing women's involvement in the Olympics, but are also part of an ever-expanding bureaucratic structure of governance. For example, the Women's Sports Foundation believes that the Olympic Movement should be doing more to ensure that NOCs exercise gender equality in their selection of female athletes. NOCs vary markedly in the levels of female representation amongst their squads. Whilst many nations, such as the British Team GB, field a high proportion of female athletes, Saudi Arabia has so far not sent any female athletes to the Games. Groups like the Women's Sport Commission (WSC) are caught up in the networks of governance of the games. They have to participate within existing regulatory frameworks, but are subject to the same risks and dangers of being appropriated, absorbed and even subsumed within existing discourse, as other bodies which combat inequality. Feminist critiques have been subverted in different ways within regulatory bodies, whether within the ironic practices of postfeminism or fixed by the classificatory systems which measure progress without permitting creative or dynamic resistance. Feminist activism can be neutralised once it becomes institutionalised (Woodward and Woodward, 2009).

The WSF also believes that the concept of gender equality should be extended to cover all female participants in the Games, whether athletes, coaches, legislators or volunteers. Specifically, the WSF recently voiced concern over the representation of female hostesses (who were volunteers) in Beijing, stating that Chinese hostesses 'were chosen on their looks, and were trained for the role by standing in five inch high heels while balancing books on their heads with a sheet of paper between their knees' (Olympics Women 2011). The WSF subsequently urged the London Organising Committee of the Olympic Games (LOCOG) to ensure that London's volunteers communicate a positive and appropriate image that adequately represents the diverse nature of the British female population.

The IOC received requests from 17 different International Sports Federations (ISFs) for modifications of events, quotas and competition formats for the London 2012 Olympic Games. The IOC Olympic Programme Commission based their decisions on key established criteria, including considerations of whether any proposed modifications would increase universality, gender equity and youth appeal (London, 2012, 2011).

Sex equality has a more public face and a visibility hitherto only framed by the binary of inclusion and exclusion. Visibility involves bureaucratic proliferation of offices, committees and subgroups which also provide a public forum for discussion, as well as fixity in the categorisation, which, once embedded and institutionalised, becomes immutable. The binary remains but with additional categories added. The additive model is one that has particular appeal within the governance of diversity, as is manifest in the proliferation of categories of persons who are seen as discriminated against or excluded. These processes are both productive and constraining (Foucault, 1981). In sport this can be, for example, black and ethnic minority, people with disabilities, disaffected youth, substance abusers, gay and lesbian people and women, all grouped together in an ever-expanding class of people (Woodward, 2007). Local government also has an ever-growing category of the socially excluded – lesbian, gay bisexual, transsexual, queer, intersex and so on (Taylor, 2010, Woodward, 2011).

The IOC World Conference on Women and Sport exists to promote women and sport within the IOC. Most recently, the Fourth IOC World Conference on Women and Sport was held in Jordan in 2008. There were more than 600 participants from 116 different countries, unanimously agreeing upon five specific developmental themes: (i) to seize upcoming opportunities to promote gender equality; (ii) governance; (iii) empowerment through education and development; (iv) women, sport and the media; and (v) women, sport and the (WSFF, 2011).

Organisations like Women in Sport Commission, which was set up in 1994, but did not become a fully fledged commission until 2004, advise the IOC executive on the policies to deploy in the areas of promoting women in sport.

In the United Kingdom, the Women and Leadership Development Programme (WLDP) has been developed by UK Sport in partnership with the British Olympic Foundation (BOF) and the Central Council of Physical Recreation (CCPR) to help tackle the issue of women's representation within the highest ranks of British sport. The programme is a key part of UK Sport's work in building a high-performance system of 'world class people' through its People and Development programmes.

Strategies include the following objectives designed to promote, firstly, participation, secondly, performance and excellence and, thirdly, leadership. They have targets: 5 per cent increase in the participation of girls and women, in the embodied practices of a range of sports and in physical education. The target is to increase the number of women performing in the World top 20 by 10. In leadership, the target is to attain at least a 30 per cent representation by women on strategic sports boards and committees.

The programme was established to address the low level of women in senior administrative positions in sport by providing periods of intense training and continuous support to build leadership skills in order to enable the participants to maximise their potential. Designed to create a level playing field for women in a competitive environment like the sport industry, it forms a key part of UK Sport's commitment to gender equality in sport (Gender Equality Sport, 2011). There has been a significant shift in the regulatory framework to recognise the need for change especially in leadership. The overarching aims of the UK project are described as fourfold:

- To increase representation by women in leadership positions in sport.
- To build the competence and confidence of women in decision-making positions.
- To increase support among organisations for the contribution women can make to sports leadership.
- To foster networking between women leaders, both in the United Kingdom and internationally. (UK Sport, Leadership 2011)

Participants are provided with a Personal Development Plan which identifies skill and knowledge requirements and sets out how these will be met, and a variety of learning methods are utilised, from workshops and presentation, to attendance at relevant international events. All participants are also teamed up with a mentor, usually an established woman leader, to provide additional support.

In addition to equipping individuals with leadership skills, the programme also contributes to each organisation's influencing work in terms of international representation, developing excellence in sports leadership and advancing governance in sport (UK Sport, Leadership 2011).

Leadership and equipping women with the strategies and networks that facilitate their taking on leadership roles which men have so successfully utilised is one of the ways to develop women's profile in sport. Another is to diversify sports and include a wider range of activities. One avenue for change is the addition of new sports which could replace some of the traditional male sporting activities with what have been called alternative or extreme sports (Rinehart, 2005, Wheaton, 2004).

The IOC receives requests for the inclusion of new or different sports in the interests of promoting greater equality, although this sometimes means replacing men's events with women's since it is not possible to stage an infinite number of competitions. The Executive Board (EB) agreed to the request made by the International Canoe Federation (ICF) for the replacement of the men's canoe sprint C2 500 m event with the women's K1 200 m. The three Federations governing wrestling, swimming and cycling (Fédération Internationale des Luttes Associées (FILA), Fédération Internationale de Natation (FINA), and Union Cycliste Internationale (UCI), respectively) submitted requests for new events, which were all accepted by the EB on the condition that any new events should lead to an increase in participation of women at the Games, and on the condition that these events should replace existing events already attributed to these sports, whilst maintaining the same number of athletic participants within the respective sports.

A route which also has some purchase is to include those women's events in sports that have been very male sports and are closely enmeshed with hegemonic masculinity (Woodward, 2006, 2009). Boxing is an excellent example of one of the last bastions of male sport which is explicitly macho and invokes opposition based on ethical and emotional grounds rather than the challenge of numbers in a finite series of sporting events. Joyce Carol Oates' claim that boxing is for men what childbirth is for women and her suggestion that women's boxing is parodic and not real (Oates, 1987) illustrates how deeply embedded gendered attitudes are within the sport.

The EC's decision to include women's boxing constituted recognition of the substantial progress that the sport had achieved in recent years in both universality and technical quality (the sport was last proposed unsuccessfully as an addition to the Olympic programme in 2005).

Fighting our corner

There is something about boxing that makes it troubling in the twenty-first century. The sport is controversial for men as well as women, but its genealogies of struggle and the problems of racism and poverty and heroic narratives of escape allied to the enfleshed intensities of its encounters make it a particularly interesting sport. Amateur boxing is very different from the professional sport but some of the excitement and much of the high degree of control and enfleshed discipline impact upon the amateur sport too.

Men's boxing is one of the oldest and most popular sports in the Summer Games, having first been presented in 1904 in St Louis. It may have been popular but it has always been controversial. Boxing was banned from the 1912 Stockholm Games because the sport was not legal in Sweden at the time. It made a comeback in 1920 and has been popular ever since. Unlike some other Olympic sports, men's boxing has been a place where amateurs can turn into superstar professionals; Muhammad Ali (then called Cassius Clay) won light heavyweight gold in Rome in 1960, George Foreman won heavyweight gold in Mexico City in 1968, Sugar Ray Leonard made his debut with light welterweight gold in Montreal in 1976 and, for British fans, Amir Khan won silver in Athens in 2004 and then turned pro. It is worth noting that Khan lost to the Cuban fighter Mario Kindelan who at 34 was still an amateur from a country where men's boxing remains an amateur sport which is pursued for national glory. It is hardly surprising that women boxers might want some of this action and especially the recognition that goes with the sport. In spite of all the charges of corruption, the exploitation of boxers and the medical concerns about injury, boxing retains some impact through its stories of heroism and of triumph over tragedy in the routes its heroes have taken out of poverty and racist exclusion (Sammons, 1988, Sugden, 1996, Marquesee, 2005, Woodward, 2006).

In 2009 the IOC decided to add women's boxing to the list of Olympic sports for the London Games in 2012. Boxing had been the only sport reserved for men at the Games, so it is not surprising that debates raged about this decision. The furore and moral panic in the media was framed by similar issues which are raised in critiques of men's boxing, but with the added dimension of frail, enfleshed femininity and fears of the voyeurism of the spectators at women's fights. Boxing demands an understanding of sex, sexuality and sexual difference and the centrality of flesh as well as embodied practices. The ambivalences between the homoerotic dimensions of boxing (Woodward, 2006) and the sexualisation of women's engagement in the sport are concentrated on boxing's enfleshed encounters and the relationship between boxers, spectators, commentators and promoters and their social worlds. There was much more media coverage given to medical and ethical concerns, however, and little public recognition of what might drive spectators to women's bouts. Questions were raised about whether boxing should be an Olympic sport for anyone, especially women. Women struggling for recognition wanted the inclusion of their sport as a sign of progress and in the interests of gender equality.

One of the loudest sources of opposition came from other athletes and competitors who felt that the inclusion of women's boxing meant creating a new sport at the expense of some existing sport. Mostly the debate centred on whether women should engage in a sport the main purpose of which is to inflict damage on an opponent and, in the professional game, to knock the other person unconscious. Within the debates that preceded the final decision to include women's boxing, however, there seemed to be more concern about the sensitivity of women's breasts to blows in the ring than the fragility of men's brains. The contradictions of such arguments soon rendered them insubstantial and ineffectual but these are the kind of strands of thinking which underpin the debate and demonstrate some of the ambivalences of the discourses of sex gender that are played out in sport. These tensions also highlight the need to retain the materiality of enfleshed capacities of sex as well as the cultural affects of gender.

Popular pubic reaction implied that boxing must be a new Olympic sport for women and people seemed to know little if anything about the history of women's boxing that stretches back to the eighteenth century in many parts of the world, although in the eighteenth and nineteenth centuries prize fighting would be a more accurate description of the activity which often took place at fair grounds and exhibition halls in Europe. When boxing became one of the Olympic sports at the third modern Olympics in St Louis in 1904, women's boxing was a displayed event, a brief moment in the twentieth-century Games. Its invisibility during much of the twentieth century does not mean that women were not boxing. Women's boxing continued to be practised through the twentieth century, even though it was not broadcast on television nor was women's boxing a professional sport with big prize money. The more public visibility is expanded, for example, through the media representations, the more invisible women and women's sport appear to be.

The history of women's boxing is somewhat different from that of many other sports, which may account for some of the controversies which have surrounded it. Women's boxing can be seen to have started in England in the 1720s in the form of prize fighting (Hargreaves, 2006, WBAN, 2011)). In the nineteenth century women's boxing was prohibited in many US states and in Europe; it was banned in Britain in 1880, not very long after Queensberry rules had been implemented, in 1865. Up until the mid-twentieth century there were, however, exhibitions and bouts on both sides of the Atlantic with popular fighters like 'Battling' Barbara Buttrick, who actually did have a fight screened on television in 1954. During the 1970s several US states allowed women to box, permitted new licences and approved bouts with more than four rounds and in 1993 women's amateur boxing was integrated into the rules of the US amateur programme. It was not, however until 1996 in the United States that women's professional boxing was formally accepted and Christy Martin's bout with Deirdre Gogarty marked the birth of modern professional women's boxing in the United States. It was another two years before Jane Couch won her legal battle on grounds of sex discrimination with the British Board of Control in the United Kingdom (Woodward, 2011b).

Boxing like most sports is gender specific as formulated by its sporting regulatory bodies. There are three types of women's boxing: amateur, professional and unlicensed. Boxing's regulatory bodies cover women's and men's sports. Amateur and professional boxing are two officially sanctioned codes of boxing, regulated by internationally recognised bodies (Woodward, 2009). At the end of the twentieth century, the International Amateur Boxing Association accepted new rules for women's boxing and approved the first European Cup for Women in 1999 and the first World Championships for women in 2001.

Boxing remains controversial, both for women and for men, and new regulations have been brought in to make the sport safer, although boxing is far from the top of the tables of risk of severe injury. According to an Australian survey in 1998 reported by AIBA (2011) boxing came tenth in a league table of sporting injuries with rugby league well ahead, followed by sports such as rugby union, motor cycling, cricket and soccer.

Amateur boxing is a long way from prize fighting. In the twenty-first century, there is considerable interest in the sport at all levels. Boxing is a highly regulated sport which many women enjoy (Women Boxing, 2011) as a means of keeping fit, as disciplined regime through which you can gain self-esteem and feel good about your body and as a competitive sport in which you can not only achieve a personal best but also gain pride in representing your country and engaging in global sport, for example, at the Olympics. It is a highly disciplined, rigorously policed and tough sport, but women have fought for the right to join in and in 2012 they can at the Olympics in a climate of transition.

Boxing can be surprising. It may be embedded in discourses of hegemonic masculinity but women's boxing can emerge in very patriarchal situations.

Twenty-five women from Afghanistan trained to box at the 2012 Olympics. The sport was approved by the Afghan Women's Boxing Federation but and the International Boxing Association has sought to accommodate and facilitate the participation of Muslim women in sport by approving the wearing of hijabs beneath their headgear and clothes that cover their bodies in order to meet Islamic religious requirements. What this does illustrate, however, is a different route of resistance and an alternative narrative in the archaeology of sport. Boxing might actually offer women a means of challenging patriarchal constraints and of subverting hegemonic masculinities. The Iran Boxing federation too has approved training for women boxers, suggesting the beginnings of change, both in the sport and in the regulatory frameworks and wider social terrains in which it is enacted.

In the twenty first century it is becoming possible within the discourses of kinship, community and sport for women, like four times world amateur boxing champion, minimum weight boxer, MC Mary Kom of India, who received very positive coverage in the run-up to 2012 to achieve acclaim and success in boxing. Change may be slow and incremental but MC Mary Kom is an interesting example of a boxing hero. She is, according to her official website, of humble origins in India, a farmer's daughter, now married and the mother of two children (Mary Kom, 2011). There are elements of the conventional route for boxers who frequently belong to migrant communities and take up boxing as the route out of poverty, but Mary Kom's journey has been more measured and modest. She has become a heroic figure without the dramas of the narratives of male boxing heroes.

Conclusion

This chapter has shown that it is impossible to disentangle shifts in the details of regulatory bodies and their charters and the rules which make up the governance of the games from the embodied practices of sport and the trajectories of social and cultural change in which they take place. The rules change according to social change and what might be called the rules of the game are ways of being in sport and the body practices of those sports which constitute the Olympics. The Games recognise the interconnections between the regulatory bodies, especially the IOC and the Olympic Charter and the wider social context of which the Olympic Movement is part. There has been limited progress on new sports but permitting women to participate in traditionally male sports offers one way of looking at resistance to change as well as change itself.

There are also powerful synergies across time as well as space. Whilst sex gender classifications are clearly contingent, and change, for example, through the proliferation of regulatory bodies in the games and social, economic, cultural and political circumstances, there are continuities and connections between the making of sex gender as in the Ancient Games and in modern times. Ways of looking at and explaining social divisions and social relations through intersectionality provide an understanding of temporal as well as spatial forces

There has been an explosion of committees, groups and organisations in the regulatory bodies of the games, all of which contribute to putting women in sport into discourse. The range of mechanisms through which the Olympics are governed are increasingly making women visible in the discursive regimes of the Games as well as on the field, track circuit and in the pool and, in 2012, in the ring.

Governments, intergovernmental organisations, multinational sponsors, national sponsors and professional leagues, teams and athletes are all part of the mechanisms of governance of the Games. Thus these processes incorporate a diverse range of actors, networks and practices, all of which are caught up in the regulatory mechanisms of the Games. The Olympics along with other sporting events occupy and are constitutive of social, economic, political and cultural practices which make up historical moments and movements in which women are becoming more visible. Visibility is not entirely unproblematic however. Being categorised, listed and measured does not necessarily create autonomy or the capacity to exercise power and control.

The regulatory framework of the Games demonstrates the relevance and importance of the intersection of different aspects of social exclusion such as those based on disability and race. Sex gender manifests particularities in sport which are embedded in the rules. Because of the separation of women's and men's competitions and the binary classification of sex, gender can be problematic. Each aspect of marginalisation and social exclusion and each dimension of diversity has enfleshed features and capacities which suggest that there are specificities as well as consonances and intersections between them. Boxing illustrates particularly well the connections between regulatory bodies that govern the Games and the enfleshed bodies which participate.

Sex includes these enfleshed bodies and encompasses sexuality in ways which the concept of gender does not always perform adequately. Sex and sexuality are not identical and interchangeable and neither is gender. Gender is often underpinned by or implicated in sexuality in ways which can be confusing and contradictory as Chapter 3 shows. Sex retains the corporeal and the interrelationship between the social and cultural field in which the rules are made and embodied through sporting performance, which, however assisted and enhanced by cultural practice, is always enfleshed. In sport, enfleshed bodies matter.

Chapter 3 picks up the story of sex power and the games through the attempts of regulatory bodies to ascertain truths about sex through its gender verification strategies which are themselves constitutive of those categories.

3
Finding the Truth: Hoping for Certainty

The previous chapter focused upon the regulatory bodies which have developed within the organisational frameworks of the Olympics and the relationship between these bodies and the wider social and historical contexts in which the games have been performed, experienced and structured. Chapter 2 set up the importance of classifications and definitions of sex gender within the disciplinary mechanisms of the Olympics and the Olympic Movement and the evidential traces of the Ancient Games in those of the modern period and the endurances of gendered ideologies, especially in relation to whether or not women were allowed to participate at all. If women were included, which sports they might be permitted to play and the rules of their engagement were often distinguished from male competitions, for example, through shorter distances, as was manifest in the controversy about the 800 metres, which was for a long period in the Modern Games deemed to be too exhausting for women. The Games have been characterised by transformations and the persistence of classifications based upon sex within the regulatory mechanisms which make up the governance of the Olympics. The rules of the Game and the sex gender of the participants have been co-constitutive. The regulatory bodies of sport declare what embodied practices are permitted and which bodies can participate and thus constitute appropriate embodiment for athletes, and those who are not permitted to be athletes in these competitions.

The governance of sport presents a discursive field in which regimes of truth (Foucault, 1981) about sex gender are re-created in which enfleshed selves engage in prescribed body practices. These are material enfleshed bodies which are made in and part of a wider field of social, political and cultural life (Woodward, 2009). Femininity and masculinity are constituted through the interconnections between different materialities which include flesh, but it is largely the enfleshed body which is seen as the source of certainties and which might reveal some incontrovertible 'truth'.

Embodied practices and enfleshed selves change and are changed through the activities they perform and, through political activity those who have been excluded intervene to change the rules. Women's enfleshed bodies are transformed in size and shape through engagement in intense competitive sport, just as the musculature and make-up of men's bodies are. Even Olympic women gold medallists are expected to conform to heterosexualised criteria of glamour on, and especially off, the field. For example, British women swimmers and cyclists who achieved gold medals at Beijing were then photographed facing the challenge of killer heels. Athletes like swimming gold medallist Rebecca Adlington, who illustrates this assemblage of contradictory femininity, embodied success, the incredibly demanding training regimen required to achieve so highly and the ordinariness of both a local girl who made good and a woman who wants to look sexy and wear stiletto heels.

The relationship between embodied sex gender and sexuality is problematic for women because, whilst sport enhances the corporeality of masculinity by exaggerating the capacities and qualities that constitute its definition, sporting practice rarely – probably never – enhances equivalent femininities. As Jennifer Hargreaves has argued,

> Sports have been classified as masculine- and feminine-appropriate because of fiercely defended heterosexist traditions. Conventional femininity does not incorporate images of power and muscularity. (Hargreaves, 1994: 171)

It is not only the *images* of power that are implicated in these patriarchal and heterosexist traditions, it is their enfleshed materiality and their embodied practices. Although Hargreaves does not state the relationship between representation and corporeal materiality, it is suggested by her use of the verb to incorporate. This is resonant of the Deleuzian alternative to semiotics which posits that the representation merges with that which it claims to represent (Deleuze, 1994); the symbolic is in the embodied. A feminist critique such as Hargreaves's also raises questions about the relationship between sex and sexuality as she suggests in the conceptualisation of sex gender, which is particularly highlighted in the field of sport.

The inclusion of women's boxing for 2012, which was discussed in Chapter 2, raises important issues and questions about how sex gender is constructed and reconstructed and the relationship between the connections and disconnections between the governance and culture of sport, as evidenced by the Olympics, and the lives and practices of enfleshed selves, who are caught up in the social and political forces that make up the Olympic Movement. Flesh and embodiment are central to boxing as is the polarised binary of two sexes, which underpins regimes of knowledge and practice in sport. Not only is the perceived machismo and aggression that is popularly linked to boxing masculinities counter to cultural conceptualisations of femininity, so too is the corporeal violence of the sport, its one-on-one combat and stated aims of imposing physical damage (Woodward, 2006). Sex and sexuality are incorporated into this ambivalent mix of forces.

The female male binary is troubling, however, not least because it can create difficulties for the measurement and classification of gendered performance. What happens when you are not so sure? What criteria can be invoked to ascertain membership of either a female or a male category of person – and are there only two categories? This chapter looks at how the Olympics have addressed strategies for finding out what might be 'true' or 'real', focusing upon what is perceived in the troublesome and troubling business of gender verification.

This chapter uses the example of gender verification testing as a case study of the processes and intersections of power axes which meet in the materiality of enfleshed selves, corporeal systems and genetic make-up and bone structure as well as comportment and body practices. In sport other classificatory systems are invoked, including psychological testing (Ljungqvist et al., 2006). This chapter also uses the example of the athlete Caster Semenya who was subjected to extensive media coverage in 2009, more due to having to undergo gender verification tests than for her considerable athletic achievement in the 800 metres at the European championships. (Semenya showed no signs of exhaustion in the competition, only athletic prowess and speed.) This chapter explores media coverage of the case in the summer of 2009 and recent developments and the athlete's eventual reinstatement as a woman within the discursive certainties of the regulatory bodies of athletics, a category of sex which Semenya and her family had never doubted.

The matter of sex gender is central to these debates and this chapter uses the example of gender verification in sport to develop discussion of the terminology and its conceptual implications and to progress the debate about the philosophical and empirical bases of sex which can acknowledge the materiality of sex. This chapter takes on the debate about 'what is sex?' using the example of sport and in particular gender verification in the Olympics and in athletics to engage with some of the theoretical problems that the sex gender debate has generated, especially within feminist thinking. The discussion is always attentive to the materialities of the enfleshed self, which is central to the debate.

Boundaries of certainty: defining dis/ability

Whereas certainties about sex gender are usually situated within powerfully entrenched traditions and appeals to the longevity and universalism of the dual categories of female and male, upon which contemporary science can elaborate with some detail, other categories of person are more problematic; the question of disabled sports presents a more complex problem. Disabled sportspeople are not explicitly banned in any sense from the Olympics, but they have to achieve specific minimum standards of performance. The Paralympics present a compromise solution achieved by the efforts of the disability sports movement. This is another binary logic which appears to divide human beings into disabled and able-bodied, but the relationship between the two movements remains contested and the dividing lines between disabled and the able-bodied have become ever more difficult to determine with embodiment at the centre of the political debate.

The case of Oscar Pistorius raises questions about the nature of certainties which appeal to technologies of scientific expertise that are implicated in the change which the regulatory bodies of sport have to address and which are relevant to the discussion of sex gender and in particular gender verification testing. The South African runner Oscar Pistorius, whose science fiction epithet Blade Runner derives from the Cheetah flex-foot blades which enable him to run very fast, is a double amputee with highly specialised state-of-the-art carbon fibre prosthetic limbs. He won the right to compete in the Olympics at Beijing and to compete against able-bodied athletes even though he had hitherto competed only in the competitions for athletes with disabilities, having been disqualified from able-bodied athletics meetings by the IAAF because his prosthetics qualified as technical aids. In the end Pistorius failed to qualify for the Olympics and ran in the Paralympics but his case raises several questions about the classificatory systems of sport and the measurement processes through which categories might be secured, whether of dis/ability or sex gender.

Firstly, the promise of the objective certainties of technology are, at least partly, subordinate to other materialities, notably the social and the economic. In the intersection of power axes, there remains a hierarchical weighting which challenges the fluidity of the systems within this assemblage and re-affirms elements of a more determinist paradigm. Pistorius was able to access such superior technology only as an affluent white, male South African. Secondly, technologies offer possibilities that transcend an essentialist notion of embodiment but the body is inextricably implicated in the constitutive aspects of subjectivity and retains some of the limitations of corporeality, what de Beauvoir describes as the ways the body as situation limits as well as enables our projects ([1949]1987). Technological advances may contribute to enhancement of capabilities but they disrupt certainties and transgress boundaries, which do not necessarily offer criteria for measurement and evaluation which could then secure knowledge. Without underplaying the massive advances of technology and science and their liberating potential for bodies that are impaired, damaged, frail or sick, it might be possible to overstate the guarantees technoscience might offer for evaluating its sown success or its own outcomes. In the case of Pistorius as an example of setting the boundaries around disability and able-bodiedness and deciding what constitutes corporeal performance enhancement there is also the problem of essentialism. Essentialism is, however, only a problem if it is construed as the opponent of progress and change and rejects all avenues of reconstruction and complexity. Thirdly, arising from the ghost of essentialism, the Blade Runner example poses a question about the classification of difference and how it is constituted, if, indeed, the concept still has any purchase.

Boundaries of certainty: interventions

Another mode of enhancement in sport is one which has more explicit implications of injustice and taking unfair advantage is the use of performance-enhancing drugs. The IOC's policies towards drugs has been highly contentious. For example, critics (Simson and Jennings, 1992 Jennings, 1992, 2000) have pointed out that the IOC has hidden behind a rhetoric of disapproval of drugs such as anabolic steroids and other banned substances and 'the creation of "artificial athletes" but they cite the epidemic of drug use as proof of the insincerity of statements such as those made by Samaranch as CEO of the IOC' (Guttmann, 2002:178). Guttmann defends some aspects of Samaranch's position, but the point here is that he was CEO at the time of the explosion of criticism about performance-enhancing drugs as a problem which not only raised a huge number of questions about bodies in sport, but also raised political questions about how pharmaceutical interventions could be regulated. In spite of the IOC's efforts in the 1980s, testing of banned substances was largely ineffectual, although the IOC did take action against some of those detected, the most notable and famous of whom must be Ben Johnson at Seoul in 1988. The instances of drug use raise similar questions to those with which this chapter is primarily concerned because existing systems of measurement and evaluation prove problematic and the crossing of boundaries in relation to flesh and embodiment have always to be addressed in relation to the political and social context to which they appertain.

To what extent does technoscience dematerialise the body and render the enfleshed body with all its limitations redundant? New technologies and the development of pharmaceuticals clearly have enormous potential for enhancement; the problems, however, are measurement and morality. Whatever the level of intervention, the body of the athlete retains its human dimensions; athletes are actual, lived bodies or bodies as situations in de Beauvoir's sense (1987), whereby the athletic body is the site and situation of the intervention and transforms performance and is itself transformed accordingly.

Real bodies; virtual bodies

Some of the debate about bodies and embodiment in the 'corporeal turn' (Howson, 2005) especially in feminist theory (Butler, 1990, 1993, Haraway, 1985, 1991, Gillis et al, 2007) in the latter part of the twentieth and into the twenty-first century has stressed the fluidity of boundaries and subverted distinctions between what is real and what represented. However, artificially reconstructed bodies may seem no longer to fit the naturalistic paradigm, thus creating the Foucauldian paradox of simultaneously being everywhere and very visible and also disappearing in the shift from flesh and blood into technological constructions. Pistorius as Blade Runner might conform to some of this configuration. Deleuze challenges the very idea of signification and representation, which has been so central to the semiotic critiques of visibility , for example, in the spectacles and media coverage of sport. Representations are, of course, crucial to the meanings that are attached to sport, but Deleuze suggests an alternative to semiotics by bridging the divide between the representation and what it is claimed to represent by merging the two. For example, Deleuze suggests that all becomings are real even through being an actualisation of the virtual. The virtual is opposed not to the real but to the actual:

> 'real without being actual, ideal without being abstract'; and symbolic without being fictional. Indeed the virtual must be defined as strictly a part of the real object – as though the object had one part of itself in the virtual into which it plunged as though into an objective dimension. (Deleuze, 1994: 208–9)

If this means that the symbolic is in the embodied it could create an assemblage that incorporates enfleshed and discursive bodies, but Deleuze's disavowal of the actual makes this unlikely in a Deleuzian approach.

Technologies are strongly associated with change and especially the speed of change in the contemporary world and much of the theoretical developments on both embodiment and identities and selfhood have sought to challenge notions of fixity and essentialism in espousing the liberating possibilities of change. The search for certainties and clear boundaries in sport seems inimical to postmodernist critiques, including the work of Foucault and Deleuze.

Feminist approaches which draw upon Foucault's work have stressed social constructionism (Butler, 1990, 1993, Gillis et al., Grosz, 1994, Lloyd, 2007). What have somewhat loosely been called poststructuralist critiques start with a fragmentation either of the unified subject or of the idea of multiplicities which challenge the view that the embodied self is a given or has essential qualities; with unity goes the notion of an essence, both of which are rejected within such approaches. Some feminists have taken up a Deleuzian approach in order to show how transformations occur and to provide a radically new theoretical framework that can accommodate the speed of technological and scientific change. In sport this might lead to a free-for-all in the advance of technology were it not for the restrictions of economic and political operations of power which clearly show that not all athletes would have equal access to enhancement whatever form it took.

Rosi Braidotti argues for the benefits of Deleuzian approaches which rethink the human subject in a non-essentialist but vitalist philosophy that deploys the idea of nomadology as a philosophy of immanence resting on the notion of sustainability as a principle of containment and development of a subject's resources, understood environmentally, affectively and cognitively as systems within the assemblage

(Braidotti, 2002). This philosophy purports to combine the specificities of the subject that is aligned to the mobility of becoming. Thus a non-unitary subject inhabits a time that is in the active sense of continuous becoming. Deleuze argues against linearity so that 'becoming is a movement by which the line frees itself from the point and renders points indiscernible...Becoming is anti-memory' (Deleuze and Guttari, 1987: 291).

This philosophy is anti-hierarchical and suggests that becoming is a mapping and a connection rather than a linear hierarchy; thus difference too is not oppositional or weighted. Difference is construed as a mutual becoming. However, it is worth noting that 'becoming' applies to women and animals. Deleuze and Guttari present the notion of 'becoming woman' because they take man as 'the ground of becoming' (1987: 291), which clearly presents problems for feminists becoming Deleuzian. Braidotti, however, asserts that what Deleuze formulates is a philosophy rather than a mode of description. Braidotti argues for the use of Luce Irigaray's theory and politics of difference as a means of using the radical rethinking of change and becoming in Deleuze, but retaining the understanding of difference that is part of Irigaray's work (1991). The question for theorising techno bodies is how the notion of becoming could be applied to the transformations of enfleshed selves in the field of sport and what this concept can deliver in explaining how the boundaries of the body can or cannot be subverted and transcended.

Deleuzians stress the primacy of change and of the crises which characterise the contemporary world with human becoming at the centre of technological and scientific advances that question what makes up life itself. As Brian Massumi says, 'the "human" is more closely akin to a saleable virus, neither dead nor alive, than a reasonable animal standing at the pinnacle of earthly life-forms, one step below the divine on a ladder of perfection' (Massumi, 1998:60). The seemingly posthuman disorder of such a claim of constant flux is both alarming and exaggerated and there is some degree of hyperbole in such claims that so overemphasise the extent of constant change. However, what does appear to be a major challenge in the contemporary world is the centrality of technoscientific interventions, which provide opportunities for creativity and invention as well as subversions and constraints. Some of the complex interfaces of technologies that have life as their focus do challenge traditional ideas of being human. As Anne Fausto-Sterling argues, 'We live in a geno-centric world' (Fausto-Sterling, 2000: 235). Genetics constitute a branch of science that is often invoked in gender verification testing. Sex gender is also subject to technological and scientific interventions, often in relation to the search for certainty in re-establishing traditional categories as well as in opening up possibilities for enhanced performance. Opportunities and possibilities, however, tend to be linked to unfair practices, which is one of the unfortunate dimensions of gender verification which is so often based on the assumption of attempting to gain unfair advantage and the premise that it is men who might be pretending to be women and is still framed by the binary logic of two sexes.

Olympics and gender verification

Regimes of truth in the world of sport are much less fluid and mobile in relation to sex gender than in many other social worlds, whatever the possibilities of transformations that technoscience promises in relation to performance. Sport is premised upon a sex gender binary which informs its regulatory framework and the embodied practices of practitioners. There are women's competitions and men's competitions and very few that are mixed, especially at the highest levels. Mixed doubles in tennis is one of the few competitive mixed sports with public recognition, unlike foursomes in golf which are more low-status, leisure activities with the high prizes and kudos going especially to male top golfers. Mixed competitions are still based upon the supposed balance of the female male binary and take difference on board in all its dimensions – enfleshed difference and that of cultural practice and recognition – which means that male athletes top the table in terms of rewards and mixed activities are mostly relegated to the lower echelons of both status and reward. However fluid gender categories may be in parts of contemporary Western cultures, in sport they remain firmly entrenched in a clear dichotomy of difference, which is also one which privileges one aspect of the binary, notably that of the male and the attributes of masculinity (Cixous, 1980).

The IOC introduced sex testing, as it was then called, in 1968 at the Olympic Games in Mexico City, apparently after claims about the masculine appearance of some competitors. The development of broad shoulders, flat chests and muscular bodies is very likely to have been inevitable as women's events became more competitive with more events and consequent increased participation of women in elite sport. Sex gender cannot be separated into artificially constructed terrains of material, anatomical bodies in cultural practices. Enfleshed selves are always both.

The gender polarities long sustained through competitive sport became blurred as female athletes generally became bigger and stronger. (Wamsley and Pfister, 2005)

The debate about the masculinisation of women athletes that had been raging for several decades in the twentieth century, both before and after the institution of gender verification testing, and persists in different forms into the twenty-first century, was greatly intensified during the Cold War. On the one hand, women in Eastern Bloc countries had greater freedom to compete in sport and sport was a catalyst for social change (Guttmann, 1991, Riordan and Hart Cantelon, 2003), but on the other they were vehicles for Communist ideology. Women played a key role in making the Eastern Bloc's sporting a success story. Female athletes thus became political tools (Pfister, 2001) as a means of enhancing the role of Eastern Bloc countries in world sport.

Some instances are more explicitly politically motivated, like Dora Ratjen, a man who was forced to compete at Hitler's 1936 Olympics and who ultimately lost the gold medal in the women's high jump, having been later found to be Herman Ratjen, a member of the Hitler Youth.

These instances of gender ambiguity are framed within ethical discourses with the implication of cheating and moral transgression. They usually involve either a reassertion of the masculinity to which women mistakenly aspire in sport because they cannot attain it without being masculinised or a sense of pity. Yet again in the field of sport, women are classified as victims and the poor relations of hegemonic elite masculinity.

More recently, prior to the unification of Germany, in the former East Germany it is estimated that as many as 10,000 athletes were caught up in the attempt to build a race of superhuman communist sports heroes using steroids and other performance-enhancing drugs. The shot-putter Heidi Krieger was given steroids and contraceptive pills from the age of 16 and she was European champion by the age of 20. Her overdeveloped physique had put a huge amount of pressure on her frame, causing medical problems, while the drugs had caused mood swings and depression and had resulted in at least one suicide attempt. Later Krieger underwent gender reassignment surgery claiming that she had been confused about her gender, but felt that the drugs had pushed her over the edge.

The US-based, Polish-born sprinter Stella Walsh, who won gold and silver at the 1932 and 1936 Olympics and set over a 100 records, was found at her death to have male genitalia, although she had both male and female chromosomes, a genetic condition known as mosaicism.

Rather than the heroic narratives of male athletes' achievements, women's stories seem to have featured tales of enfleshed exploitation. Women remain victims or are corrupt. Women's bodies in these narratives are the target of organised deception and corruption. Sex became a tool for the manipulation of sporting success in a process in which women's bodies were deeply implicated.

The stated aim of gender verification testing was to prevent any man from masquerading as a woman in order to gain advantage in women-only athletic competitions. Gender-determination tests were degrading, with female competitors having to submit to humiliating and invasive physical examinations by a series of doctors. Certainty was to be achieved through the common sense of visible difference, but at the expense of women's self-esteem and human dignity. Later the IOC used genetic tests, based on chromosomes. Geneticists criticised the tests, saying that sex is not as simple as X and Y chromosomes, and it is not always simple to ascertain, because, for example, it is thought that around 1 in 1,600 babies are born with an intersex condition, the general term for people with chromosomal abnormalities (Blackless et al., 2000). It may be physically obvious from birth – babies may have ambiguous reproductive organs, for instance – or it may remain unknown to people all their lives. Human beings may exhibit a variety of chromosomal and physiological characteristics, such as androgen insensitivity syndrome (AIS) when a child is born with XY chromosomes but feminine genitalia, or those with congenital adrenal hyperplasia who have XX chromosomes but masculine genitals.

The Spanish hurdler Maria Patino underwent mandatory gender verification testing at the World Student Games in 1985. She was found to have androgen insensitivity, which meant she had Y chromosomal material and had small testes inside her body. Patino refused to withdraw or feign injury and was discredited and lost her studentship and her Spanish athletic residency. She had lived her life as a woman and, as she told the press after being dismissed, 'If I hadn't been an athlete, my femininity would never have been questioned' (Schweinbenz and Cronk, 2010). Sport reproduces the binary differentiating logic of sex gender. The embodied selves caught up in these events are assumed to have some agency and the capacity to make decisions, for example, about whether or not to take the drugs and, if detected, whether or not to withdraw.

At the Atlanta Games in 1996, eight female athletes failed sex tests but were all cleared on appeal; seven were found to have an intersex condition.

There was considerable resistance to gender verification testing from different constituencies which included medical scientists and doctors all of whom challenged the reliability and validity of such tests. They were also, of course, strongly criticised by the women athletes who had been subjected to the tests and on ethical grounds. As a result, by the time of the Sydney Games in 2000, the IOC had abolished universal sex testing but, as has continued to happen, some women still have to prove they really are women. The IOC, however, was slow to make the decision to abandon the tests.

The IAAF seems to have acted more proactively at this stage in the field of gender testing and at least recognised the diversity of sex gender. In 1990 the IAAF became the first major international sports body to recommend allowing transsexuals to compete, with some restrictions, which were agreed in 2004. Athletes who have sex reassignment surgery before puberty are automatically accepted as their new sex must have all surgical changes completed, be legally recognised as their new sex in the country they represent and have had hormone therapy for an extended period of time. For male-to-female transsexuals, this generally means a minimum of two years.

Transsexuals who have had a sex change from male to female can compete in women's events in the Olympics, as long they wait two years after the operation. The reasons for the timescale are not entirely clear and the possible explanations range from the assertion that athletes have to prove that they have learned to be real women to women having to show they have the necessary stamina and can survive in the world and pass as women, before they can compete. Another element in this mix which relates to the materialities of enfleshed sex is the period of time it takes for the balance of 'male' and 'female' hormones to settle in order to secure an authentic female make-up.

The humiliation of gender testing is evident in several of the high-profile cases of recent years. For example, Santhi Soundarajan, a 27-year-old Indian athlete, was stripped of her silver medal for the 800 m at the Asian Games in 2006. Soundarajan, who has lived her entire life as a woman, failed a gender test, which included examinations by a gynaecologist, endocrinologist, psychologist and a genetic expert. It appeared likely that she has AIS, where a person has the physical characteristics of a woman but the genetic make-up includes a male chromosome; the trauma of the testing led her to attempt suicide while awaiting the results. Edinanci Silva, the Brazilian judo player born with both male and female sex organs, had surgery so that she could live and compete as a woman. According to the IOC, this made her eligible to participate in the Games and she competed in Atlanta in 1996, Sydney in 2000 and Athens in 2004.

The IAAF set out its approach in a paper in 2006 (IAAF, Gender verification 2006) in order to establish a policy and mechanism for managing the issue of gender amongst participants in women's events. According to this paper, if there is any 'suspicion' or if there is a 'challenge' then the athlete concerned can be asked to attend a medical evaluation before a panel, comprising a gynaecologist, endocrinologist, psychologist, internal medicine specialists and experts on gender/transgender issues. The medical delegate can do an initial check, which could be construed as a pragmatic strategy or a reprise of the focus on visible difference and gendered corporeal characteristics (IAAF, Gender verification 2006).

The legacy of humiliation that accompanied gender verification testing endures in much of the discussion about setting a high degree of certainty about the sex of sporting competitors. Gender verification tests presented a mix of cultural, social and political inequalities which intersect with embodied, enfleshed materialities. Masculinity has not been subject to the same doubts, perhaps because men and masculinity have been seen as the yardstick of normality by which standards and classification of sex are judged and it can be proved that women are not men. Also, women are unlikely to want to masquerade as men in athletic competition because of their enfleshed differences. If there are two sexes there can be no obfuscation. Establishing criteria by which a person's sex can be incontrovertibly ascertained also suggests that finding certainty and the truth is the morally superior route. The IOC has always insisted that gender verification tests were designed not to differentiate between the sexes but to prevent men pretending to be women and winning unfairly. Ethical questions may have appeared to be paramount but control of women's gender and sexuality also informs these claims.

The debate was situated within a discourse of 'fair play' and the prevention of the possible advantages which male athletes might gain by participating in women's competitions, barely concealing patriarchal discourses which masculinise any successful female athletes and fail to recognise the possibility of women's athletic achievement; if they are any good they must be men.

Although the introduction of gender verification testing by the IOC at the 1968 Summer and Winter Games was apparently to ensure that all female athletes faced equal competition, such tests have been criticised throughout their history in sport, not only by feminists and critical social philosophers but also by the medical community more widely and by geneticists and endocrinologists (Schweinbenz and Cronk, 2010).

Humiliation remains a powerful component in the mix that makes up gender verification and resonates with the victim status of those who are classified in the under-represented groups which are the target of charitable discourses of social inclusion (Woodward, 2008). Whatever progress might have been made in acknowledging complexity and some of the power relations in play in the making and remaking of sex gender, entrenched attitudes persist. The IAAF may have been more active and more progressive than the IOC and one of the first regulating bodies to address the challenge, but in 2009, they proved one of the least progressive bodies in sport.

Caster Semenya, 800 m Champion Athlete

In August 2009 the Berlin World Athletics Championships were shaken by another controversy. Caster Semenya, an 18-year-old from South Africa, won the 800 metre title by nearly two and a half seconds, finishing in 1:55.45. Only three hours after winning the gold medal, Caster was at the centre of a harsh, very public contestation concerning her gender. A bitterly disappointed Italian runner, Elisa Cusma, who finished sixth, was reported as saying, 'These kinds of people should not run with us. For me, she is not a woman. She's a man' (Kimmel, 2011). It is noteworthy that the rival competitor's use of pronouns reflects the ambiguities of what is so troubling about this dispute, for 'these kind of people' the subject pronoun 'she' is used with both the object 'woman' and 'man'. Cusma was not the only confused commentator on the case, as is evident in the enormous coverage given to the 800 m gold medallist Caster Semenya. She is fast, so fast that other athletes questioned whether she was a woman, leading the IAAF to instigate gender verification tests, albeit in a procedure that, contrary to guidelines, was leaked before the final at the World Athletics Championships in August 2009. The case started badly with the victory of the athlete being so quickly followed by this procedural offence by the IAAF in disclosing information about the tests prior to the results. Perhaps ironically, Caster Semenya did not break the 800 m record of 1:53.28 that had been set by the Czech athlete Jarmila Kratochvila in 1983. Kratochvila too had been subjected to chromosomal sex testing at the Olympics in 1980 on grounds of her strongly muscled shoulders, arms and thighs. There are significant endurances in the experience of women athletes, although the Semenya case achieved considerable significance because of the volubility and visibility of the debate and its condensation of so many diverse factors.

I was fortunate to be asked to comment on the case to a variety of news media, if depressed that many of the media interviews were prefaced by some reference to Semenya's 'masculine' appearance'. For example, in one case the journalist reiterated his views pressing me to agree with his own, repeating, 'Yes, but she looks like a man, doesn't she. You can't say she doesn't. You wouldn't fancy her if you were a man would you', reiterating and reinstating yet again the female male gender dualism and the heterosexual matrix of assumed heterosexuality.

I was interviewed by a number of agencies ranging across Canadian radio stations, including a Toronto-based student station, to the BBC and Sky News and the *London Evening Standard* besides being reported in a range of UK newspapers.

The focus on Caster's visibly corporeal appearance was ubiquitous in each of the interviews, but Sky News was the least directed by these, what appeared to me, prejudiced factors restricted by a rigid sex gender binary. I found this surprising as I would have expected the commercially driven corporation to stress the kind of controversies that might appeal to a mass audience and secure more viewers through populist appeal. Sometimes the profit motive can have democratising side effects through opening up different dimensions of popular appeal. For example, the 2006 men's World Cup in football recruited a wider audience of spectators from previously under-represented ethnic groups, albeit from more affluent South Asian supporters, when tickets became available to a wider constituency that was no longer limited to traditional fans who could prove their club allegiances (Woodward, 2008).

Many interviews sought expert commentary and construed expertise as within the discipline of medical science. Some media agencies, notably those who were most firmly located within a restricted sex gender dualism, seemed disappointed that, in spite of being a professor and a doctor, I was not a medical scientist, or at least a psychologist or psychiatrist, reflecting the popular equation of hard science (any science?) with knowledge and expertise, and social science with opinion. Concomitant with this synergy between expert knowledge and science is the assertion that science has the answers and that not only is there an absolute truth but also science is the route to establishing what that truth is. Science can thus secure certainty and questioning is devalued, as the admission of uncertainty must connote lack of knowledge. Popular understandings of knowledge as refracted in the discursive field of media systems are not based on the need to ask questions in the sense that the philosopher Karl Popper suggested (Popper, 2002, [1959]), nor of Foucault's understanding of knowledge as both regulating and constraining, and enabling and productive (Foucault, 1973a, 1973b, 1977). The media are thus part of the mix of reinstating and creating certainties and truths, where possible based on a binary logic, which may be designed to reassure, but, in itself, opens up gaping lacunae of ignorance. Nor is there anything new about women's bodies being the site of the expression and inscription of ignorance (Irigaray, 1991, 1984, Howson, 2007).

Bodies are shaped by sporting practices and these practices shape sport, but bodies are gendered through the commonalities of flesh and women in sport have to negotiate racialised, heterosexist stereotypes. Caster Semenya's raised levels of testosterone (BBC news, 2009) are also generated by the embodied practices of an elite athlete and may not confirm certainty about a sex gender category. Testosterone level was, however, cited as a major factor in the scientific discourses which dominated media coverage of the debate.

The debate, especially as manifest in media coverage, invoked expert scientific and medical commentary in its path from claims of unfair practice and a body variously described as 'manly' and with a 'strikingly musculature physique' (Daily Mail, 2009) to sympathy for defiant resistance to the humiliation of gender verification testing (Los Angeles Times, 2009) and the claims that this very fast woman must be a man.

Gender testing has a long history in sport, even though compulsory tests were abandoned at the Olympics in 1992. Tests have changed from those based on the embodied features which those classified as experts can perceive to DNA and chromosomal tests and the current, more complex panoply of procedures that include psychological testing. There is some acknowledgement of the complexity of gender identities and the weakness of a distinction based on the categorisation of human beings into two sexes; intersex and a range of different forms of development mean that many people than we imagine do not conform neatly to the clear genetic and physical criteria that the regulatory bodies of sport deploy. Intersex is itself deeply problematic (Kessler, 1998) and the term is disputed (Merck, 2010) although there are strong arguments for the recognition of more than two sexes; as Anne Fausto-Sterling argues there may be at least five (Fausto-Sterling, 2000). What is most telling

cultural shifts and some repositioning in relation to sex gender and a more open approach than that of some more traditional, paternalistic media organisations. The more local press, like the free Evening Standard, for example which is modelled on the search for immediate response for readers and the conflictual drama of the moment, seemed more keen on sexualised hyperbole and the reinstatement of stereotypes and a rehearsal of the polarities of conventional visible difference in a discourse of fixed characteristics of either femininity or masculinity. This version of sex gender also invokes sexuality with this powerful avowal and instance upon heteronormativity. Sporting identities are firmly located within the heterosexual matrix. The femininity that accompanies being a woman is also assumed and asserted to be heterosexual through the embodied practices, comportment, dispositions and visible appearance that confirm it.

Discourses of sex gender have been questioned, as have been the stereotyping of the characteristics of sex and the reiteration of visible difference embedded in a discourse of fixed traits of masculinity on the one hand and femininity on the other. In 2011, when interviewed by an avowedly sympathetic Observer broadsheet journalist, Caster expressed her reluctance at being in the public spotlight and her desire only to be famous for being fast and especially for winning (Kessel, 2011). Even in a newspaper article written by a journalist who deplores the treatment Caster received at the hands of the Western popular press in 2009, it is noted that Caster has grown her hair, has beautiful smooth skin, soft features and wears a tiny bracelet covered with diamante hearts (Kessel, 2011:10), all information of the sort that was largely absent from coverage of men's 100 m world record holder until 2011, Usain Bolt. Sex gender is deeply implicated in experience and situation and it is difficult to extricate the diverse factors through which it is made and to separate sex and gender, but it remains the case that sex gender is more often applied to women than to men.

Sex, gender and sexuality

> Bodies in sport highlight the problem of gender and the interconnections between sex and gender and about how sexuality is incorporated into this mix. Feminist work on intersectionality has highlighted some of the distinctions between sex and sexuality and the need to engage with a critique of sexuality in the operation of power in the making of social divisions. (Taylor et al., 2011)

Debates about difference have often centred upon gender, initially as a discussion of sex and gender, for example, within feminist theory, especially in relation to the problem of bodies and in the context of the hierarchical nature of that relationship when the two are presented as separate concepts. Whilst the mind and the soul might be rated above the body in soul/body, mind/body dualisms, in the sex gender debate, embodied sex has greater weighting as a determinant of gender, for example, in shaping its capacities. Liz Stanley (1984) described the argument as being one between biological essentialism, which prioritises biological, embodied sex as the determinant of femininity or of masculinity, and social constructionism, which focuses on gender as a social, cultural category. The ambivalent relationship between feminist activism and biological arguments about sexuality has led at different moments to a distancing of sexuality from both sex as corporeal and anatomical and gender as social and cultural. Sex was associated with biology which has largely been the subject of IOC gender (the recently preferred term) verification tests and gender with social and cultural practices which might have been seen as the outcome of anatomical sex. Sex and gender have been combined, but there has still been a strong assumption that sex as a biological classification is privileged over gender as covering social attributes, in terms of the certainty it affords in relation to identity. Secondly, where the two have been explicitly disentangled, the influence of sex upon gender has been awarded priority and higher status than any influence gender as a cultural and social construct might have over sex. There is also a normative claim involved in this hierarchy, namely, that sex *should* determine gender. Incorporating flesh into the critique has the advantage of reducing the normative elements of gender.

Sex and gender have also been elided to women's disadvantage, whereby cultural expectations of what was appropriate or possible for women were attributed to some biological law (Oakley, 1972). The notion that women should be relegated to second status, because of anatomical differences from men, in particular, the possession of a uterus, has a long history in sport. The tension between acknowledgement of women's bodies as situations manifesting particularities that require different provision of care and the subordination and devaluing of women justified on such grounds have been confused and in some ways reflects the equality difference debate. Women have been excluded from the embodied practices of sport (Hargreaves, 1994), because of their sex, which was claimed to be generative of dire outcomes such as Aristotle's 'wandering womb' and its contemporary translation into the protection of reproductive capacities. Women have been excluded from some sports, like boxing until 2012, and continue to run shorter distances, play bouts of less duration and comply with different regimes from men in sport, such as playing off different tees in golf or fighting fewer rounds in boxing, on the basis of corporeal difference. Such exclusion is premised upon enfleshed differences. Feminists sought to make a distinction between the biological characteristics of the body, the anatomical body and gender as a cultural construct. More recently the idea of an oppositional distinction between sex and gender has been challenged, most powerfully by postmodernist feminists such as Judith Butler (1990, 1993) and for many the term gender is largely preferred.

This preference is also manifest in the discourse of the regulatory bodies of sport like the IOC. Track and field athletics bodies like the IAAF also use gender, perhaps reflecting cultural change but also possibly to mask the oversimplification of the binary logic of sex testing which as gender verification appears to combine the certainties of science with social and cultural factors. Gender has, however, achieved a theoretical and conceptual hegemony and is now ubiquitous with sex being relegated to a crude biology, rather than being the main descriptor, determinant and explanation of difference between female and male athletes.

Sex too is discursively constructed (Butler, 1993). The meaning of 'sex' is strongly mediated by cultural understandings that, it is argued, make it impossible to differentiate between sex and gender and it is increasingly recognised that they are mutually constitutive. The use of gender permits an acknowledgement of this powerful cultural and social mediation (see Shildrick and Price, 1999). Gender may provide a satisfying theoretical account of difference which fails, however, to accommodate the everyday experience of sex and lived contradictions of sex. The contradictions and ambivalences are all too evident in cases like that of Caster Semenya, and Merck argues that experience is distorted by the social insistence upon and persistence of the dichotomous categories of female and male (Merck, 2010). Just as the feminist writer Shulamith Firestone claimed over 40 years ago, liberation for women will never be possible until not only male privilege but also the sex distinction itself is eliminated (Firestone 1970). There are strengths in this argument except it remains largely premised upon the philosophical categories of sex and its corporeality, rather than the empirical experience which combines lived experience and situatedness with the enfleshed actualities of the body as a situation.

Stella Sandford argues for a trans-disciplinary conceptualisation of sex which can be critical of the routines of the everyday, which has some purchase in the field of sport, even though Sandford's own argument is not applied to this empirical field. Sport is characterised by routine and everyday practice as well as the spectacular moments of public display (Woodward, 2009). Rather than being the last bastion of entrenched binaries, sport might offer a site for the reinstatement of sex as a category in order to challenge the rigidity and inflexibility of an ontology in which sex is said not to exist and sex is dismissed as a discursive fiction. Sport also offers a means of engaging with the empirical everyday of enfleshed experience.

Toril Moi suggests the 'lived body' as an alternative to the categories of sex and gender, (Moi, 1999, de Beauvoir (1989). This concept provides a non-essentialist synthesis of corporeality by situating the physical body and its experiences in the social world around it. The embodied self can initiate action in different situations which can thus be differentiated. Bodies do exist out of time and place (the exceptionality of "out of body" experiences notwithstanding). Even in the transcendence of sporting experiences that are 'in the zone' (Csikzentimihalyi 1975, Rinehart and Sydnor, 2010, 2003), the material body is still temporally and spatially located. The body is always located in a given environment so that, as a 'situation' incorporating the physical facts of its materiality, such as size, age, health, reproductive capacity, skin, hair and the social context, Moi's 'lived body' is not biologistic, that is, it is not reducible to its corporeal parts, subject only to general laws of physiology and divided into two categories of gender. This eliminates the constraints of other binaries too, such as nature/culture; the body is always part of culture, inculcated with habits, acting according to social and cultural rules, but retains the possibilities of addressing what is enfleshed (Woodward, 2009).

> To consider the body as a situation...is to consider both the fact of being a specific kind of body and the meaning that concrete body has for the situated individual. This is not the equivalent of either sex or gender. The same is true of "lived experience" which encompasses our experience of all kinds of situations (race, class, nationality etc.) and is a far more wide-ranging concept than the highly psychologizing concept of gender identity. (Moi, 1999: 81)

The idea of the 'lived body' provides one route for addressing difference without reductionism and for the exploration the othering that arises from the marginalisation that accompanies difference. However, as Iris Marion Young (2005) points out, although the lived body avoids the binary logic of sex/gender, it may pay insufficient attention to the structural constraints which shape experience. Consequently, she argues for the retention of the concept of gender.

Sandford traces the genesis of sex through its philosophical and empirical narratives and argues that the recent preference for gender, some of which derives from the sex gender distinction that is assumed to have been made in de Beauvoir's *Second Sex* (1989 [1949]), is largely based upon a misunderstanding. Sandford suggests the mistaken idea that de Beauvoir is separating sex as biological from gender as cultural is a misrepresentation of de Beauvoir's exposition of women as the second sex arises from a problem in translation, especially from French to English. The issue is one of how de Beauvoir has been read in the anglophone world and because of the endurance of these interpretations which are part of a wider intellectual movement, it seems unlikely that the more recent translation of the entire original text of the *Second Sex* (2010) makes a great deal of difference to this aspect of the debate.

In French *sexe* signifies the sexual life and sex and sexual difference are synonymous. The sexual life includes sexuality and its expressions. In English, sex and sexual difference refer to the material reality of the human (Sandford, 2011). This is more than a matter of language, although translation explains some of the misunderstandings.

The everyday difference between women and men is probably more marked in sport than in many other areas of life. Sexual difference is evident in all aspects of sport and sex informs the segregated practices and regulations of sport as a set of social relations which enable the recognition of women and men in a hierarchical relation of inequality. Thus sex is material (Delphy, 1993[1992]).

Embodied difference is not only a constituent of subjectivity and the formation of the self and part of the explanatory framework through which gendered identities can be understood, it is also part of the sexual division of labour and requires the possibility of collective action, for example, in challenging social exclusion and its embodied consequences.

The possibility of collective action is, however, further subverted by Butler's assertion that the category 'woman' is itself unsustainable and only serves to limit feminist projects. The feminist subject is generated by its representation. Gender identity is unstable because it relies upon performativity which involves the repetition through acts and gestures. Thus Butler has challenged the idea that gender is predicated upon sex; sex, gender and desire are all effects, that is, none of them are natural or essential. This has some purchase in an interrogation of the performativity of heteronormativity in sport although it is problematic in the political project of feminism if there is no category of "women", not even one based on a strategic essentialism as advocated by Gayatri Spivak (1988). It is also problematic because material, empirical, enfleshed sex is absent. This raises some important issues for theorising difference and sex gender. On the one hand, gender seems to offer the possibility of change that holding on to the corporeality of sex cannot deliver. Gender has thus been enthusiastically embraced by feminists and activists. On the other hand, gender, especially as deployed by the regulatory bodies of sport like the IOC and the IAAF, merely opens up new disciplinary regimes of regulation that are still haunted, or perhaps more emphatically underpinned, by the rigidity of objectivism that accompanied traditional binary logic.

Irigaray's politics of difference has been recuperated to address gender within a range of theoretical positions including the Deleuzian (Braidotti. 2002). Irigaray's earlier work is in dialogue with and in opposition to Lacanian psychoanalysis in asserting a non-essentialist version of difference and presenting a challenge to the patriarchal claims of the Oedipal complex and the Law of the Father, which like de Beauvoir encompasses sex and sexual difference. Contrary to Lacan and to Freudian universalism, Irigaray argues that Western culture rests on the death of the mother and that sexual difference is both embodied in its specificities and cultural in its manifestations and impact. Irigaray demonstrates the absence of the female pre-Oedipal imaginary and of representations of the mother–daughter relationship and of the mother in Western thought, which offers a dynamic and powerful assertion of difference and of the female imaginary deriving from female corporeality ((Irigaray, 1991, 1985). Irigaray transforms the relationship between bodies and culture in a politics of difference that, although sport was never part of her empirical brief, has enormous resonance with the politics of sex gender as played out in sport through bodies and discursive regimes, regulatory bodies and bodies of regulation.

Women and especially the mother–daughter relationship is absent from much of Western culture, for example, in psychoanalysis that draws on Classical mythology for its tropes and metaphors and in the regimes of truth which circulate in the field of heroic narratives of the state, public life and the military. Such absences are also startling in sport where so many heroic legends are based on male kinship networks and the father–son relationship (Woodward, 2006) and rarely that of mother and daughter. Motherhood maybe be an absent presence (Woodward, 1997) or tied up with the mechanisms of control of women's sexuality and reproductive capacities, for example, where participation in competitive sport might be construed as dangerous and deleterious to women's capacity for childbearing.

Conclusion: the case for flesh

The sex gender binary of female and male is deeply embedded in discussion of truth and authenticity and invokes a certainty and authenticity which scientific verification principles might guarantee. Science is the resource for guidance with the objectivism to inform a series of tests which could bestow certainty. The binary logic of the system posits two bounded categories of sex based upon genetic, anatomical criteria, which if correctly applied following prescribed procedures could determine to which sex a person belongs. Sex, however, is too messy even in sport to be susceptible to the application of simple criteria of assessment, or even the increasingly complex criteria which have been developed in gender verification tests. A proliferation of categories of expertise or of sex gender does not in itself address fluidity or break down boundaries; more expert witnesses may merely create more boundaries. Sex gender seems to defy regulatory mechanisms designed to fit people neatly into pre-given sexes and the criteria that have been developed are not fit for purpose and are addressing the wrong questions in seeking medical, scientific certainties.

It is not only a matter of people deciding for themselves what sex they are, sex is enfleshed and lived and the sexed self is situated within a gendered social world where sex matters. Empirically, the majority of people live their lives as female or male and there are enfleshed differences which contribute to the classificatory system which is in place and has genealogies and archaeology (Foucault, 1974, 1988a, 1988b).

Flesh is implicated in sex gender and how it is understood, represented and experienced. The concept of being enfleshed offers a way of acknowledging and embracing commonalities among people, as well, of course, as between humans and non-humans, whether in relationships between species or between animate and inanimate matter (Haraway, 2003); for example, in the case of disabled athletes and the use of protheses, other forms of matter can substitute for and act as flesh. Flesh is less bounded than the body and affords more materiality and connectiveness through the capacities of flesh to encompass diversity. The separation of mind and body embedded in Cartesian dualism is not the only issue at stake in engaging with corporeality and the materiality of bodies.

There is some confusion between philosophical and empirical categories of sex gender which could be clarified by exploring some of the specificities of lived experiences and the plasticity of flesh, by combining flesh and experience, perception of self with the perception of others and of situating enfleshed selves within the social world.

Material bodies are the target of sporting practice and the subjects of sporting success and celebration but they are also troubling and troubled by the gender binary which underpins all sporting practice. There are anatomical, corporeal differences between women and men as well as cultural differences. Whilst these may be recognised by a feminist politics of difference, however, it is often only particular differences that become the focus of attention within sport. Social construction can overemphasise the plasticity of bodies and by concentrating upon the body as socially inscribed may miss the inequalities that are at play. Sex rather than gender may offer more purchase for embracing difference whilst highlighting sources of inequality and the material operation of power. Sex has to acknowledge the potential of transformation through embodied practices and their intersection with the materialities which include culture class, race, ethnicity and the technologies through which changes take place.

Gender is also tied up with compulsory heterosexuality, and although sex and sexuality are not synonymous, there are points of connection and synergies which are productive in focusing upon sex as a key concept in explaining inequalities and women's experience of sport and its practices.

The IOC and other sports bodies were so alarmed at the plasticity of flesh and the transformations in women's bodies through elite sport that the tests could have been seen as offering reassurance that heterosexual normativity was secure and that it could be secured. Even into the twenty-first century, as the case of Caster Semenya shows, for a woman to challenge patriarchal norms and the gendered sexual attractiveness of the heterosexual matrix is much too subversive to be tolerated. A woman athlete who as an enfleshed being has the capacity for speed, does not receive the acclaim of male elite athletes; she is suspect because her performance challenges the hegemony of masculinity in sport and because subversion of the rigidity of the sex gender binary is too troubling and unsettling as it defies the certitudes of truth and the reliability of verification. Men are subject to testing too of course but the rigours of science and technology are applied in cases of disabled athletes or when performance enhancement is involved.

Although the introduction of gender verification testing at the Olympics was intended to prevent men from competing as women, such tests also serve to reinstate patriarchy, ethnocentricity, normative heterosexuality and nationalism. It is noteworthy that the tests were called gender rather than sex verification. It is contradictory given the scientific, objectivist approach taken by the regulatory bodies of sport, like the IOC, that the organising body should have opted for the more culturally inflected term, rather than a more biological version of the sex. The aim may have been to create a more comprehensive version of proof which took on board the cultural and social and psychological dimensions of being female or male which gender was seen as more likely than sex to deliver. The cultural practices of athletes and their visible appearance certainly play a large part in decisions about who was to be tested; a masculine comportment and outward appearance suggests the need for proof that this person is a woman and not a man. Science and technoscience generate as many, if not more, uncertainties as they purport to clarify in the regimes of truth that encompass and recreate sex gender.

The discussion in this chapter demonstrates the centrality of sex gender in sport as one of the axes of power which intersects with other axes of power through which social relations and inequalities are forged and identifications made by enfleshed selves. Sex gender is also part of the assemblages of collectivities in which identifications are made, including the national and the transnational which are taken up in the next chapter. Sex connects to other materialities such as wealth and poverty, race and place. The example of Caster Semenya's experience highlights the centrality of racialisation, which is spatially and temporally inflected, in these debates about gender verification, where science meets sex, race and ethical judgements. The processes and points of connection and disconnection are spatially located, which is further explored in relation to nation, diaspora and transnational identifications in the next chapter.

4
Nations, Host Cities and Opportunities

Inequalities between nations are manifest in the systems of engagement in the Olympics and in sporting outcomes – success or failure in the binary language of sporting competition. Economic and financial capital are major contributors to the possibilities and achievements of sporting success, but cultural, social and physical enfleshed capital are also at play. These inequities are also evident in competing arguments about the processes of bidding for the Games and the politics and economics of the city (Gold and Gold, 2007, Guttmann, 2002, Jennings, 1996, 2000, Lenskyj, 2000, Preuss, 2002, 2008, Sugden and Tomlinson, 2011) and in the diverse ways in which hosting a mega sporting event mobilises space. The topologies and topographies of Olympic cities demonstrate the relational dimensions of inequalities in a number of different systems and processes which include the relationships between places, objects and people and the relational dimensions of inequalities in a number of different systems, including the economic. The contours of the topological encompass space, materialities, time, power, affect and change in each of which sex gender is deeply implicated, and provide a means of looking at coherence and continuity as well as instabilities. For example, the narrative of change in the development of the Games and the way power operates is not even, or linear, in its trajectory. It is, however, necessary to address stabilities and endurances as well as change and disruption to see the persistence of inequalities, such as those implicated in patriarchy and racism.

Hosting the Games provides employment opportunities and the potential for a vastly enhanced infrastructure, as well as for creating enormous debts through the expanding demands for finance. The history of host cities also raises questions of corruption in the history of the Games (Guttmann, 1984, 2002, Jennings, 1992, 1996, 2000,

Lenskyj, 2000, Preuss, 2002). This chapter presents an evaluation of these contradictions and tensions within the context of debates about social inclusion, equalities and inequalities and the different power systems which intersect in the re-production of inequalities which operate at different levels including transnationally and nationally.

The Olympics are closely tied to national identifications (Hill, 2002, Guttmann, 2002) through the processes of social inclusion and the participation and success of national teams and through the kudos that can go with hosting the Games. Spatial identifications are central to the Games but these operate in complex ways at the Olympics; medals are awarded to individuals as representatives of nations, but early versions of amateurism and national identities have long been abandoned in the Olympics as in the rest of global and national sport although there are traces, one of which is present in the case of football in 2012, when a G.B. British team was proposed rather than separate national teams from each of the nations which makes up Britain. This chapter maps some of the historical changes that have taken place in the Games in modern times against a background of reframing the nation at other sporting sites. The chapter uses the example of football, as a sport which is not as central to the Games as athletics, to explore how national identifications are changing and how the Games can accommodate these changes in a sport that is increasingly popular among women, but dominated in the public arena by the men's game (Caudwell, 2007, Goldblatt, 2006, Hargreaves, 2002, 2006).

Bidding for the Games: cities and processes

Bidding to host the Olympics is itself an industry, a massive accumulation of systems and processes that are implicated in the endeavour to secure success, albeit at considerable cost. The mechanisms and apparatuses of bidding to host the Olympics offer some insight into the iterative practices that assemble the connections between nations, systems of governance, enfleshed sporting practices and regulatory bodies, sponsorship and economics.

Although the focus on the host city suggests a local focus, central government support of all kinds has to be very substantial; the city is not only cosmopolitan and transnational, it is global and global/local. There are multiple axes of power which intersect in the processes through which decisions are made. It is, however, possible to identify particular operations of power, notably the mechanisms of commercial interests and sponsorship and the ways in which they draw in the involvement of nation states and the regulatory apparatuses of global sport, including those of the Games.

The Olympics are not only central to any history of global sport (Sugden and Tomlinson, 2011), they are also central to any under- standing of globalised modernity or postmodernity. As Maurice Roche has argued, the complex processes of the Olympics involve intercon- necting elites and combine the interests of political and economic elites and professionals from the increasingly supranational cultural indus- tries (Roche, 2000). The bidding process for London 2012 featured celebrities who occupy places in different elite systems and networks, embodied particularly effectively in the popular celebrity figure of David Beckham, former England and Manchester United men's football captain, more recently of LA Galaxy, partner of Victoria Beckham and national hero. These connections and the differential weighting of the operations of power are evidently present in the processes of bidding for the Games as well as hosting them.

As is evident in the discussion so far in this book, the Games have been characterised by increasing levels of bureaucracy and regula- tory mechanisms, many of which are implicated in attempts to secure cohesion, equity and democracy. One of these bureaucratic systems which involves prospective Olympic cities is the candidature file which is the official marketing bid document, in recent years running to several volumes, submitted by shortlisted candidate cities to the IOC. It is prepared by the bidding organisation to set out the case for their particular city (Warde, 2007). The file is assessed by technical adjudi- cators who may reject unsatisfactory bids, and forms the basis for the final voting by IOC members. At its core are technical details about the projected budget and how the various sports events and participants are to be accommodated comfortably and securely. Although much of the file is very specific, it also has to display the city's capacity to host a large international event successfully. Logistical considerations about how the movement of people will be handled involves broader-scale matters such as transport. The report also includes a general volume or section that markets the city and its wider setting. This part of the submission is structured to showcase the city's attractiveness and openness in a way that also tries to communicate a more general sense of a wide and deep local commitment to sports and to hosting a successful Olympics (Warde, 2007), thus framing the Games as a democratic regime.

London's 2012 bid was powerfully configured around claims of multi-culturalism and social inclusion by celebrating the multi-ethnic community of the United Kingdom (somewhat ironically as the day after the Games were awarded to London was the day of the terrorist attack targeting London's transport system, 7/7), as well as more routine matters such as the logistics of transport networks and accommodation.

Building the wide and deep commitment within the city and the nation involves a great deal of public and media relations work by the group initiating the bid to win support from newspapers, television and radio. Media executives, editors, journalists, business leaders, politicians and other prominent figures have to be drawn in to make material contributions through marketing strategies such as advertising locally and through the production of glossy corporate brochures. LOCOG was particularly effective in utilising such means, however modest the claims of Beckham and the London red double decker bus at the hand-over event after Beijing in 2008 (Sugden and Tomlinson 2011).

Provided they can be convinced that the candidature will be competently advanced, many corporations and companies associated with a bidding city are likely to see benefits in the wider exposure that will result, even if the bid eventually is unsuccessful. For example, despite their city's humiliating defeat in consecutive final IOC voting to decide the locations of the 1996 and 2000 Games, much of Manchester's business community would have welcomed a third bid to host the Summer Olympics. It was this support which was translated into what became the city's successful bid to host the 2002 Commonwealth Games.

Engagement with the community, locally and more widely, is also required to win the backing of key individuals and gain at least the semblance of widespread popular support. Any local organisations or individuals in sporting networks, especially Olympic sporting networks, are likely to be harnessed in some way to the bid, For example, London 2012 secured David Beckham and, especially Sebastian Coe, now Lord Coe, the 800 and 1,500 metre medallist, elite athlete and Conservative politician to so successfully lead the London bid for 2012. Typically the bidding organisation sponsors local sports and cultural events to raise awareness and is often involved in the distribution of personal marketing items such as tee shirts, flags, balloons, pens and key-rings that bear its logo.

The logo itself forms a key identifier for the bidding campaign, usually embracing a combination of Olympic imagery with various signifiers of the bidding city. Another promotional device that has occasionally been used at this stage has been the Olympic mascot. In most cases mascots have appeared after the award of the Games, the best known being Moscow's 1980 bear cub mascot, Misha. An exception was Barcelona's bid team who launched a competition to design a mascot to build youth involvement (COOB, 1992). The 2012 logo was controversial on all counts, including its aesthetic and cultural impact and significance, which many felt were incomprehensible; people got used to it through the familiarisation of reiteration in its routine exposure which made it accepted and acceptable.

Candidature files also constitute and reproduce figures through portraits and brief statements of support from key individuals from business and the community, along with figures from politics and government and those with an international profile so that the bidding organisation can ensure that it can meet, and impress its case on, anyone likely to be able to advance the bid and affect its success.

Until 2002, a key marketing moment was when the predominantly male IOC delegates exercised their rights to inspect would-be host cities at an extraordinarily demanding period for bidding teams. Delegates were reputedly entertained in a manner that approached the care lavished on official visits by leading heads of state (Warde, 2007) and suggest some of the practices whereby hegemonic masculinity is reiterated. Sydney, for example, ensured that all traffic lights encountered by visiting IOC groups were changed to green on their approach, to avoid delays or any sense of traffic congestion (McGeoch and Korporaal, 1994).

The ostensible purpose of these visits was to show delegates the city, its sporting credentials and its capacity to stage the world's biggest sporting event. There were parties in the homes of leading members of the bidding team or other prominent citizens of the host city all informed by appropriate sensitivity to language and cultural affinities, underlining the openness of the city to visitors from all parts of the world.

Such display might have been too visible and the Olympic Movement began to prohibit the most extravagant forms of hospitality by bidding cities in 1991 to 1992, although it was not until 1998 that sufficient evidence emerged to cause the practice to be comprehensively changed (Jennings and Sambrook, 2000, Miller, 2003). The occasion was the IOC delegate visit prior to the selection of the location for the 2002 Winter Olympics, which was hosted by Salt Lake City. In spite of the city's reputation for religious adherence and morality, it was the site of large-scale bribery with several delegates and their families allegedly bribed with holidays, medical treatment and other favours. When these allegations from a Swiss IOC member began to circulate that there was an IOC investigation which resulted in the resignation of three delegates, ten replaced, ten warned and only two exonerated. Following this scandal, delegate visits were banned by the IOC. Instead, it has strengthened the demands for technical and financial information from bidding cities, to provide a more evidence-based rationale for decisions. From the choice of London for the 2012 Summer Games, this still did not seem to have given primacy to the candidature file, although it did produce extensive promotional material from sponsors.

The economics of hosting

For most of the early decades of the Modern Olympic Games, the economics of the IOC and the Games were both fragile and under-developed. Sponsorship was, nonetheless, central from the very beginning. The 1896 Greek Olympics were only made possible by the gift of over a million Greek drachmas from businessman George Averoff and proceeds from the sale of souvenir stamps and coins. The 1900 and 1904 Olympics have no recorded accounts as both were subsumed into the World's Trades Fairs being held in Paris and St Louis, but neither made any profit, all of which conformed to de Coubertin's ideological position on amateurism and the Olympic Movement. The 1908 Games in London were less disorganised, with the British government paying for the new Shepherd's Bush stadium. Similar publicly funded stadium construction was carried out at Stockholm 1912 with a new athletics venue and Antwerp 1920 where a new aquatics centre was constructed. Paris 1924 cost approximately 10 million francs, but took only just over half of that in receipts. Amsterdam 1928 was the most successful early Olympics, in terms of balance sheets.. With half of the £1.2 million cost underwritten by the Dutch government, the Games as a whole appear to have broken even (Guttmann, 2002).

The Berlin Olympics of 1936 generated new precedents economically, politically and ideologically. Estimates suggest a total budget of US$330 million and a programme of urban redevelopment and venue construction then unparalleled. Berlin in 1936 presents not only a well-resourced spectacle and a demonstration of considerable financial investment, but also political and ideological investment on a massive and extreme scale. The 1936 Games is most well known as Hitler's Olympics, which highlights the extremities of this version of German nationalism and the constraints of Nazi political ideologies. The 1940 Tokyo Olympics, cancelled because of the war, however, had planned a level of expenditure that was at least equal to that of 1936, London 1948 broke the pattern with its postwar austerity budget with an athlete's village, housed in old Royal Air Force (RAF) barracks and both Helsinki

1952 and Melbourne 1956 were understated and bore no resemblance to the mega spectacles that emerged later in the twentieth century. The 1948 Games was the austerity Olympics. However, by the late 1950s the costs of even these relatively modest Olympics were steadily rising as the number of athletes, sports and sporting facilities increased. The cultural capital and social capital generated by the Olympics were productive in facilitating such expansion. The arrival of global media and the world's TV cameras and an ever-bigger press contingent made new and additional demands, which also created the ever-growing phenomenon of the Games.

The Olympics were sustained over the next 12 years by hosts who were all caught up in the interconnections between political self-interest and securing financial resources. The Olympics have been characterised by the tensions between political narratives and those of economics (Preuss, 2004) and points of connection and disjunction between them. Rome 1960, Tokyo 1964 and Munich 1972 marked the return of the defeated Axis powers to the inner circle of the international community. Mexico City 1968 served as a vast public announcement by the ancient regime in Mexico that its brand of political authoritarianism and state capitalism had succeeded. There is a long history not only of the Games being affected by economic and political contingencies, not the least of which was World War II, but also of it always operating in relation to those circumstances.

Montreal was implicated in the generation of political affects, as the hub of French-speaking Canada in an era of massive constitutional, cultural and linguistic upheaval. The 1976 Montreal Olympics were however, a financial disaster, with gigantic cost overruns which the taxpayers of Montreal were compelled to finance. Yet again there was a mismatch between expectation and resource recovery, but this was on a grand scale. The financial crisis of the Montreal Olympics was so serious that other nations were deterred from attempting to stage the event, and Los Angeles was the sole bidder for the 1984 Games. Moscow was only able to support the burden of the 1980 Games with the concentrated resources of the highest levels of the Soviet state behind it. In this case it was the state rather than the market.

Beijing n 2008 was situated in a different global political world, but the resources of the state were again relied upon to deliver a new political and cultural message, one of which was designed to promote China's global markets and political networks as well as to demonstrate national competences and success. By the twenty-first century the relationship between state and market was much more complicated and messy.

Conflicting discourses

In the discursive regimes of hosting and financing the Games there has always been at least a stated reluctance to engage with market forces and capture commercial support because this might jeopardise Olympic ideals. Commerce and sponsorship were conspicuously absent at the first Olympics after the Second World War. Although the then president of the IOC, Avery Brundage, a US business man with right-wing political affiliations, vehemently opposed moves to develop the Games on a more commercial basis. Even when he retired, at the Munich Olympics in 1972, Brundage was declaring that the IOC 'should have nothing to do with money' (Barney et al., 2002: 100) and argued that arguments over the distribution of money were destructive, threatening to 'fracture the Olympic Movement' (ibid: 275). These tensions had been evident from the start of the modern Olympics. De Coubertin, speaking at the University of Lausanne in 1928, opposed the escalation of construction of stadiums stating that 'all stadiums built in recent years are the result of local and, too often, commercial interests, not Olympic interests at all' (de Coubertin, 2000:184). What has been read into this is the overt idealism of the founder of the Modern Games as a man who opposed athletics as display and a show, implying that commercially based large-scale events would corrupt the amateur spirit of the Olympics; 'these over-sized showcases are the source of the corruption at the root of the evil' (ibid: 184). De Coubertin's acclaimed idealism might have been construed as naïve optimism, although it is also historically and discursively situated as one of the regulatory mechanisms at play in the nineteenth and early twentieth century (Foucault, 1981, 1988a, 1988b), which also gained some purchase in the field of sport, especially in relation to the Olympics. The disavowal of commercialism, made explicit in de Coubertin's statements, is also part of a nineteenth-century moral and religious regime of truth which located commerce and morality as contradictory.

Amateurism is a male version of white, middle-class female morality as embodied in the idea of the Victorian poet Coventry Patmore's 'Angel in the House' who, as the model of moral femininity, is the guardian of morality in the Victorian household, responsible for the excesses of the pursuit of profit by men in the public arena of capitalist endeavour. The separation of commerce and trade from morality and high mindedness was familiar rhetoric within the discursive regimes of the bourgeoisie. In the case of masculinity the discursive field of play is commerce where greed must be regulated and policed. Femininity carried the responsibility for controlling, moderating and containing male sexuality and its excesses, largely through being kept in ignorance, but, nevertheless, within a framework of morality.

The contradictions were inevitable, because the project would have to attract sponsors, although in an age before the globalised visibility of television the Olympics were not a global product. There had been some early advertising, for example, of Parisian sporting equipment in 1901 and Benedictine brandy in October 1902 in the publication *The Olympic Review*, the official bulletin of the Olympics,(Barney et al., 2002). By 1924 in Paris the stadium was bedecked with advertisements for Ovalmaltine, Dubonnet, Cinzano and many other commercial products (ibid.). Rather than explaining the dangers as the IOC being naïve, the committee was caught up in changing times and the movement of different forces which created new demands and new possibilities which were, nonetheless, difficult to reconcile with some of the founding principles of the Olympics. Barney et al. describe in some detail the difficulties in these processes and the possibilities of exploitation by the forces of profit and commerce when set in relation to the principles of amateurism (Barney et al. 2002).

These examples illustrate how the economics of the modern Olympics had again been transformed through different relationships and connections and through discursive tensions which materialise at different points, temporally and spatially: Firstly, these materialisations are effected by global commercialisation and, secondly, by an increasing emphasis on the wider, long-term economic benefits of holding the Games, rather than a simple immediate profit-and-loss account. The economics of the Games, for example, as manifest n the bidding process, are always connected to other political and cultural aspects of the operation of power. Over the last 25 years, the debate has been framed by the influence of commercialism and the need to balance Olympic ideals with economic and commercial factors but always in some relationship to the state and to the apparatus and ideologies of governance. The interconnections between these factors underpin the bidding processes that shape the mechanism that inform the bidding by host cities. They are part of the assemblages of synergies and dissonances which collide and coincide rather than two rigidly opposing views.

Change and continuity

One of the most heavily weighted axes of power which shapes change and reinstates endurances, is the economic. Economic structures and forces connect to social, political and cultural materialities. Change is not regular or routine but the economics of the Olympics were transformed in two key ways. Firstly, under Juan Antonio Samaranch, its seventh president between 1980 and 2001, the IOC embraced the model of mega-event sponsorship pioneered by Fédération Internationale de Football Association (FIFA) in the selling of the men's football World Cup. There are several points of connection between FIFA and the IOC, not least in the bidding for the 2018 and 2022 men's competitions, which were won by Russia for 2018 and Qatar fir for 2022, amid accusations of corruption and bribery that resonated with earlier stories of corruption at the IOC. The origins of these links might be more benign; beginning with the 1982 tournament, FIFA sold expensive but exclusive sponsorship deals to the biggest transnational companies in return for controlled and immense television coverage. In turn, the value of TV rights was steadily pushed upwards, massively accelerated by the arrival of new forms of television technology and the Internet in the 1990s (Sugden and Tomlinson, 2011).

The second key event was the organisation of the 1984 Los Angeles Olympics, which actually generated a considerable financial surplus (Ueberroth *et al.*, 1985). Los Angeles extracted huge profits from the sale of television rights, getting US$225 million out of ABC and another US$112 from Japan alone. Value was also extracted from sponsors by restricting their numbers. Whereas the Winter Olympics in Lake Placid had received US$9 million from 381 sponsors, Los Angeles received US$130 million from just 30. Expenditure was trimmed to the minimum. Corporate America undertook much of the stadium work; Southland Corp built the Velodrome and Atlantic Richfield renovated the Coliseum. In a new form of product placement, General Motors provided official cars and Xerox, the organisation's copiers. New and carefully policed licences were created for product categories giving, for example, official Olympic hamburgers and chocolate bars (ibid.).

Held during the Reagan administration which was marked by a particular confluence of ultraliberal economics and ultraconservative foreign policy, the LA Olympics could be construed as an all-American triumph. This was national identity conflated with neo-liberal democracy defined in opposition to Soviet Communism. In the absence of the USSR, who had repaid the Americans for their boycott of Moscow 1980, the United States was the dominant force at the Olympics, producing wall-to-wall domestic TV coverage with fantastical advertising revenue – ABC made a US$435 million profit on the deal and the hosts achieved a US$200 million profit. Since the 1980s, it has become possible for OCOGs to be confident that they would be able to host the Games and produce a surplus of revenues over operating costs (Preuss, 2004). However, this has not been a straightforward economic success story and costs of staging the Games remain extraordinarily high. There are losses as well as gains, and although OCOGs may be more confident, host cities are not.

The Olympics have, nonetheless, become an enormously high-profile phenomenon that attracts the world's most prominent cities to bid for the privilege of hosting the Games, especially the Summer Games. It is not surprising that the nation is frequently subordinated to and subsumed by commercial interests, although in the case of the United States they seem to have elided, with free markets, global capital and the pursuit of profit being the defining features of national identity; freedom is market liberalism. Beijing in 2008 opened up new possibilities for reconfiguring national identity through acknowledging the specificities of Chinese cultures and histories at a point of engagement with global market and economic forces and, in particular a global economy ready to embrace Chinese markets more fully.

The history of bidding for the Games does not present a linear narrative, although the processes that are implicated have followed a trajectory that has become increasingly complex. The Games themselves have continued to include an ever-growing line-up of events, participants, media coverage and media personnel with a global audience. Early Games after Athens in 1896 were linked to trade shows which celebrated international trade markets. The Games were not particularly high profile or even successful cultural events, for example, in Paris in 1904, although the efficient management of the AAA and the newly formed British Olympic Association (BOA) succeeded in utilising the Franco -British Exhibition in London that year to attract spectators to the marathon on the final day where the crowd reached 90,000 (Sugden and Tomlinson, 2011). The longer story is one marked by disconnections as well as synergies but from the start of the Modern Games, links with trade have played a part in securing success for some cities and some nations over others. Most bids have negotiated a middle ground between public and private spheres but there have been cases where the impetus has been predominantly private. This has been especially so in the United States with Los Angeles, which has hosted the Games twice (1932 and 1984) and seven other shortlisted bids building its case more completely than that of any other large American metropolitan city on promotional puff. Los Angeles paved the way for the resurgence in competition to stage both the Summer and Winter Olympic Games from the 1990s. Subsequent Games have not been quite so completely privatised in their approach (Warde, 2007), although as Sebastian Coe said of the London bid for 2012, someone has to pay for the Games and, however important the role of national governments, there has to be private-sector sponsorship (Coe Torch 2011). LOCOG acknowledged this. Funding for the Organising Committee comes mainly from the private sector. A total of £2 billion will be raised from sources including sponsorship, broadcasting rights and selling merchandise (LOCOG, 2011).

Hosting the Games: pros and cons

Cities and nations bid for the Games because there is prestige and kudos attached to hosting the biggest show in town but, as has been demonstrated above, bidding and hosting incorporates a diverse accommodation of materialities which make up the success or failure that are implicated and promised in the process.

Potential host cities have to demonstrate a reliable infrastructure; they must have realistic plans for building stadiums, housing for athletes and officials and transport systems. Infrastructure promises may create a good bid but costs notoriously and inevitably rise and delivery is central to the project, but this element of a coherent bid depends on both resource and the credibility of the potential host city as a key player.

Decisions are contingent as well as political and timing and politics work together. Historical specificities are central to success which is contingent upon power geometries and political and cultural forces. In 1964, the Tokyo Olympic Games were the first to be held outside Europe or former European-populated colony, such as America or Australia. Since then, the Olympics have rotated around the world, making it unlikely that a European city would get the Games immediately after another European city or an American city after another American host. Democratisation and social and political inclusion generate the transnational dimensions of the Games.

Every Olympic bid has to formulate a convincing narrative about what the Olympics are going to mean to the host city, the host country and the IOC. Sydney's bid focused on featuring claims to having the distinction of being the 'greenest Games ever'. This too was temporally specific and contingent upon the circulation of ecological discourses within the wider social and cultural terrain and became politically acceptable. At a moment when environmental concerns were globally mainstreaming, it allowed the Olympic Movement to acquire some green credentials.

Beijing 2008, by contrast, was sold and accepted as the centrepiece of China's great modernisation coming-out parade also configured within the possibilities of global capital and its market potential.

Host cities do not operate in a vacuum. Bids must also have absolutely unequivocal backing of host governments at every level, and if there is an opposition, from the opposition too. The city is the spatial focus but the wider state is implicated at every point. Popular support too has to fit into to the process, or at least the acceptance and public perception and expression of consent. Winning over the populace and creating a public may involve manufacturing consent. The IOC claims that the bids are more than bureaucratically generated elite projects, although in the contemporary world this is a very accurate description. They also like to see considerable, mobilised, if manufactured, support from host cities' and countries' publics. Publics are made and make the process of bidding and are called into being through the systems that make up the bidding so that collective support is caught up in the this stage of the Games too.

There are, of course, other currencies of less commendable influence in the IOC. Histories of the bidding process demonstrate the well-known and well-established practice of lavish gift giving, through receptions, holidays, donations to governments and charities, and, if necessary, even cash to IOC members in order to help secure votes towards winning a bid. The work of British journalist Andrew Jennings was instrumental in uncovering this in the 1990s, a process that culminated in the exposure of the large-scale corruption involved in Salt Lake City's bid for the 2002 Winter Olympics (Jennings, 1996, 2000). The possibilities for corruption are great because the stakes and the cost are so high.

While Los Angeles 1984 appeared to change fundamentally the economics of the Olympics, its successors have yet to repeat its significant financial achievement. Atlanta 1996 just about broke even. Both Seoul and Barcelona, buoyed by the new flows of income into the Olympic Games, made small profits on the Games themselves, but only because gigantic levels of public spending were effectively written off the balance sheets; around US$3 billion in Korea and US$5 billion in Spain. Sydney and Athens both lost money and the costs and benefits of Beijing are less easy to ascertain although the vast expenditure might suggest the inevitability of a significant financial loss but cultural and political gains. The costs of London 2012 escalated vastly in the run-up.

No bid documents or strategic plans promise to make a loss, and the language of bidding has always been based on the promise of profit.

That they do still make losses appears all the more surprising given that the income from commercial sponsorship and the sale of media rights, much of which is passed on to the hosts, has continued to rise. It seems very likely that costs have always been underestimated.

Politicians, officials, accountants, almost everyone persistently underestimate the costs of hosting an Olympics. There are both technical and political reasons for this. Technically, the growing complexity and scale of the Games and the degree of uncertainty over long timescales makes accurate costing increasingly difficult. However, in the face of that uncertainty there is a predisposition among bid cities and their elites to believe lower estimates, good assumptions and best scenarios rather than the reverse. The political process for a bid city drawing up a budget of course necessitates making a plausible case without frightening taxpayers and legislators.. In general, the forces of scepticism are less organised, less well connected and less able to argue their case than the enthusiasts, though the balance of power is shifting; scepticism and resistance are increasingly voluble.

There are some genuinely new costs associated with hosting an Olympics, notably in relation to security and the management of risk. Security costs became a major factor after the kidnapping and killing of Israeli athletes at the 1972 Munich Olympics. The bombing of the 1996 Atlanta Olympics heightened awareness of risk. Now, post 9/11, and for London, 7/7 the perceived level of terrorist threat to mega-events has climbed and the costs of securing them have escalated even further. The technical specification of Olympic facilities and environmental implications of building are becoming more stringent and expensive, as has been evident in London in the lead-in to 2012.

Perhaps most importantly, there is a spiral of expectation and aspiration. When one Olympic Games closes with the endorsement that 'this is the best Olympics ever' the pressure is on their successors to match it. The impact of Barcelona's successful rebranding exercise rooted in a show of spectacular landmark architecture has also raised the bar of aesthetic expectations at the Olympics and thus a tendency to build ever bigger, more complex facilities, which reached a peak in Beijing 2008. London could only gaze in wonder and reconstitute their bid through an avowedly modest display if not modest regeneration budget for Stretford in East London and the transport system of the city.

Given these constraints, the Olympics can at best break even but are likely to lose money and need subsidy and public financial support. Thus the economic and financial systems of the Olympics in which the

Games are enmeshed and which they generate cannot be compared to the workings of a conventional company or even a commercial sports league. The economic rationale is not to make a profit; rather, the economic case for the Olympics is made in terms of its one-off, catalytic impact on the economy and culture of a city or a country, which is a fact that makes the estimation of economic costs and benefits of the event highly complex.

A central argument in the discourse of Olympic bidding documents is the promise of urban regeneration. The infrastructural scale and complexity of a Modern Olympic Games requires, for most cities, a large-scale programme of land acquisitions, infrastructure investments and building. Not all Olympic Games, even contemporary ones, have emphasised this dimension. Los Angeles 1984 relied almost exclusively on existing facilities and renovations. London 2012 has a massive new infrastructure of transport, housing and stadiums. However, all the Summer Games since have been accompanied by the transformation of key zones of the host city. Beijing 2008 was accompanied by the perhaps the greatest wave of urban redevelopment ever seen.

The debate over the Olympics as a vehicle for regeneration falls into five categories: employment and growth, housing, urban infrastructure, sports facilities and participation and the environment.

Bid documents and politicians, the leading promoters in most Olympic bids, often claim that hosting the Games will result in the creation of jobs, an increase in levels of investment, or higher economic growth, all stimulated by the building programme and the spin-off economic effects of new roads, better telecommunications and more tourism.

However, what the headline figures often conceal and what the sceptics including anti-Olympic campaigners, opposition politicians, affected local residents' groups question are the short-term nature of jobs, the preponderance of low-paying rather than highpaying jobs. Investing in one set of projects, such as stadiums and metros, means that money is not available to invest in other projects.

Housing is a central element in every Olympics project, because the Olympic village is a huge enterprise housing over 12,000 athletes and all the officials and coaches however intimate the connotations of the 'village'. All Olympic bids argue that the village will then be transformed into a permanent residential zone with relevant amenities, but sceptics point to other housing impacts of the Olympics. In Seoul and in Beijing, especially, Olympic construction programmes were accompanied by widespread land clearance and demolition, which has resulted in the forced eviction of many thousands of residents, often with little compensation or alternative provision. Contentious land clearance has also been a feature of London 2012.

Legacy is problematic; selling off the Olympic village after the Games is another area of concern. In Barcelona, accommodation in the Olympic village, located for the most part in a series of towers by the harbour, was sold to affluent buyers. Homebush Bay, the neighbourhoods created around Sydney's Olympic village, went the same way after 2000. Social housing needs of low-income groups, where the shortage invariably lies, have largely not been met.

Perhaps the most important aspect of infrastructure investment is in urban transport systems, which offer the possibilities of benefits, especially to those who depend on public transport, such as women, mothers, young people and the elderly. Most Olympic Games are accompanied by an upgrade of international airport facilities, major road systems, new underground routes, access routes to and from major venues, new underground lines and other forms of public transportation each of which has the capacity to enhance social cohesion. Enthusiasts argue that the impact of these changes bring long-term benefits to all aspects of a city's economy, while newer public spaces and neighbourhoods, such as Barcelona's renovated harbour, help rebrand and advertise a city.

Increasingly sport is a central element of public policy agendas as diverse as education, race and ethnic relations, social inclusion programmes, and health promotion strategies and, inspired by the Games themselves, there has been a massive increase in popular participation in sport and exercise (Wagg, 2004, Woodward, 2008). The facilities that are built are invariably reserved for elite training and competition rather than for being widely used. Moreover, their locations were chosen for the one-off Olympic event with its many agendas – they are not necessarily accessible to much of the public, particularly those sectors of the public that government would like to engage. In London 2012 the Cultural Olympiad occupied a central role in widening participation through the arts and cultural activities as well as porting practices (Cultural Olympiad, 2011).

As the importance and public profile of environmental issues has risen, the environmental impact of the Games has come to be seen as more and more significant. Olympic bids have tended to emphasise their green credentials, with Sydney 2000 setting new and high standards. Social inclusion embraces values of sustainability, however far those values might be in conflict with the forces of commercialism. Rather than being a drain on the environment, a successful Olympic bid could lead to the restitution of urban green space and mini-eco systems, improve public transport and diminish air pollution, and provide a global demonstration of new environmentally friendly technologies and materials.

Sceptics have argued that often these promised benefits are rarely if ever delivered and that marginal local improvements are undercut by the enormous pollution and carbon costs of transporting hundreds of thousands of people to the Games. Whatever the advantages of hi-tech HD television technologies and the limited probability of actually being able to get a ticket for the event of choice, or even any ticket at all, 'being there' has enormous appeal and the Games are primarily about corporeal, enfleshed, sentient engagement, whether for participants or for spectators.

Perhaps the most important, though intangible, element of an Olympic balance sheet is the question of image, reputation and even brand. Berlin 1936 was the prototype of the Olympics as a political global spectacle, but the brand was national rather than urban, and ideological rather than economic.

Through their control over key elements of the Olympic programme hosts are able to articulate a central set of messages or stories about the Games, the city and the country they are held in. In Barcelona's case, for example, the Olympics were used to transform a city blighted by industrial decline into the prototype culturally sophisticated, post-industrial city which is a Mediterranean home to the creative industries and a magnet for tourists and international visitors.

Techniques of rebranding include the content of the opening and closing ceremonies and control over design details of mottos, street decoration and urban dressing and architectural statements, including the main stadiums as well as other complexes which offer a unique opportunity for giving out big messages. Munich 1972 built facilities in a deliberately low-key modernist manner as a rejection of the bombastic neoclassicism of the 1936 Olympics. The Cultural Olympiads are now included in all Olympic programmes. Cultural Olympiads incorporate a diverse range of activities with London 2012 being the most ambitious to date. In Beijing in 2008, the host committee's activities and promotions included attempts at transforming routine cultural practices in the anthropological sense of the everyday; campaigns were launched to control public spitting and encourage orderly queuing in an effort to smoothe the passage of visitors street cleansing. Most Olympics, however, have been accompanied by the removal, arrest, deportation and control of a variety of street dwellers, such as the homeless and mentally ill people (Lenskyj, 2000). In London 2012 the Cultural

Olympiad reached much greater heights in promoting social inclusion and artistic and creative regeneration and productivity.

Football: pros and ams

Football is not the first sport you would think about in the context of the Games. Football occupies other sporting public spaces more insistently and dramatically. These range from the new stadiums, like Soccer City, one of the many built for the men's World Cup in South Africa in 2010, sites that are home to great football like the Nou Camp in Barcelona, Maracana in Rio in Brazil and Wembley in London as well as traditional homes, like Old Trafford in Manchester, new homes for traditional clubs like Arsenal's Emirates Stadium in north London, to the massive media coverage of the sport and its celebrity players. Football is a popular and populist sport with genealogies of working-class local community sport (Giulianotti, 1999, Giulianotti and Williams, 1994, Houlihan, 2008, Wagg, 2004) which is also increasingly popular among women (FA, Women 2011). Football has extensive global reach, especially across Africa, Europe, South America and increasingly the Middle and Far East; men's football. Football is also a sport that can raise the spirits and rise above the everyday and the routine practices and even the iterative identifications of the sport itself. The great men's teams, Hungary in the 1950s, Brazil from the 1950s to the 1970s, Holland in the mid-1970s and Spain in the twenty-first century; clubs like Real Madrid in the late 1950s and 1960s, Tottenham Hotspur in 1961, Manchester United in 1968 and at the time of writing in 2011, Barcelona. Fifteen minutes after half time in the Champions League Final on 28 May 2011, Xavi, Iniesta and especially Messi with his irresistible goal scoring transcended the ordinary and the mechanical and demonstrated why football is called the Beautiful Game. Religious metaphors which label these three players the 'holy trinity' (Holy Trinity, 2011) are not understatement and capture the intensities and expressiveness that football has the capacity to generate. Women's football involves the same enfleshed practices and corporeal techniques and the same rules but the virtual and the enfleshed material practices are always enmeshed in ways that make it impossible to ignore the marginalisation and invisibility of much of the women's sport. Football's affects are visible and high-lighted in the professional men's game; the silence and invisibility especially in the individualised narratives off as well as on the pitch render the emotional and material affects of the women's game much less intense.

Football was introduced as a medal sport at the 1908 Olympic Games. Great Britain won the gold medal and then successfully defended their title four years later in Stockholm. The sport has featured at every Olympic Games since, with the exception of Los Angeles 1932. Football is interesting for a number of reasons in understanding some of the different power geometries of the Olympics. Firstly, football is a sport which raises debates about the relationship between amateurs and professionals and the demands of the professional Game more emphatically and dramatically than any other sport, especially as played out in the messy interconnections of the sport–commerce–media nexus. Television coverage is central to football finance and to its affects, which are material and emotional.

For 2012, football also raised questions about national identifications and issues about how meaningful these might be in the UK context in particular in relation to devolved governance and the links between politics, culture and sport. The greater the demands for independence for Scotland, the less enthusiasm there was for participating in a GB British team. Sport may matter more and it was the legacies of sporting achievement that the nations which make up Britain sought to protect, but the case study does raise some issues about sport and national identifications which might be highlighted in the context of the Olympics. Each of these aspects of football, the issues of amateurs and professionals linked to the forces of global capital and matters of national identification is closely enmeshed with the forces and flows of gendered relationships and the configurations of sex as expressive and productive of inequalities, not only in sport but within wider social and cultural terrains. Nonetheless, in football, the explicit coverage of sex gender is largely empirical in terms of women' and men's competitions with very little critique or deconstruction beyond discussion of the inequities of lived experience and lack of support and sponsorship of women's sport. The all-pervasive and diffuse operations of power (Foucault, 1980, 1982) construct women as sexualised, even pornogrified in contemporary 'raunch culture' (Levy, 2006, Woodward and Woodward, 2009) as well as marginalised and peripheral to sport's central concerns.

Football is not central to the Olympics in which track and field occupy pole positions, but football is the global game in many respects (Goldblatt, 2006), because of its capacities to combine passion, local, national and ethnic identifications and enfleshed, sentient experience, whether through participation or through spectatorship and affiliation. Football combines traditions of working-class community and support networks and configurations of sex gender with some of the most powerful expressions of feeling. It can capture the imagination, create affects of emotion and aspiration and generate extremes which are sometimes expressive of and dependent upon conflicts that are deeply embedded in communities characterised by difference. Football has its own contradictions and tensions, like other sports, but football's are often conflictual and extend beyond the investments that are made on the pitch and on the terraces. Football is the site at which religious and cultural oppositions are expressed and reiterated. Football affiliations may be expressive of other forms of social deprivation but the sport also reproduces these inequalities, notably in relation to sex gender. Football is deeply misogynist. Even in the twenty-first century there is routine acceptance of discrimination against women, which is not superficial. Women regularly appear in the news and sports media as sexual partners, for example, of male football stars in 'kiss and tell' stories, where the only cultural capital women can invest in is the enfleshed capital of their looks and their sexualised availability. For example, in the case of the Manchester United midfielder Ryan Giggs, whose status as a Welsh international status passed largely unremarked in the massive media coverage of his extra marital affair with Imogen Thomas, a former participant in the reality TV show *Big Brother*, much was made of the ubiquity of such sexualised activity. His affair was the focus of popular media coverage (Sun, 2011) although it was apparently noteworthy because he had sought a super-injunction in the courts to prevent being named. This was a debate about the power of the very rich to silence the media (UK forum, 2011) but the issues are underpinned by systems and technologies of inequality in which sex as a conceptualisation is deeply implicated. Patriarchal power systems and technologies of sex operate and intersect in other fields sand are certainly not confined to sport, as the case of the former chairman of the International Monetary Fund also demonstrated in 2011 (Strauss Kahn, 2011).

At a time when the Football Association (FA) is fighting to promote the women's game and gender equality, if there are still everyday cultural practices of exclusion and discrimination, football is becoming increasingly popular among girls and women. This was recognised in 2011 with the establishment of the women's Super League (Super League, 2011) which reinstated the professional game for women in the United

Kingdom. This was welcomed by women in football, although the cap of £20,000 per annum as the maximum which could be earned by only three players (everyone else earns even less) clearly demonstrates the inequity between the women's and the men's game where players routinely earn twice that in a week. In the discourse of hegemonic masculinity that dominates football, as it does most sports women and girls are grouped together for classificatory purposes in a manner in which men and boys are not; sport may indeed sort out the men from the boys.

There have been massive culture shifts in sport, in the anti-discriminatory legislation and activism, for example, kicking racism off the terraces and out of the ground (FARE, 2011, Woodward, 2007a), but gender bias is resolutely entrenched in the culture of a sport. Nonetheless, there have been massive increases in the number of women participating, as players, as amateurs if not professionals, it has to be said, and as referees as is manifest on the FA's website (FA 2011). In spite of the efforts of organisations which combat all forms of prejudice and legislation against discriminatory practice, football remains dominated by a hegemonic masculinity which devalues women and takes for granted the acceptability of sexist discourse and gender discriminatory cultural practices. Women are targeted as inherently incapable of understanding the rules of sport, especially football. Hostility may be expressed in the language of homophobia, racism, ethnocentrism and sexism, but men are not targeted because they are men, whereas in cases like that of Sian Massey a line referee in a men's game in 2010, women are (Woodward, 2011c). There are points, especially in the field of sport, when the networks of hegemonic masculinity carry more weight than other networks, identifications and affiliations, including those of nation. Nonetheless, because of the organisation of sport and its measurement of success and failure through not only sexed categories but the labelling of national affiliation, it is not surprising that nation matters in sport, although in football national competitions are sometimes less highly rated, particularly by players, than club events.

Footballing nations

The politics of national identities in sport are closely tied up with, and often in conflict with, in the case of the men's game, the professional sport and the demands of sponsorship and finance which may exert more powerful regulatory forces than the regulating bodies of most sports as national sports organisations. Contemporary debate about the shortcomings of the national team, especially in UK men's football, is often focused on the demands of the club, with frequent games and large proportion of foreign players, in a system in which the club is seen to take precedence over the national team. The regulatory body which governs the sport has to produce and implement the mechanisms through which sport is organised and practised. Football, however, has a place at the Olympics.

For 2012, football was billed as a major feature of the Olympic programme at the London Games. Spread across six major grounds around the United Kingdom, the London 2012 Olympic Games the football competition was promoted as promising plenty of excitement (Football 2012, 2011). The Football competition with two medal events at London 2012 was staged at six grounds around the United Kingdom, to provide some equity in the regional and national location: City of Coventry Stadium in Coventry in the West Midlands; Hampden Park in Glasgow in Scotland; the Millennium Stadium in Cardiff in Wales; Old Trafford in Manchester in the northwest of England; St James's Park in Newcastle in the northeast and Wembley Stadium in London. The 504 athletes included 216 women and 288 men with 12 women's teams and 16 men's teams. Beginning with group matches and ending with a knockout phase, the competition was claimed to offer all the drama that fans have come to expect from major international tournaments. The competition might display the embodied practices of football on the pitch but lacks the sporting mega star of the Premiership and European and South American leagues. There were two medal events at London 2012, one for men's teams and one for women's. The run-up to 2012 presented a debate about the inclusion of national teams in Britain, which had particular resonance because of the global dominance of the Premiership in the men's game.

The controversy in the lead-in to the Games was framed by concerns by Scotland, Wales and Northern Ireland. A row began in 2007 over the BOA's determination to field men's and women's British football teams at the 2012 Olympic Games. Debates were not surprisingly about the men's competitions; yet again the women's games were not so much focused on nation as on the number of events in the Games as a whole and the fear that more women's events would mean fewer men's (BBC, 2007). Football, for example, in Britain developed as a man's game, although there were many women's teams earlier in the sport's history such as the famous Dick Kerr's Ladies (Jacobs, 2004). Men's dominance was affirmed by the FA and the organisation's exclusion of women from their pitches. Football fandom and spectatorship has also been domi-nated by men but there are also powerful affiliations of kinship groups in which women play an important if less visible role. The Scottish (Scottish Football Association (SFA)), Football Association of Wales (FAW) and Northern Ireland Football Associations have all opposed the idea on the stated grounds that they feared involvement with a British team could threaten their status with football's European and world governing bodies, despite FIFA's assurances (BBC, News 2007).

The BOA started discussions with the Football Associations of England, Scotland, Wales and Northern Ireland to find a way to put together a truly British team in both men's and women's competition for the Olympics. Whilst the English and the Northern Irish were initially supportive, the FA of Wales and Scotland were not (BBC, News 2007).

When the world's first football association, the FA, was formed in 1863, its geographical remit was not clear: there was no specification of whether it covered just England, the entire United Kingdom or even the entire world. The question was answered when the SFA was founded in 1873. The third national football association, the Football Association of Wales, was founded in 1876 and a fourth, the Irish Football Association (IFA), was founded in 1880.

Football therefore developed with separate national teams repre-senting separate associations for each of the countries of the United Kingdom and no UK football association was ever formed. When foot-ball was held as a demonstration sport at the 1900 Olympic Games, club teams entered with Upton Park representing Great Britain and Northern Ireland. Upton Park won the gold medal, which has since been retro-actively awarded by the International Olympic Committee as a full gold. For the 1908 Olympic Games in London, the FA persuaded the IOC to include a football tournament, which they organised. A team, made up entirely of English players, was entered as the England national amateur football team, although sometimes this is called Great Britain. Great Britain won and an arrangement was reached with the other Home Nations' FAs, under which a Great Britain team consisting of amateur players organised by the FA would enter future tournaments.

The composition of this team varied over time, with squads predom-inantly made up of English players. Great Britain won again at the 1912 Games. The team withdrew from the 1924 and 1928 Games over disputes surrounding professionalism, which eventually led to the with-drawal of the Home Nations from FIFA, and the creation of the FIFA World Cup. Following this, Great Britain competed from 1948 through to 1972, though they failed to qualify for all Games after 1960. The last occasion on which a Great Britain and Northern Ireland team reached the Olympic finals was the 1960 Games. After the FA scrapped the distinction between professional and amateur players in 1974, no more British Olympic teams were entered. By the twenty-first century there might have been enthusiasm from FIFA as but IFA president Raymond Kennedy told BBC Sport that he would be supporting the SFA and FAW's stance, adding: 'We would not want to compromise our national identity' (BBC, 2007). The major opposition to joining a British team was the possibility that Wales and Scotland would on the one hand loose their national identities and legacies of success in the game and on the other that there would also be the demand for a British team in European competitions and the men's World Cup which might interfere with the dominance of the Premiership. There are specificities to the place of the Premiership and to the assemblage of nations that make up Britain and the United Kingdom, which are different from other spatialised situations. The former Soviet Union has been split into 15 different countries now with 10 playing in Union of European Football Associations (UEFA) and 5 in Asia, but these are separate nations and the same sponsorship media relationships may not be implicated.

The inclusion of more nations presents logistical problems too. One of the debates addressed in relation to the inclusion of women's boxing in 2012 centred upon the number of events and the contentious question of which events would have to be dropped in order to permit a fuller more equitable range. In order to accommodate the intensity of the expanded programme, the 2012 football competition was scheduled to kick off two days before the Olympic Games Opening Ceremony, with the first group matches. New regulations were established at London 2012 in which, there would be age restrictions for the women's competition, but, somewhat bizarrely, but presumably to accommodate the demands of the professional game and the Premiership, the men's competition would be an under-23s event, although each country will be allowed to include three older players in their team. Both the men's and women's competitions began with a group stage with the teams divided into groups of four (three groups in the women's tournament, four groups for the men), with the best eight teams qualifying for the quarter-finals. From here, the competitions were played to a knockout format: the two winning semi-finalists playing for the gold medal at Wembley, with the two losing semi-finalists competing for the bronze.

These arrangements for 2012 represent the changes that have been taking place, firstly in relation to the popularity of the sport allied to the dominance of the men's professional game and especially that of the Premiership. These issues are situated within a framework of IOC attempts to embrace equal opportunities, including those of sex gender and, largely abandoned in other sports, rationalities of the binary logic of amateurs and professionals and recognition of the claims of national identities, here configured around those of the nations which make up Britain. The relationship between a particular sport and the Games has to be located not only within the wider social and cultural context but also within the genealogies of the sport itself. London 2012 presents a turning point in some of the controversies that have surrounded football as a global sport, a sport with a massive, passionate following but also beset by controversy not least about corruption and the possibilities of illegal activities related to a variety of forms of corruption including the gambling syndicates which haunts global professional sport, as well as the institutional racism and exclusions of sexual politics that underpin some of the social inequalities that are both constitutive of and constituted by sport, including the Olympics.

Football matters: foul play?

Football matters for a number of reasons, many of these are included above in relation to the passionate commitment which so many fans worldwide devote to the sport as well as its economic and financial importance and the sites at which football is represented on the global media. Sometimes this media coverage is of controversy and this is one of the points of connection with the Olympics. Controversies in sport cover a diverse field of activities, but in the case of the Olympics one particular dimension of corrupt practice brings together discussion about football and the Games and challenges idealist configurations of innocent national identifications. One of the most recent incidents relates to the bidding process which is based on the synergies between IOC and FIFA and, in men's football, bidding to host the competition in 2018 and 2022, and the Games in the case of Salt Lake City.

The Salt Lake City story was a tale of massive corruption, which can be attributed to the organisation of the IOC and its capacities for individuals to operate within the bidding process. Salt Lake City, having failed in their efforts in 1991, made certain that in 2002 the Games would be in Utah by doling out the most extravagant gifts of money, presents and even jobs. They were successful in 2002 because of the enormity of the spending and bribery, and because the structure and organisation of the IOC and the bidding process made such corruption possible.

In the case of Salt Lake City there was a clash between Olympic ideals and greed and large-scale corruption in a city's attempts to secure the benefits of the Games (Calvert, 2002).

In 2011, Lord Triesman, former FA chairman, declared, before the House of Commons' Culture, Media and Sport Committee, that elements of FIFA were corrupt, based on the failure of England to succeed in hosting the 2018 men's World Cup (Sky, 2011). The bribes apparently used to secure votes, of which England somewhat humiliatingly gained only two, were described as 'certain attractive propositions, whether it be women or cash, or in the case of one member, according to Lord Triesman, a knighthood honour from the Queen' (Ronay, 2011). There is more money in the men's game and football, like most other sporting practices, is part of the heterosexual matrix (Butler, 1993) which reinstates homophobic exclusions at myriad points (Woodward, 2007). It is thus hardly surprising that women are included in the list of bribes: women as commodities on a par with cash and luxury gifts are reinstated in the discourses which generate these affects. Coverage of women in the media is also sexualised rather than engaging with women's sporting achievements. Women receive more visibility as sexual partners than sporting players. Football also has close ties to prostitution as was manifest in the debates about trafficking and the arguments underpinning the encouragement of the migration of women working as prostitutes to South Africa for the 2010 men's World Cup (Woodhouse, 2009).

These matters were publicly debated in the context of England's failure to gain more than two votes in support of its bid to host the competition in 2018. These allegations were followed by others and even FIFA President Sepp Blatter was accused of corrupt practices and widely reported as under an ethics probe (*Wall St. Journal*, 2011). All of this is resonant of Salt Lake City in late 1998 and demonstrates synergies in the opportunities that are presented within the governance of sport at the highest levels for corrupt practices. These practices are often individualised in their coverage although the solutions offered after Salt Lake City appertained to restructuring of the organising body the IOC and suggested that corruption is not restricted to pecuniary practices but involves diverse aspects of exploitation, often including the sex gender divisions and other aspects of social exclusion.

Conclusion

The Olympics present a complex arrangement of different elements. Exploring the issues that are imbricated in bidding for and hosting the

Games offers some insight into the points at which different factors connect. There are tensions between the benefits and disadvantages of hosting the Games. These range across a number of aspects of the economy and society, some of which can be recorded on balance sheets and others which are less immediately apparent. Those that are harder to quantify include the environmental degradation and longer-term outcomes in relation to the opening and closing of markets, the creation or destruction of employment opportunities and transform-ation of spatial locations, housing and architecture, which can be both damaging and beneficial.

The development of the Modern Olympic Games reveals how the culture and politics of the Games, the Olympic Movement and economic and commercial factors intersect and occasionally collide. Although the Games have their own particular interest groups which constitute their regulatory mechanisms, including IOC members, politicians in the host city and nation, local industry, national sponsors and television networks, they remain part of the global economy and are affected by changes in it. The Games present the interstitial spaces between the enfleshed practices that are specific to different sports and the economic and political systems they generate and are generated by.

There have been significant shifts in the relationship between the Olympics and economic and political forces, most notably demonstrated by the increasing commercialisation of the Games from Los Angeles 1984 onward, when commercial interests became not only more visible and voluble but also more dominant.

Sex gender remains less visible, although sex difference operates at different levels, empirically and politically. The invisibility of women is constitutive of inequalities in which flesh, embodied practices and material affects combine to recreate inequalities and social divisions. Categories of sex are mechanisms through which sport is organised, for example, the division of competitions into men's and women's events is ubiquitous and a major means of measurement and classification in sport; it is one that is more dominant and prevalent than any other, such as body size, although age categories are also part of the regula-tory systems which are universal, but less controversial. Often it is only women's competitions that are marked, although at least in athletics both women's and men's events are so classified, unlike football in the field of professional sport. It is only when women's sport becomes visible in some instances that controversy arises. For example, women's inclusion and participation, whether in football or boxing or less mainstream, or malestream, non-traditional sports that questions are then asked about whether the inclusion of women's events means fewer men's competitions and the participation of women is described as unfair as it is seen to reduce the opportunities for men. Football offers a good example of the entrenchment of sex gender difference which is often played out off the pitch in the representational systems of the media more visibly than on the field or track or in the governance of the sport.

There are both benefits and disadvantages that emerge from the economics of the Games. For example, host cities can benefit from improved infrastructure, increased levels of employment and income, and cultural advantages of an enhanced image of the city involved, which raise the overall prosperity of the area. However, these advantages may be more strongly associated with higher income groups, and the poor do not always benefit; they may even suffer. The enormous investment leads to urban restructuring, which can be divisive. The benefits of hosting the Games may lead to an enhancement of the profit margins of the corporate big players, but this can be at the expense of local communities, many of whom are not able to access any improved facilities, or benefit from the greater employment opportunities or the infrastructure that is put in place for the Games. Given the strong links between the IOC and corporate finance, this is a problem that is unlikely to be addressed. However, this is an uneven process and host cities do manage the utilisation of previously unused spaces, for example, to create new recreational spaces that everyone can enjoy.

The nation is the motor for hosting the Games; national identifications are more important than any other when it comes to gaining success as the host city. The centrality of commercial interests makes some nations more valued than others, although there is also a recognition by the IOC that hosting the Games has to be a privilege and opportunity that is shared more equitably across the globe. There are elements of equity in spreading the range outside Europe, the United States, Canada and Australia which inform decisions, but the economic imperatives of creating a satisfactory infrastructure and the interests of the state and commerce mean that this is never entirely equitable or democratic whatever the mobilities of transnationalism in the global economy. What in much of the literature is attributed to individualised self-interest on the part of IOC members, local commercial interests can be usefully understood as an assemblage of social, political, cultural and economic systems into which patriarchy is enmeshed and embedded. Sex gender as a political conceptualisation of difference is more than a descriptor of the participants in athletic competitions and events or the individuals who are IOC members and officials in the regulatory bodies of the Olympics. Empirical actualities are materially important but can only be understood explanatory frameworks of the power bases that inform the politics of difference and an understanding of the workings of the networks of hegemonic masculinity. These conceptual frameworks are also crucial to understanding the spectacles, the spectacular and sensations of the Olympics, which is the concern of the next chapter.

5
Spectacles and Spectators

This chapter develops the debates set up in earlier chapters about the measures and mechanisms of operations of power in sport that are underpinned by sex gender relations that are manifest in representation and symbolic systems. Thus it focuses on the nature of the media spectacle and the mega-event, in the case of the Games the rituals, insignia and opening and closing ceremonies in particular (Horne, 2007, Houlihan, 2008, Miller and et al., 2001, Scambler, 2005, Sugden and Tomlinson, 2011). More emphasis has been given to media coverage (Markula, 2009) and the visibility of women at different sporting sites, for example, in feminist work on the representational systems of sport (Daddario, 1998, Giardina, 2005, Hargreaves, 1994 Markula, 2009). Sex gender, or more specifically gender, has played a key part in the analyses of the coverage of such sporting spectacles (Daddario, 1998, Markula, 2009), especially in relation to the vast media coverage which the Olympics receive (Sugden and Tomlinson, 2011), although feminist work has stressed the empirical presence, or more likely absence, of women (Markula, 2009). This chapter offers a critique of the spectacle and its visibility in promoting possibilities of inclusion and includes sex gender as the conceptual basis for understanding the operation of power in making the spectacle and develops the argument already introduced about the merging of representation and the virtual with the material, enfleshed actualities of sport.

Sensation, visibility and sound are central to the making of the Games and of who is in and who is out, who speaks and how silence is configured. The IOC plays a key role, as do NOCs, and the voice of the IOC is audible, notably through is male figurehead in the actuality of the president and the preponderance of male members of the committee and most importantly the hegemonic masculinity that exceeds attempts at diversity and social inclusion in the context of gender. It is the president of the IOC who speaks at the opening of the Games and embodies the authority, which is usually coded male, as well as the principles of the Olympic Movement.

This chapter offers a discussion of spectacle and sensation as well as an analysis of how the spectacles, the ceremonies and media coverage throughout the Games are contingent and temporally and spatially located as well as governed by commercial, economic and political factors, as Chapter 4 demonstrated.

Visibility is a powerful mechanism in the production of spectacle and the Modern Games, like all sporting sites, rely heavily upon the media to make its practices visible and visual. The major spectacles of the Games are the opening and closing ceremonies and some of the events; some events and competitions are more spectacular than others and certainly elicit more interests from spectators. In the ticket lottery for 2012, of the 20 million who applied for 6 million tickets, hopeful buyers who committed substantial sums aspired to getting one of the 'big three', that is, the opening or closing ceremony or the most prestigious of all the events, not surprisingly a men's event, the 100 metres final. The visibility of the Games involves enfleshed presence too; you are seen to be there in the assemblage of sport, spectatorship and the status afforded to attending particular events. It is little wonder that the realisation that the majority of tickets (reputedly in a ratio of 6:4) went to corporate bodies created a challenge to the democratic ideals of the IOC and expressions of egalitarianism from LOCOG as voiced by Lord Coe who had led the London bid.

Although the visible and visual have centrality and primacy in the constitution of spectacle, other senses are invoked and through sensation which is unmediated through the affects generated by the spectacle; the senses are part of the process through which the sporting event is both experienced and represented (Woodward, 2009). Rather than being just a show to be viewed, an event like the opening ceremony of the Olympics is a spectacle which sweeps up the performers, the participants, the sounds, objects and symbols as well as those who watch and cheer into the intensities of the event.

As the opening and closing ceremonies demonstrate only too well, the sounds, symbols and things that are caught up in the spectacle are not arbitrary and provide links between the nations participating, the nation hosting, the IOC and the sponsors of the Games. What is not arbitrary is the power sources of what is seen and unseen, rather than conspiratorial, individualised agency.

States, like corporations, have brands that are used to promote identifications through the Olympics. It is hard to imagine the Games without the paraphernalia of transnational as well as national, commercialised postmodernity.

Sociologists of sport have recognised the centrality of the Olympics in the historical development of sport as part of popular culture. Toby Miller demonstrates how the visualisation and visibility of sport as television-based popular culture provides a crucial site where populations are targeted by different forms of governmental and commercial knowledge power (Miller et al., 2001). Miller invites the reader to imagine the spectacles of the Olympics without the familiar political and cultural symbols with which worldwide audiences have become so familiar:

> No comprehensive media coverage, no national flags flying, no playing of national anthems, no politicians involved in ceremonies, no military displays, no tables comparing national standings and athletes competing in whatever clothing they desired instead of national uniforms. (Miller et al., 2001:2)

All these symbols and practices combine to make the Games visible and visual, however uncritical media commentaries on such displays have been in terms of social relations and divisions which underpin them. Discussion is more usually centred upon how effective the spectacle is in relation of viewing figures and sensational properties. One area in which visibility and the power of looking have been interrogated is in feminist theories which have devoted considerable attention to both the lack of visibility of women in sport and the explosion of images of women in popular culture, not only in celebrating women's achievements but also in presenting women as objects rather than subjects of desire.

Gendered looking; sexed practices

Feminist approaches have frequently addressed problems of silence and invisibility, where women are seen to have been denied a voice and a presence, hidden from history in Sheila Rowbotham's (1974) terms, or an absent presence in feminist cultural studies as in the work of E. Ann Kaplan (1992) or lacking a voice, words or visibility as in Luce Irigaray's (1984, 1991) and Hélène Cixous's (1980) early work. Feminist work on representation has often focused upon visual images whether in the field of artistic representation or within the field of popular culture, especially within the media and with desire (for example Kaplan, 1992, McRobbie, 1994, 2008, Gorton, 2010), rather than sport. What in second-wave feminism was called objectification has been translated into pornification or pornogrification (Levy, 2006) in the third wave (Gillis et al, 2007). Gendered lives are lived, experienced and re-constituted, especially in contemporary societies that have such powerful tools for visualisation and where the senses are invoked in so many ways which do not require a physical, corporeal engagement in the space in which the activity is being enacted and the pornified images of popular culture have migrated into sport. Women are more likely to occupy media space as cheer leaders or some kind of mascot or card girls, so-called rather than women, because infantilisation often accompanies pornification in boxing.

The Olympics offer a more egalitarian space in many ways. The athletes in the opening and closing ceremonies wear the uniform dress of their national identification and on the track or field, and the podium if they succeed, they wear sports gear. Nonetheless, women, although benefitting from Lycra technologies and those of the sports clothing industry as well as high-specification equipment, still have to negotiate the demands of spectatorship and the cultural imperatives of the heterosexual matrix and be attentive to their make-up and appearance, even in elite athletic performance.

Reality and representation suggest that there are mediating processes in play and that mediation is gendered as in the original concept of the male gaze whereby women see themselves through a male gaze and desire is the prerogative of the male and not the female gaze; in psychoanalytic terms a female gaze would be an impossibility since desire is premised upon male subjectivity (Berger, 1972, Mulvey 1975, 1981, Gammon and Marshment, 1987). Counterarguments have suggested that the gaze, rather than routinely involving women always seeing themselves and being seen through the male gaze, could mean that women themselves look as well as being always looked at; there might be a female gaze, a European gaze, a queer gaze and the possibilities of a democratisation of the gaze, to mention but a few of the permutations. Feminist elaborations of objectification which have drawn upon Mulvey's original theories have largely eschewed the psychoanalytic underpinnings of her earlier work but retained the objective subjective binary. Feminist developments have the advantage of stressing the politics of looking and of visibility and invisibility. They allow exploration of the operations of power and its patriarchal implications in order to highlight some of the contemporary contradictions of the explosion of liberatory discourses of sex and sexuality, which were highlighted by Foucault (Foucault, 1981). Foucault saw psychoanalysis as implicated in instating and producing (Foucault, 1981), but which reinstates traditional sex gender binaries which sexualise women and are far from 'empowering' in the language of postfeminism (Woodward and Woodward, 2009). In sport, as in other fields of popular culture, the gaze and looking raise the problem of voyeurism and the mechanisms of power through which some spectators are privileged and some constituted as other or are objectified. Recent re-articulations of the gaze have been translated into a feminist politics which identifies the iterative objectification of women through representational systems which mimic pornography, hence the ubiquity of the pornification of representational systems and of the processes through women can look and be looked at have relevance to debates about the culture of sport.

Spectacles and symbols

> The symbol of the Olympic Games, the five rings, is the most readily identified image in the world. The rings are recognised by over 90% of the world's population, which is even higher than the logos of the megabrands such as Shell and McDonald's. (Gregory Andranovich, quoted in Morgan and Pritchard, 1998: 140)

In terms of branding, such massive corporations present august company for the Olympics. Although links with multi- and transnational corporations have become ubiquitous as well as controversial, for many sporting bodies like the IOC and FIFA the Olympic Movement was not so strongly interconnected until well into the second half of the twentieth century A previous IOC president, Juan Antonio Samaranch, was captured on videotape at the Atlanta Games in 1996 clearly saying that the Olympic Movement was 'more important than the Catholic religion'. Samaranch subsequently claimed he was misquoted: 'I said maybe the Olympic movement has more followers than any religion in the world. I did not mention the Catholic religion.' American TV networks, however, remained adamant that he had (Sandomir, 1996). What is relevant about this anecdote is the invocations of the spiritual and the transcendent which permeate the apparatus of spectacle and especially of the rituals of the mega-events that the Modern Olympics have become. The fervour of religious commitment is another strand of the interrelationship between sport and religion which is also expressed as community and shared interests, as in the example of the Commonwealth Games in Chapter 1. At points religion and politics dominate aspects of the mix, but the relationship between economic, social, cultural and political forces is always contingent upon time and space.

1936: a spectacular case study

The birth of the Modern Olympics into a world in which forces of warring empires and nation states were central meant that the event would inextricably be shaped by political flows. Sport does not exist in a political vacuum, whatever the reiteration of platitudes about sport and politics not mixing, but is part of its time and place and is also constitutive of these temporalities and spacialities and sporting spectacles incorporate political forces. De Coubertin' vision was of the Games as a global spectacle with an ethical message. The Belgian organising committee of the 1920 Antwerp Olympics, for example, had been allowed to refuse participation to the defeated central powers of the First World War. The creation of the Olympic oath and the Olympic flag, both of which made their debut at Antwerp, suggested that the process of fashioning a global ritual was under way. However, when in 1930 the right to host the 1936 Olympic Games was awarded to Berlin, a massive shift in the nature of the Olympic spectacle and its permanent overt and explicit politicisation was put into discourse in some spectacular ways.

The Olympics have been used for specific political purposes, none more so than the 1936 Berlin Games, the so-called 'Nazi Olympics'. Although other aspects of power were in play, notably economic forces, there was particular emphasis on political forces in 1936. The spectacle involved militaristic display based upon an aggressive, disciplined masculinity, mass enthusiasm and the reconstruction of figures eliding sporting heroes with the Nazi state and its future imaginings. The Berlin Games were set in context as:

> Born of a nationalistic age, from their beginnings in 1896 the modern Olympic Games had been played amid a martial display of flags, military marches, patriotic anthems and nationalistic rivalries. The Nazis did not create this atmosphere; they merely carried it to its absurd limits. They cloaked the Olympics of 1936 in political and military garb, using them as a showpiece of German engineering skill, cultural taste, and athletic prowess. (Baker, 1982, p. 251)

The celebration of disciplined militarism is widely enmeshed with racialised, ethnicised masculinities. What is most striking is the bellicosity and rigidity of the military discursive regime of truth in this scenario, but it is also powerfully gendered through its enactment of masculinity, the performance of which is not entirely restricted to those who are men but at this historical moment and in the context of sport it is largely the realm of enfleshed and very visible men.

The Olympic Congress held in Barcelona in 1932 had experienced difficulties in making a decision on the 1936 Olympics, and Berlin's success was the result of the postal vote. It was a vote, in effect, for fully accepting a stable, peaceful Weimer Germany back into the international community. The local organising committee for the Games was formed on 24 January 1933, six days before Adolph Hitler was appointed chancellor of Germany, which presented problems for the IOC. Although one wing of the Nazi movement had embraced sports as an instrument of Aryan racial regeneration and social regimentation, traditional English sports were largely despised and nationalistic *Turnverein* gymnastics were celebrated within a racialised, racist discursive regime which was inimical to the Olympic Movement. Contradictions in relation to the patriarchal underpinnings of Nazi ideologies were less apparent but the overt racism might have been expected to be perceived as problematic. However, the initial contacts between the IOC and the new regime did not seem to have been as troubling as might have been expected.

The events which make up the negotiations are usually presented as a narrative with central characters (Guttmann, 2002), with stories such as those about Hitler's own lack of enthusiasm for most sport as well as his overt racism, and agentic figures like Goebbels, who was in charge of official propaganda and reputed to have recognised the extraordinary opportunity that the Olympics presented for transmitting the Nazi political message. Stories require central characters and protagonists but these are figures made possible by the coalescence of political, cultural and economic factors from which they emerged and through which they were made. The Nazi cultural machine and state provided the financial support a spectacle that announced the beginning of the 1,000-year Reich in Germany; they were also conscious of the damage that protests from abroad could create. Led by Jewish groups in the United States, there was a global campaign to boycott the Games on account of the racial policies that Germany was implementing in domestic sports. The IOC, led by Avery Brundage, campaigned tirelessly to prevent the boycott and, but for some limited opposition, he succeeded. Brundage travelled to Berlin and was satisfied by his

German hosts. Allen Guttmann reports that Brundage went so far as to say that he demanded 'Jews and communists keep their hands off American sport' (Guttmann, 2002: 61). Nearly 4,000 athletes went to Berlin, making it the biggest Games ever, and it was, by a factor of at least four, the most expensive Games yet put on (Guttmann, 1984).

The torch lit at the sacred altar at Olympia 12 days before the opening ceremony on 1 August and transported by 3,075 runners was synchronised to arrive at exactly the right moment at the Olympiastadion, which had been built at the site of the Deutches Stadion in Berlin for the 1936 Games. More than 110,000 people listened to the 30 trumpets that announced Hitler's arrival. Pageantry was an elision of disciplined militarism and large-scale emotional expression, which drew upon and reproduced religious practices and symbolism.

An aging Richard Strauss led the orchestra in a rendering of *Deutchland über alles* and *Horst Wessellied*, followed by his own 'Olympic Hymn'. Sixty year old Spyridon Loues, winner of the marathon in 1896, headed the Greek team's march-past, after which a further 51 national teams, paraded by, some giving the Nazi salute, some not. A recorded message from the terminally ill Coubertin was played... Hitler departed at 6 p.m., again to a fanfare of trumpets, and the evening was then given over to a no less grand festival of Olympic Youth. Outside the stadium the Jewish population enjoyed a temporary respite from anti-Semitic slogans. (Scambler, 2005: 58)

Spectacles incorporate the visibility of some and the invisibility of others. The embodied presence of black athletes, for example, the majority of the US track and field winners were African American, was problematic for the Nazi regime. Hitler is reputed to have refused to speak to the brilliantly successful medal winner Jesse Owens, who won four gold medals in 1936; for the 100 metres, for the 200 metres, the long jump and the as a member of the 1×400 metres relay team. The Berlin Olympics highlight the more extreme versions of a political project manifest in the Games and in considering who is included and who is excluded, whose achievements are recognised, as well as the visual displays and performances.

Berlin 1936 was the first Games to build an Olympic park of such grandeur and obvious political symbolism, the first Games in which a consolidated ideological machine was actively engaged in staging the Games. Berlin was also the first Games to be covered by television; it received the highest level of media coverage yet received and it was the subject of the innovative and deeply politicised film-making of Leni Riefenstahl, whose film of the Nuremburg Rally, *Triumph of the Will* which was released in 1934 as an explicit propaganda vehicle for the Nazi party, was followed by filming of the 1936 Olympics *Olympia*. *Triumph of the Will* had not only set a precedent for future films documenting and glorifying the Olympic Games, but the synergies between this film and *Olympia* merged the two events, the rally and the Games, since both were explicitly and directly political in their creation of spectacle. Riefenstahl was one of the very few women film makers of the time and her involvement in films that so overtly, and technically effectively, expressed Nazi propaganda has been highly controversial. Her work is highly regarded for its technical competence but strongly criticised for its message, the more so because she was a woman, although what seems more relevant to a critique than the empirical gender of the director, beyond endorsing the view that women cannot be the sole bearers of moral principles, is the combination of forces which make up the political movement of which the films are expressive. These forces include those of political ideologies, the breakdown of economic systems, enduring cultures including those of militarism, bellicosity and masculinity.

Each film presents a cinematic version of the intersecting forces of Nazi politics, the technologies of film and photography, militarism, cultural, elitism, racism and racialisation and patriarchy which is extremely unsettling as a powerfully manipulative experience of explicit Nazi propaganda which situates the viewer not only as a spectator but also as member of the crowd which endorsed Hitler's politics. This version of disciplined militaristic masculinity is also evocative of the sporting masculinities that have informed the Modern Olympics, from the very start with de Coubertin's conceptualisation of the Games as a challenge to feminised failure in war. Spectatorship is central to the film. *Triumph of the Will* privileges the viewer with an impossible, perfect view of the proceedings, in a troubling disconcerting way, such that viewers become, for the duration of the film, the protagonist of Nazism, resonant of the processes through which Hitler generated affects of control among large numbers of ordinary German people. Sensation is unmediated in that sensation occupies the interstitial spaces and the to and fro of affect between film and spectator.

In the orchestrated editing and vast, abstract human landscapes of the outdoor sequences, considerable weight is invested in the individualised figure of Hitler. The figure of Hitler is reconstituted and re-presented as expansive, laughing and joking with his people, but the next moment, he is abstracted, so lost in the apparently deep responsibilities of leadership that he seems not to be able to hear the ecstatic applause as he looks over his notes. The central figure of Hitler is made from the first minutes of the opening stanza of the film, when he appears to descend from the clouds, transubstantiated from a Teutonic heaven to the earthly precincts of Nuremberg appearing to be invested with both divine authority and populist ordinariness. What the film most effectively generates is disquiet about the extent to which Riefenstahl's films in the 1930s, in particular the cinematic spectacle which explicitly brings together politics and the Olympics in particular, can be caught up in a politics of deception and destruction through the engagement with spectacle. Similar technologies of production and presentation are involved in Olympia, which has the added dimension of sporting practices and the mechanisms of investment in sporting success which makes up sport.

No Olympic Games had presented such a coordinated spectacle as Berlin. The Olympic Torch Relay was a ritual initiated by the Games organiser Carl Diem, in order to anchor Germany's civilising missions and give cultural weight to its Hellenic roots, whether real or imagined. On the opening day of the Games, an open-air breakfast concert was presented for the IOC, after which 28,000 members of the Hitler Youth celebrated the arrival of the Olympic torch in a city centre park. In the evening, the IOC and the upper echelons of the Nazi party entered the Olympic Stadium together to the strains of Wagner, whose work has been haunted by and haunts the historic contradictions of its sublime and transcendent musicality and its political associations. Later in the evening, Goebbels entertained 2,000 Olympic and foreign dignitaries in a mansion recently confiscated from a Jewish Berlin family. Over the course of the Games, the most ambitious and expensive cultural Olympiad was staged, accentuated heavily on German music, opera and health rather than 'degenerate' modern art.

There was a strong strand of neo-medievalism in the aesthetic of the Nazi regime. Faux medieval orders, flags, pennants and crests were an essential part of the visual vocabulary of the great mass rallies that the party staged as well as of the day-to-day adornment of state offices and uniforms. The 1936 Olympics gave the regime a gigantic canvas on which to project itself, utilising insignia which connect the Aryan visions of the regime with the Olympic spirit and demonstrating the power of spectacle in promoting political ideology.

Sporting spectacles and mega-events

The media have played a role, especially in recent years, in transmitting knowledge about sport through making visible and audible particular sporting practices and connections. Sport always stands for something more than itself, 'always both representing and being represented' (Miller et al., 2001, p. 61). Sport lends itself to spectacle and sensation; it is more than kicking, hitting or catching a ball, or running or jumping; it is about success and failure, and hopes and aspirations. These may be personal, they may be linked to community, such as a particular team or club, or they may be national, especially as expressed in international competitions. The Olympics are such international competitions, and are prime examples of what have come to be called 'mega-events' (Roche, 2000).

Miller et al. suggest that rituals such as the medal ceremonies at the Summer Olympic Games epitomise 'national identification and affect'. Such rituals are a tableaux of bodily dispositions. The athletes, their bodies draped in the colours and insignia of nation and corporation, are led to the ceremony. Olympic Games' opening ceremonies as rituals are illustrative of sporting mega-events where the culture of sport is represented and reproduced, especially through the media coverage that transmits these events across the globe.

In the contemporary world, the label of mega event is increasingly associated with sport or popular entertainment, because of the sponsorship they invite and the profits that can accrue to investors. It is impossible to disentangle the spectacle from the levels of sponsorship, although the relationship is not straightforward or singular in its trajectory. At some points the sponsorship and the product being sponsored can become disassociated. The product provides the spectacle, as, for example, the Olympics do on a large scale every four years, or other sports do throughout their season each year, as, for example, football does. However, as has been demonstrated in the case of football, there is no direct relationship between the sponsor and the product and the regulatory bodies of the sport, like FIFA, are also involved. In 2011 the sport and its sponsors, including Coca-Cola (which also sponsors the Olympics), became so disconnected that the sponsor called into question the integrity of the governing body of the sport, some of whose members are also members of the IOC. This is a far from simple story of a healthy wholesome product, sport, benefiting from the albeit profit-motivated support of commerce; sponsors too can appeal to the moral high ground and cast aspersions at the integrity of sport. The escalation of sponsorship has, however, had significant impact upon sport and the Games in particular, especially in relation to their display and the processes of making spectacles and what counts as spectacular.

While the Berlin Games of 1936 were explicitly political, the 1984 Los Angeles Games, the 'capitalist games', were more directly commercial:

> Led by the dynamic Ueberoth, the LAOOC sold television rights to ABC for $225 million; the European networks Eurovision and Intervision together paid another $22 million, and the Japanese added some $11 million to the coffers. The LAOOC raised another $130 million from thirty corporate sponsors, including American Express, Anheuser-Busch, Canon, Coca-Cola, Levis, IBM, Snickers and Sanyo. (Guttmann, 2002: 160)

No fewer than '43 companies were licensed to sell "official" Olympic products, such as the McDonald's Olympic hamburger and the Mars Olympic snack' (Scambler, 2005: 65), and the opening ceremony has been described not only as 'show-biz' but as Disneyland. There are different elements in the construction of a sporting spectacle, which include the processes of production, choreography and performance. Sporting events now increasingly involve the display and pageantry of the entertainment industry and at times there is little to mark out the sporting event from the mass appeal rock concert. This trend in the production of big sporting occasions has been called 'spectacularisation' (Gruneau, 1989). Through these processes, colour, variety and drama are added to the sporting narrative being represented by 'packaging the product' (Stead, 2008: 341).

The Modern Olympics have become ever more dependent on sponsorship and on television companies, as has indeed become the case in much sport across the globe. Commercial sponsors donate money in order to advance their own businesses through the global publicity afforded by advertising at the Olympics. NBC contracted to pay the IOC US$3.7 billion over the 12 years from 2000. Audiences are vast and it is the media coverage of the Games that attracts sponsors and television companies. The Olympics are big business. At Athens in 2004, when there were 11,000 athletes from 201 nations and 12,000 media personnel, an estimated 3.9 billion people watched the Games (Horne, 2007). Domestic sponsorship raised over US$600 million, more than 3.5 million tickets were sold, generating US$228m. The television rights to the Games made US$1,476,911,634 (Robinson, 2008). At Beijing there were 11,028 athletes from 204 NOCs who competed in 28 sports and 302 events. In 2009 the Beijing Organising Committee reported that expenditure would be on a par with Athens in 2004, that is $15 billion, but other sources suggest it was more like $40 billion, making the Beijing Games the most expensive to date (Guardian, 2008, 2011).

The Olympics certainly have international appeal and are conducted on a very large scale. Maurice Roche argues that mega-events are best understood as large-scale cultural (including commercial and sporting) events, which have a dramatic character, mass popular appeal and international significance (Roche, 2000: 1), claiming that mega-events in globalised modernity have become not only more complex but also more contradictory in the relationships between sport, commercial enterprise, sponsorship and governance (Roche, 2006).

Sport is included in the category of culture, along with a whole range of activities and interests ranging across not only music, art, drama, literature and sport, but all the different ways in which human societies are distinguished and make sense of themselves. Culture includes the material culture of artefacts and the culture of ideas and beliefs. Sport has synergies with religion, especially in its affective elements; it has even been claimed that sport could be a religion, so powerfully held are the beliefs and commitments attached to sport. It is in the mega-events that such claims might have most resonance. Ellis Cashmore argues that the opening and closing ceremonies at the Olympics, like half-time at the Super Bowl, offer the most staged, 'stupendous, elaborate displays of ritual and liturgy' (Cashmore, 2005: 110), which he compares to religion which was certainly supported in 2008 with the most spectacular opening and closing ceremonies at Beijing, albeit within an overtly secular framework.

Beijing featured stadiums that have become architectural landmarks (Rogge, 2008, 2011). The Beijing National Stadium, the now famous Bird's Nest was full to its 91,000 capacity and provided a stunning display of Chinese culture. The ceremony was directed by Chinese filmmaker Zhang Yimou, who was the chief director. The director of music for the ceremony was composer Chen Qigang. It was noted for its focus on ancient Chinese culture, and for its creativity, as well as for being the first to use weather modification technology to prevent rainfall. The final ascent to the torch featured Olympic gymnast Li Ning, who appeared to run through air around the membrane of the stadium. Featuring more than 15,000 performers, including the famous terracotta warriors, the ceremony lasted over four hours and was reported to have cost over US$100 million to produce. The opening ceremony was lauded by spectators and various international presses as spectacular and spellbinding and by many accounts the greatest ever (Brownell, 2008). The handover of the Olympic flag from the Mayor of Beijing to the Mayor of London Boris Johnson, followed by a performance organised by LOCOG, which included performances by guitarist Jimmy Page, and recording artist Leona Lewis in a closing ceremony presented something of a contrast between Beijing and London. Whereas Beijing had deployed a vast panoply of visual, aural, sentient techniques whereby to celebrate Chinese cultural inheritance, encompassing art, opera, dance, albeit all prior to the communist era, London relied upon more modest icons of popular contemporary culture, a London bus and David Beckham, who, nonetheless, embodies a pinnacle of the sports mega star. Celebrity is a crucial component of Western cultural practice, increasingly manifest in sport.

Cashmore suggests that in the Western world, sports stars are better known than religious leaders and the spectacular displays associated with contemporary sport may even imply transcendental properties previously reserved for religion. His other argument about sport relates to the enthusiasm of its followers and the claim that sport provides direction and fills a vacuum for individuals and communities in the contemporary world. The spectacle of the Games suggests that this claim might have some purchase, although the comparison between religion and sporting allegiances is greatly exaggerated in claims about the spiritual qualities of sport that are likely to be unacceptable to religious believers. However, the rituals of the sporting spectacle, the scale of the display and its flamboyance all make the significance of the opening ceremonies of the Olympics in the modern world central to an understanding of the processes and power systems in which sport is implicated and how sport generates and legitimises power relations in the wider political and cultural terrain. Cashmore's argument suggests rationality and agency in the performance as well as the creation of the event which can be better construed as generative of emotional, political, economic, social and cultural affects in itself, that is, in its performance.

The scale of the Olympics and their ceremonies, and the global networks, through which they are transmitted, make the Games megaevents. It is the potential that the Games offer for economic growth and financial gain, and the sport–media–commerce nexus through which this is made possible, that opens up the massive investment and commercial promise of these sporting spectacles. In sport, the megaevents can be seen as those that, firstly, are deemed to have significant consequences for the city, region and nation in which they are held and, secondly, attract considerable media coverage thereby attracting global investment. The commercialisation of the Games as well as their political potential and the scope they provide for enhancement of the host city and nation, in terms of both economic infrastructure and cultural kudos, further contribute to their large-scale, 'mega' status.

The torch: 1948 and 2012

The Olympic torch is a key object in the events which make up and inspire the Olympics. Although the torch is largely represented as symbolic it can also be seen as having the expressive capacities to go beyond discourse (Massumi, 2002) as an object which generates affects and is itself generated by political, cultural and social forces. The torch itself creates light and movement and generates inspirational affects. The object of the torch is always related to its bearer, or bearers, and to the spaces through which it moves as well as its own materiality and the technologies used to light it, with the method of lighting the cauldron having the capacity to create as much anxiety as inspiration, such as the archer in Barcelona 1992 or the flying gymnast in Beijing 2008. The torch and its bearers carry enormous cultural and political weight in the make-up of the Games: Muhammad Ali in Atlanta 1996 and Cathy Freeman in Sydney 2000.

Much has been made of the torch relay with its opportunities for 8,000 torch bearers at the 2012 Olympics. The torch was of equivalent importance in the Austerity Games of 1948 (Ampton, 2009) and a comparison of the two moments and the events through which they were constituted is interesting in exploring the spectacles and sensations of the Games, especially within the context of promoting social inclusion and addressing inequalities. The London 2012 presentation of plans for the torch offers a particularly useful and interesting way of exploring how the torch as an object is caught up in the event and how different elements combine to generate excitement and intensity, which has much in common with 1948, even though the two Olympiads are separated by 64 years.

London 2012 is in sharp contrast to the last time the Games were held in the city in 1948, although both had torch relays. In 1948, there was no 70-day extravaganza and it involved nothing like the 8,000 torchbearers to carry the Olympic flame around the United Kingdom in 2012, although the London 1948 Olympic Torch Relay was greeted with wild rejoicing and a mobbing of the torchbearer, even when he (and they were all he) ran on by in the dead of night (BBC News 1948, 2011). Ahead of London's 1948 Austerity Games, the organisers, led by Lord Burghley, continued the pre-war tradition started by the Nazi regime at the 1936 Berlin Games to set up what was then only the second torch relay of the modern Olympic Games; 2012 may be post global economic crises, but in 1948 post-war budget, Britain was struggling with rationing, which would be in place for another six years (Hampton, 2009). Lord Burghley, however, in 1948 (like Lord Coe in 2012) wanted to stage a relay to 'capture the imagination of the public and the spirit of the Olympic torch' (BBC News 1948, 2011).

The scale and scope of the event, like the torch itself, had to meet the stringent demands of an austerity budget. Britain could barely afford to stage the Games so the scope of the relay and the torch itself had to be affordable. The 1948 Olympic torch was a relatively simple artefact, fairly hefty with a plain stem topped with a wide cup that held the burner. Capital letters in the style of the 1940s spelt out 'With thanks to the bearer' and the Olympic rings are punched out on the bowl.

The designer of the 1948 torch Ralph Lavers had been required to create something inexpensive and easy to make, but still 'of pleasing appearance and a good example of British craftmanship'(BBC News 1948, 2011).The torches used in the 1948 relay were made of aluminium, a relatively cheap material , and ran on solid fuel tablets, except that used in the final leg at the opening ceremony inside Wembley's Empire Stadium, which was stainless steel and housed a magnesium-fuelled flame designed to be easily visible by the watching crowds and cameras.

In 2012, the torch covered the United Kingdom, aiming to come within one hour's journey of 95 per cent of the population. In 1948 the domestic plan was less ambitious. However, issues of equity and democracy were still caught up in the 1948 as well as in the 2012 event. The 1948 relay had a wide scope and was located within the boundaries of Britain. In 1948 there was a European leg, with a Relay of Peace starting from Greece, through Italy, Switzerland, France, Luxembourg and Belgium through to England.

This enterprise was situated within the context of reiterating and reconstructing European unity after the devastation of a continent shattered by World War II and still in turmoil. The Games' Official Report of the XIV Olympiad relates how on 17 July in the ancient stadium at Olympia, the first runner, Greek Corporal Dimitrelis, stepped forward. Laying down his arms and taking off his uniform, he appeared clad as an athlete and thus having symbolised the tradition that war ceased during the period of the Ancient Games, he lit his torch and set off (Torch 1948, 2011). These were not only the Austerity Games they were the peace games and there was a clear division within this stage in the 1948 event between militarism and athleticism, even if the torch's arrival at Wembley stadium was greeted with a 21 gun salute.

After years of stress, the report recalled, 'a gleam of light, the light of a Flame, which crossed a continent without hindrance, … caused frontiers to disappear, … gathered unprecedented crowds to see it pass' and 'lit the path to a brighter future for the youth of the world' (Torch, 1948, 2011). When the torch arrived at Dover late on 28 July, 50,000 people welcomed it and a five-mile-long caravan of traffic followed the start of its overnight journey towards Wembley. Janie Hampton, however, reports a shaky start for the torch's arrival in Dover after its 11-day journey; the flame blew out for the first time as soon as it landed in Dover, only to be relit not by the back-up flames from Olympia, but by a cigarette lighter, and later on, by a firework (Hampton, 2009).

In 1948 there was no mass television or satellite coverage of course and the relay was many people's only contact with the Olympic Games and a sufficient attraction to bring people out onto the streets, even at night, in an era of few televisions. In Charing, Kent, at 1.30 a.m., 3,000 people reputedly mobbed the torchbearer; in Guildford, Surrey, every available policeman.

In 2012 the context was very different; an extended period of peace in spite of military activity in Iraq and Afghanistan in which the British participated and a global cultural economy saturated with media capacity to record and transmit images and massages across the globe at alarming speed. The speed and flows of media networks so closely enmeshed with sport are unprecedented. Nonetheless, the plan for 2012 was to create embodied connections and to make the experience of the Games local as well as global within the United Kingdom. The London Olympics torch relay beginning on 19 May 2012 at Land's End and ending 70 days later at the opening ceremony in the Olympic Stadium was to follow an 8,000-mile route in order to encompass as much of the UK community as possible (BBC News Torch, 2011).

At the press conference in 2011, which launched the relay route, Lord Coe talked about LOCOG's decision to extend the democratic approach which London had taken to the presentation of the Games from the start of the bidding process, with its emphasis on social inclusion and diversity. The process was one of participation, through the technologies of the Internet where, as with ticket purchase, citizens could become torch bearers (BBC News Torch, 2011). Seb Coe spoke of how the torch would travel through communities, being carried by different people and 'the galvanising effect he expected the tour to have on communities as the Olympic spirit coursed through them and they hosted their own celebratory events' (Coe Torch, 2011) deploying a discourse of charitable cohesion and traditional community values which are resonant of the Queen's speech discussed in Chapter 1. 'Coe spoke affectingly about a husband and wife team who sold their house so the community gym they run in south-east London could survive – his nomination for one of the 7,200 out of 8,000 torchbearer slots reserved for members of the public' (Coe Torch, 2011).

The torch, its movement and progress are, however, also enmeshed with the economic and political forces which make up the Olympics. Coe's press conference was also attended by representatives of the three presenting partners, Samsung, Coca-Cola and Lloyds TSB, whose companies' logos necessarily and inevitably are displayed at all opportunities. 'The man from Coca-Cola alone promised to bring "happiness and celebration" to the route' (Coe Torch, 2011). The torch relay is one of the few events at which the IOC permits overt branding, in the symbiotic relationship necessitated by LOCOG's need for the sponsors to contribute £700 million towards its £2 billion budget, and the sponsors require value for their investment. Elements of bathos intruded when the press conference began with Coe invoking the loftiest of Olympic ideals and ended with the defence of Coca-Cola Coke and questions on how many fizzy drinks his own children consumed. All three sponsors have also invested in the idea of using the relay as a means to run campaigns offering worthy members of the public the opportunity to participate in Olympic history and run a short distance with the torch. The global/local actualities of the relay include local media coverage of the back stories of those running and the celebratory events that will take place every night thus generating enthusiasm for the global event that is the Olympics.

Democracy and community

Spectacles are as much about absences as presences. Women were excluded from the first Games of the modern period and not permitted to enter until 1900, and even then women were restricted to a very limited number of competitions. The resistance to women's inclusion can be attributed to the misogyny of patriarchal Victorian value systems, which drew on the fear that too much athleticism, like too much intellectual activity, might impair women's reproductive powers. De Coubertin had also expressed anxiety about the inappropriateness of women's bodies being on public display. Things have changed and the Olympics have more recently offered a much fairer playing field, even showcasing women's athletic triumphs to be configured within the games' heroic narratives. International sporting festivals, such as the opening and closing ceremonies of the Games, provide rare opportunities for women athletes to gain recognition. One instance of this is the case of Cathy Freeman, the Aboriginal sprinter who carried the torch at the Sydney Games in 2000 and won Australia's one track gold medal. However, although Aboriginal culture was central to the opening ceremony in Australia, the historical and contemporary situation of Aboriginal peoples was not and remains marginalised in mainstream Australian politics. The points of inclusion at the Olympics may belie the role of women and black and minority ethnic peoples in sport (Phillips and Magdalinski, 2008).

The range of scope of the Games carries egalitarian meanings, especially given the framework of the Olympic ideal, however tarnished at times, and the spectacles of these mega-events can be seen as creating new and more democratic possibilities. There are opportunities for diversity in location, for example, through staging the Games across the globe, through the inclusion of over 200 nations and a vast range of sports and the focus on the athletics as a sport with more egalitarian capacities and representation. The opening ceremonies include the march past of each nation, without hierarchy in alphabetical order, except for some priority to the host nation while the medal ceremonies celebrate meritocratic achievement albeit based on resources which privilege some nations over others.

Whatever the purpose of the organisers of the Games or of the IOC, the delivery of the Olympics has to be orchestrated. Cultural meanings and practices are created and performed in elaborate, complicated and costly processes whereby the ceremonies are constructed and presented as well as emerging and transforming through iterative practices and performances. Music is selected to connote particular meanings, often because it is linked to national belongings, militaristic practices and patriotic stories. Cultural practices which form the stratified deposits of common sense (Gramsci, 1971) appear organic and taken for granted, but they also have to be reproduced and recreated, and the Games offer an entertaining illustration of cultural reproduction in practice. Beijing in 2008 used highly regimented disciplined displays to invoke and perform traditional Chinese cultural practices and histories without any explicit deployment of China's more recent Communist inheritance but with the military precision that legacy had made possible (Beijing 2008, 2011).

The realisation of de Coubertin's dream was from the very beginning a betrayal of an ideal: a version, like amateurism in sport for much of this century, of what the American sociologist Robin Williams (1963:391–5) called a cultural fiction, in which lip service is paid to values which do not match with or prescribe the limits of everyday action. It is no less a cultural fiction today. In the song to round off the Los Angeles Opening Ceremonies (both pre-Opening and once the Games were officially open), the stadium swayed to the tune of *Reach Out and Touch* with adapted lyrics stressing international friendship:

> Reach out and touch somebody's hand,
> Make the world a better place if you can;
> Come join the celebration as we salute the unity of every nation....
> That we all care and it's love and people everywhere...
> We can change things if we start giving;
> Why don't you... Reach out and touch?
>
> (Tomlinson, 1996: 602)

Not every nation was there in Los Angeles to be saluted. For example, the USSR, as it then was, withdrew from what have also been called the Cold War Games. In such ways are cultural fictions concretised, and global political and cultural histories enmeshed with an ever-adaptable set of Olympic ideals and a recurrently revisionist account of Olympic history (Lenskjy, 2008).

Conclusion

The rituals and spectacles of the Olympic Games are conventionally seen to offer particularly opportunities for the promotion of cultural values as well as products through the visibility of spectacular displays. The presence of the world's media and modern technologies make them especially attractive to sponsors and entrepreneurs as well as governments; this is a global stage on which sports stars perform and goods and values can be promoted through performance, association and display. However, different sites involve different specific practices and different Olympics are generative of different affects which are temporally and spatially situated and configured.

The values that are implicitly and explicitly expressed at these ceremonies, especially the opening ceremonies, are frequently configured around the nation and, in particular, the nation state, which has a powerful position in the assemblages of the Modern Olympics: the games offer a stage for the performance of a nation which is often denied in other political arenas. The culture of the Games as expressed at the ceremonies is also framed by the Olympic Movement and its ideals, although these are ideals that have largely been betrayed, especially in terms of the celebration of peace and a peace movement for young people (Lenskyj, 2000, 2008, Tomlinson, 1996).

The ceremonies demonstrate that sport is to be taken seriously: sport matters. Whatever the hyperbole and the razzmatazz of these mega-events, what is at stake is more than 'just entertainment'. Not only are the Games big business, they are also seriously political and offer a site for the enactment of political conflicts, which demand the generation of sensations of emotion and sentient as well as material affects. Sport is also crucial to representation and assemblage of culture and is constitutive of culture through the modes of commerce, politics and nation. The virtual and the representational are inseparable from the enfleshed practices and material dimensions and forces of the games. Materialities such as financial and economic flows and sponsorship are shaped by as well as shaping the virtual processes of sponsorship.

The Games largely present a very particular version of the nation and the nation state, as bounded and contained, rather than a more open transnational, globalised source of identity. The rituals and symbols deployed at the ceremonies reinforce, reinstate, remember and create traditional national identities which are strongly evocative of the militaristic disciplined body practices of masculinity by which they are performed. This is clearly a place for national patriotic identifications and for political as well as sporting contests, but, although sport is so transparently based on the binary logic of sex, the opening and closing ceremonies are far from transparent in their enactment of masculinity and hegemonic masculinity as performance elides with athletic, enfleshed achievement and, in the big ceremonies, militaristic nationalism.

The Games are global through the range of nations participating and, even more importantly, through the involvement of global corporations and the world media. The opening ceremonies of the Olympics demonstrate the impact of globalisation in all its manifestations and the links between sport, politics, economy and culture, and the inequalities of the contemporary globalised world.

The culture of sport is closely connected to global politics and economics, which is particularly apparent in the sport–media–commerce nexus which plays out in the opening ceremonies of the Olympics to demonstrate the inextricable interconnections between the media and sponsorship, and some of the contradictions as well as synergies between the mega-event and the Olympic ideal. Performance of the big events of the Games are as competitive as the enfleshed athletic activities, with each host city and nation attempting to present a spectacle that surpasses all others, Beijing in 2008 being a good example in both the politics and the display of the events and the synthesis of the virtual with the material. The massive displays in which individual people were subsumed into collective waves of light, movement and colour provided a demonstration of the massive scale of population and change in China.

The Modern Olympics offer an accumulation of new technologies through which cultural changes take place, all of which is closely enmeshed with the creation and performance of the spectacle and the experience and relationship of spectatorship. This is not a linear narrative of change and progress, although there have been pivotal moments of drama and disruption in the Games. There are remarkable endurances in the disciplined marching of the national groups of athletes, the iteration of the Olympic ideals from the IOC, the magnitude of the stadiums with tiny figures in blocks of nation and similar but more mobile collections of the artists and performers. Spectacles are orchestrated and designed but they also generate and are productive of new relationships and configurations that have political, economic, social and cultural affects as well as reacting to and being formed by them. Spectators and the performance of the event are all caught up in the processes of being, doing, remembering and becoming, where the rituals of the Olympics are experienced in the enfleshed presence of 'being there' or viewed at a distance on television.

Some of the processes of cultural production are manifested in the organisation and management of the opening ceremonies in which media play an important role, not only in the transmission of sporting spectacles, but also in their creation. The use of symbols, images and signifiers of nation and athleticism, the choice of music and visual images are all affects of and are affected by current popular cultural forms as portrayed in the entertainment industry, as well as the narratives of national pride and athletic achievement that make up the memories as well as the imaginings of the Olympics. Cultures are reproduced and formed through a mix of technologies, symbols, representations, memories and stories that come together in sporting mega-events and spectacles to which visibility and sensation are central.

6
The Art of Sport

The spectacles such as sporting competitions and events and the mega spectacles of opening and closing ceremonies which were discussed in Chapter 5 are all part of the processes of display which characterise the Olympics and create its visibilities. Art is another display system and in the run-up to 2012 art as display took on a very different form from that which is most usually associated with art and sport. This chapter focuses upon a different set of processes from those that were the subject of Chapter 2, and develops those of Chapter 5, namely, the processes that are involved in looking and spectatorship and at debates about representation. What happens and what is the relationship between looking in art and looking at sport and how is sport represented in art?

Rather than exploring art as a visual reflection upon and reconstruction of a sporting event, this chapter addresses some of the points of connection between art and sport in projects that explicitly engage with widening opportunities and promoting social inclusion in order to offer some understanding of how different systems can be assembled to create sporting events and experiences which are central to the Olympics. The links between art and sport offer a different dimension of widening participation which might challenge – or reinforce – social inclusion as a charitable project which constructs its constituents and recruits as the beneficiaries of altruism.

The art of sport can relate to the competences of sporting activities and practices; sport especially at the highest levels demands both supreme technical skills and the creativity to go beyond routine, competent performance. Elite sport requires a very high degree of skill as well as aspiring to the very highest levels of human achievement so that the performance of sport can be indistinguishable from artistic performance, embodied in the description of boxing as the Noble Art.

London 2012 is also distinctive in its embrace of the Cultural Olympiad, the website of which (Cultural Olympiad, 2011) outlines the celebration of the London Games in events spread over several years in order to sustain and secure a lasting cultural legacy and covering a range of categories of activities, places and movements; literature, libraries, museums, galleries, music, outdoor events, theatre, dance and comedy all coming together in the 2012 London festival, the biggest ever such festival. The Cultural Olympiad, like global sport, is explicitly dependent on sponsorship, listed on its site: the Arts Council England, Legacy Trust UK and the Olympic Lottery Distributor. BP and BT are Premier Partners of the Cultural Olympiad and the London 2012 Festival, The British Council supporting the international development of the London 2012 Cultural Olympiad projects and Panasonic are the presenting partner of Film Nation: Shorts (Cultural Olympiad, 2011). The project has been aimed at promoting maximum participation and social inclusion through the arts as well as building upon Britain's canonical inheritance, notably as embodied in Shakespeare through events at Stratford on Avon, Shakespeare's birthplace at the newly rebuilt theatre, at the Globe in London and in a new BBC film series of his plays. In the field of promoting widening participation through the arts there is always a tension between those elements which are concerned with making the canon and what is situated at the higher end of the high/low spectrum of tradition in the arts, available and accessible to everyone and on the other hand opening up possibilities for new creators of the arts. Art, like sport, is also widely imbricated in the power axes which generate inequalities as well as opportunities.

Other tensions relate to the individualism of both fields and the idea that artists work for themselves to achieve personal acclaim in the same way that athletes seek a personal best and individual celebrity, whatever the language of being a team player. At the announcement of the 12 leading British artists commissioned to design artwork for 2012, Michael Craig-Martin, the veteran conceptual artist selected, who is probably best known as a tutor at Goldsmiths College in London where he mentored a cohort of the much acclaimed Young British Artists (YBA), was reported as saying:

> If art and sport have something in common it's that both are about personal achievement and obsession. (Hudson, 2011)

He went on to observe that while designers, for example, of Olympic posters do so as a work assignment, 'artists bring something different ... a personal language, a personal vision' (Hudson, 2011: R4).

Obsession and individual creativity relate to the psychic investment that artists and athletes make as well as the dedication and commitment that is required to achieve success. It also points to the creativity and passion that are elements of both sport and art, but the emphasis upon individualism is inimical to the collective project of widening participation and promoting social inclusion. Nonetheless, the contemporary cultural stress on celebrities means that diversity programmes inevitably draw upon the idea of the celebrity role model as well as the notion that the move from obscurity to fame is possible for anyone whatever their social situation.

Art and sport are not easy companions and the relationship can be underpinned by an antipathy between the aesthetic more cerebral practices of art that affect sport as corporeal and unthinking. The ancient Greek culture which informed the Ancient Games involved the perception of both art and sport as sacred activities to be revered and respected equally. Twentieth-century cultural practices of common sense suggested divisions between the two fields with each constituted in part through the specificities of the other, art as effete and removed from everyday life, sport as hearty and philistine. Craig-Martin reinstates this from his position as an artist, through his reference to having no interest in sport 'probably because I was very bad at it' (Hudson, 2011: R4), thus re-iterating the everyday observation that not only are art and sport diametrically opposed but natural talent in one might preclude engagement with any success in the other. Art and sport, however, might be able to offer more, and this is what informs some of the 2012 Cultural Olympiad and, on a smaller scale, the Art of Sport project which I researched for this book. In the twenty-first century the United Kingdom already has a legacy of popular British art represented in the work of contemporary artists like Tracey Emin, Rachel Whiteread, Chris Ofili all members of the group that was called YBA and who are members of the group of 12 whose work has been commissioned for 2012 and the festival of the Cultural Olympiad. These are also artists who live in the host city and are part of its culture, as Martin Creed, the minimalist artist who has actually sent sprinters hurtling through the galleries of Tate Britain as part of his work and who has also been chosen, noted, 'art helps fix the games in time particularly if you use artists that are of the time and local to the place' (in Hudson, 2011: R4).

This chapter narrows the empirical focus on art in the context of representation, but widens the remit by linking art to the discourses of social inclusion and equal opportunities. Celebrity is still implicated, but The Art of Sport project is slightly unusual because it highlights the need to work at success and counters the X Factor or Big Brother television game show, reality TV formula of picking people from nowhere to occupy starring roles. The Art of Sport programme brings in local heroes in sport who were already training hard but who had not yet made it along with artists in similar positions as well as more publicly recognised figures in art and sport. I also suggest an alternative conceptualisation of the materialities of art through different genres, interpretations and images of sport and in particular use the deconstruction of the 2012 project, The Art of Sport, sponsored by Lloyds TSB bank, which brings together young artists and young athletes in a promotional fundraising venture. This is achieved within a project which seeks to attract investment by some of the bank's more affluent personal clients. This project involves a somewhat different version of the sponsorship process which occupies not only the private arena of personal, individual clients as sponsors, but also a more private, intimate sphere of relationships that are not named in the public arena; this is private money and private people who do not want to display their names in public.

Art is considered as material, that is, as an object which has affects and is affected (Clough, 2008, Deleuze, 2005). Art objects themselves generate affect and are affected by spectators and instigators of such projects as The Art of Sport (see figures 1–6). The participation of a big bank in a role that draws on a legacy of patronage, reconfigured in a particular economic climate of recession (the project began in 2008, with exhibitions through 2009), demonstrates some of the points of connection and disconnection and the affects of art and of sport.

Art and the Games

There has been a long tradition of links between art and sport in the Olympics. De Coubertin developed ideas for an art competition which involved awarding art works in the various fields that were directly inspired by sport. In fact, the emphasis on art inspired by sport was spelt out in invitations to the Art Competitions by organising committees and was encoded in the Regulations of the Contests Literary and Artistic for 1912. However, momentum gathered over the twentieth century for a shift from the holding of arts competitions to the arts festivals which became the Cultural Olympiads, which developed the connections between sport, cultural policy and urban regeneration (Garcia, 2008, Inglis, 2008).This idea was strongly supported by Avery Brundage when he became President of the IOC in 1952 (Stanton, 2000). In a 'circular' published in July 1953 Brundage set out the case as to why he believed that Olympic arts competitions had seen their day. One reason was that the arts awards tended to go to professional artists and Brundage saw this as being at odds with the amateur ethos of the Olympic Games.

Another strand in the link between art and sport in the Games is the use of posters. Posters have largely been seen as utilitarian, a means of advertising the coming Games, which host cites and nations would exploit as best they could to promote themselves and the Olympics and also, as suggested above as being produced to order, thus lacking the spontaneity and creativity of the 'personal vision' of art (Hudson, 2011). Some critics claimed that advertising was the enemy of art and clearly, from this perspective, the aesthetic pretension of the poster is corrupted and tarnished by its associations with the impure realm of advertising and commercial promotion. However, in many fields of sport, none more so than in the Olympics, posters have been designed by recognized artists and have deployed techniques more usually encountered in the field of art that is uncontaminated by advertising. The trend within advertising too of course has been to play with artistic technologies and aesthetic tropes of fine art. For example, the poster for the Stockholm Olympic Games of 1912, designed by a member of the Swedish Royal Academy, Olle Hjortzberg, provides a relevant illustration of such collaboration. Hjortzberg was a decorative painter well known for his murals of church interiors (Timmers, 2008). He was also a passionate believer in the poster as art form, being a member of the 'Artistic Posters' society. Hjortzberg's poster for Stockholm 1912 is described by Margaret Timmers as follows:

> His composition represented a parade of nations, each athlete bearing a billowing flag – with Sweden's at the forefront – and marching towards the common goal of the Olympic Games. It was also a celebration of the nude male body as an ideal, a symbol of athletic perfection in the classical tradition. (Timmers, 2008:21)

Posters clearly have the capacity to connect art and sport in dynamic ways which could be framed within the democratising rhetoric of the Olympic Movement, but which, nonetheless, reflect and reproduce social divisions, notably those of gendered corporeality and elitism.

Five series, each containing seven posters, were published in conjunction with the 1972 Munich Games, when the organising committee set out "to engage the best [international] artists" in a poster series that would "relate artistic activity to the Olympic Games" (Timmers, 2008:82). Some versions of posters were produced on high-quality paper as limited editions to generate interest in the collectors' market and the artists were selected by an appointed art commission with the brief to target artists who would deliver avant-garde work. Artists contributing to this series included David Hockney, Tom Wesselmann, Jacob Lawrence, Horst Antes, Max Bill and Eduardo Chillida (ibid.: 84–87). Artwork more accessible to a sports audience was presented in what was called the 'sports series' of posters which offered images of 21 different sporting activities. The series included the official poster for the Munich 1972 Games, featuring 'a photographic modification of the architectural model for the Munich Olympic Stadium' (ibid.: 88–89).

Posters have the advantage of immediacy and intensity and of being in the present whatever memories or becomings they may embrace in their symbolic systems. The artwork in a poster directly engages with sport by virtue of its purpose and so offers a particular expression of the synergies between art and sport. Posters are art objects which present unmediated sensation and a mix of the egalitarian and elements of elite sport and high culture in the arrangements of the different strands which make up the poster and its artistic and sporting capacities, which are so frequently concentrated on flesh and embodiment and aestheticised, racialised, sexed bodies. Posters, like other art forms in this context, generate affects and sensation and deal in contradictions.

Affects and sensations

The concept of affect presents alternatives to narrative and mediation and presents a route into understanding the relational processes which have affects and are affected (Clough, 2007, Gregg and Seigworth, 2010). The concept of affect has been increasingly deployed in order to redress some of the inadequacies of poststructuralism and deconstructionist theories in relation to both emotion and the relationship between people and things, which include the spaces in between. For example, these spaces occupy what is between seeing and the seeing subject; between the object that is seen and perception and what is perceived. Objects neither exist in the eye of the beholder as in idealist philosophy nor only in the material objects as in empiricism, but in between through 'the same movement which creates at once the intellectuality of mind and the materiality of things' (Bergson, 1911: 216).

Bergson's conceptualisation of creative evolution counters materialistic or mechanistic notions of the evolution of life in nature and provides the impetus for Deleuzian notions of the relationship between objects and perception which contributes to much current thinking about affect. Bergson's originality lay in the connections between a theory of evolution and a theory of knowledge. Bergson drew a distinction between the character of people's conceptual knowledge of the external world and consciousness as known from within. The intellect in its study of the external world proceeds by analysis and classification of objects which are assumed to be static, arranged in a series of static affairs or events, which is in contrast to human self-consciousness, where change in time is experienced without awareness of a series of states; stages of before and after are interconnected not separately spatialised are the classificatory systems of the external world. These internal states which use neither concepts nor metaphors become feeling, that is, in more recent language, affect, which is made through the movement between internal and external worlds and occupies these interstitial spaces. Feelings can be seen as the conversion of an affect into what, according to Stephen Frosh, can be symbolised and which involve being moved or touched (Frosh, 2011). Feeling can be emotion put into words, or into other communicable forms, which include art forms as bodily states caught up in processes of perception and of putting emotion into words or images or some symbolic form.

The idea of affect also offers a particular perspective on the agency of people, living things and objects that moves away from notions of intention to a consideration of the relational force of things, the unconscious and the capacity of events to intervene in social processes. Agency is in the event: an affect gathers diverse materials and sweeps them up into a new consistency, a transformation for the duration of the affect. This can be applied to the sporting event as in the Games themselves and in the relationship between sport, art and spectatorship or viewing.

Events, like a sporting performance or competition, or a painting encompass a wide range of materials, and how they are arranged is central to the discussion of affect. The arrangement of people, places and things and the affects they generate are understood through sensation, which is central to explanations of affect. A focus on events invokes the relationship between objects, perception and subjects; sport is viewed by spectators as are art objects and it is through spectatorship as well as the enfleshed activities of athletes that affects are generated. It is manifest in the events that are most popular at the Games that there is an interrelationship between what is happening on the track, for example, and how this is both affected by and affects what is seen and enjoyed. It is these affects that work through sensation which art attempts to reconstruct and demonstrate.

Sport and art are both made in relation to the past and to memory, however. Different and diverse materials include their pasts, which generate consistencies and duration and raise questions about representation and memory in relation to objects. Sport is made and re-made through memory and re-constructions of past events, none more so than at the Olympics and memory is an important component of affect. Sporting events are made through their pasts in terms of records previously set and hopes of record breaking and new standards. The networks of sport are also made through memory and through the rehearsal of past triumphs and disappointments. In order to be a sports fan or aficionado you have to be able to remember the genealogy of your team or your hero. Artistic events and art object are understood and constituted as well as classified through the traditions, trends and movements of which they are part.

Although some aspects of the event, especially as represented in a painting or artistic work, may seem static, they incorporate movement; even objects can be arranged so that they develop their own consistencies and intensities and thus sensation, especially in sculpture which embodies the movement of bodies in sport.

The representations of sport are not as distant from its enfleshed practices as might be expected. What artistic representations of sport seek to reproduce are the intensities and expressions of flesh through other materials such as marble, stone or oil paint on canvas. Flesh is implicated in sensation, as material, having its own affects and being affected, but also as having specific capacities and properties which contribute to sensory processes. The whole event is sensory through the organisation of light, movement and matter as in art and expressive systems.

The movement of light and bodies plays a key role in the drama of artistic representation wherever it is enacted and experienced, that is, in the flesh or in an art form. Different senses are evoked and, for example, some are more present in different situations. Being present at the stadium encompasses all aspects of sentience, but the senses are connected through movement and light even when the spectators are not physically present and this is what artistic objects in sport are about even if they seem to be, as objects, far removed from the event in the stadium. Even at a distance we are caught up in the maelstrom of the event and movement develops its own consistencies and intensities and thus sensation (Sobchack, 2004).

Flesh is implicated in sensation, as material, having its own affects and being affected, but also as having specific capacities and properties which contribute to sensory processes none more so than in boxing for spectators and viewers as well as for boxers. Movement takes place within sensation which includes the embodiment and enactment of thought through sensory media. There are particularities to sporting events, not least in relation to the involvement of corporeal activity. Enfleshed selves are implicated in what counts as sport or sporting activity at whatever level in particular ways. There is a connection between participants, even, for example, among runners who pass in the park or on the road, which may not be there among visitors to the museum or the gallery.

The affects of the art object, like the sporting event the intensities of which it seeks to capture, reproduce and create, include the past, which generates consistencies, for example, in the making of heroic masculinities in particular in the sport. Art is productive of sporting affects too although performances of sport have wider circulation on television than in artistic technologies and the Internet. Nonetheless, the relationship between art and sport is implicated in understanding the currency of sport as constituted by and constitutive of culture. An investigation of the processes is also instructive in exploring how different axes of power intersect and the ways in which social and cultural inequalities are at play in the field of sport. Sensation is implicated in these intensities in that the sporting event itself is drama, representation and enfleshed. What is spectacular, for example, through sporting moments, whether live or embodied in a cultural form like the art object, brings together the enfleshed practices of sport and the excitement of spectatorship. The processes, however, are still located within the social context in which art is made and sport is performed and enacted within cultures of inequality and difference.

Art and sport: sport as art

The links between art and sport are not new as was demonstrated above and some sports lend themselves well to different and particular art forms. There are an increasing number of projects linking art and other cultural practices to the Games, many of which are what make up the Cultural Olympiad. The 2012 Cultural Olympiad also recognises the changing technologies and practices of artistic engagement that might recruit a more diverse and youthful constituency, for example, through its combination of film and digital innovation and community art events. The Cultural Olympiad is also interesting in relation to the concerns of this book as it explicitly addresses matters of widening participation and the promotion of social inclusion:

> Spread over four years, it is designed to give everyone in the UK a chance to be part of London 2012 and inspire creativity across all forms of culture, especially among young people.
>
> The culmination of the Cultural Olympiad will be the London 2012 Festival, bringing leading artists from all over the world together from 21 June 2012 in the UK's biggest ever festival – a chance for everyone to celebrate London 2012 through dance, music, theatre, the visual arts, film and digital innovation and leave a lasting legacy for the arts in the UK. (Cultural Olympiad, 2011)

The visual arts are one element in the remit of this project which aims to establish and build upon the links between art and sport. London 2012's Cultural Olympiad builds upon the splendour of the memorable opening ceremony at the 2008 Beijing games, in spirit at least. What can art do and what are the connections between a set of artistic practices, images and the materiality of art as an object for sport and what can sport do for art? What's the relationship between art and sport as modes of display, spectacle, practice and experience? The Olympics are a series of events which have affects and are affected by different dimensions and modes of being which connect to it, including art. There are specific points of connection between art and sport and synergies between art and sport that make art an attractive mode for engaging with the intensities and the emotions of sport. One of the questions that this raises is that of the relationship between emotion and representation and whether what is involved is the representation of emotion in and through art or whether there are alternative ways of explaining the interconnections. Was demonstrated in Chapter 5 some of the intensities of sport have been translated into cinematic representations and sport has been used to promulgate political messages as in the controversial Leni Reifenstahl films in the 1930s, notably her film of the 1936 Olympiad. There are, however, more complex correlations rather than direct causal links between art and sport which are implicated in different kinds of relationships.

Not everyone is enthusiastic about the synergies between art and sport, or uncritical of the Olympic Movement's rhetoric. The argument of David Inglis (2008), amongst others, is that the relationship between sport and the arts has suffered from the modern differentiation between art and sport, for example, as is evident and most apparent in the disjuncture between the Games of the Olympiad and the Cultural Olympiad. The Games organisers have largely failed to see Olympic sport and the cultural programme as being an essentially united endeavour rather than two separate components needing to be somewhat artificially and laboriously linked together. If a clear distinction is made between the arts and sport, the cultural core of the nexus goes unrecognised and the cultural or artistic programme tends to be regarded, whatever rhetoric might be bandied about, as primarily a corporate operation focused on presenting the host city in what the organisers perceive to be the best possible light to an international audience, in the public arena of the global mass media.

According to Beatriz Garcia:

> Rather than separate identities that must be 'blended', sport, culture and education should be seen as dimensions of the very same principle. The sports and recreation science literature understands sport as a cultural manifestation and an activity through which education takes place. Thus, it is not possible to understand the concept of sport or Olympic sport, without reference to the concepts of culture and education. For this reason, the concept of a cultural programme separated from the sporting and educative programmes seems to be redundant. One would expect all of them to be integrated and perceived accordingly by everybody involved within the Olympic experience, from athletes to coaches, organisers and spectators. However, the lack of an integrated sporting cultural discourse perceived as such by average Olympic audiences and promoted as such by Olympic organisers, supporters and media, reveals that the idea of a perfect and evident integration of these concepts within people's minds is far from being a reality. (Garcia, 2008: 366)

Sport and art do, however, have the capacities to generate powerful emotions and strong identifications and there might be meeting points wrought through these affects. The exhilaration and sense of being transported either through participation in the enfleshed activities of sport or even of spectatorship might even go beyond emotion that can be expressed in words and art might over the means of giving expression to such affects.

Affect offers another way of thinking about the processes that are involved. As Brian Massumi argues, although not of sport, there are intensities and affects that are outside the discourse of emotion and representations of feeling but which art as an extradiscursive, transcendental plane could capture (Massumi, 2005). Alternatively, such extradiscursive affects can be understood within a psychoanalytic framework which invokes the concept of jouissance, for example, as developed in the early work of Luce Irigaray to engage with affects that are extra- or prediscursive and outside the patriarchal symbolic (1985). Within sports studies this has sometimes been translated into the idea of 'being in the zone' although much of the work that has used the concept of the zone has focused upon much more individualised dimensions of the experience (e.g. work inspired by Csikzentimihalyi, 1975) than the social aspects which are implicated in Massumi's work and in the approach which I am taking in this book.

The social context in which art and sport are experienced in within the discussion in this chapter is one in which a point of connection between the two is the programmes promoting social cohesion, widen participation and create citizenship.

A sport in which widening participation has been a particular concern, especially as construed as anti-racism programmes, is football, albeit a sport that is not central to the Olympics. Football provides a useful example, however, because of its global reach and appeal and because of its working-class affiliations. Football emphatically puts social class into the mix. Football also features campaigns to eliminate racism, especially in the United Kingdom (KIO, 2011) and increasingly across Europe (FARE, 2011). What is called anti-racism, for example, in the Football against Racism in Europe organisation and its campaigns (FARE 2011) now embraces recruiting and protecting women, gay people, disabled people and disaffected youth and those with drug or alcohol dependencies (Woodward, 2008). The following case study has particular relevance because it highlights issue of social class, the tensions between high and low culture which haunt sport and the troubling matter of how those recruited by widening participation programmes are classified and thus constituted.

The purpose of this example is to locate art and sport synergies in the context of widening participation and to bring social class divisions and configurations of masculinity in sport.

The beautiful game: art and social inclusion

Art provides a means of both displaying and accessing some of the powerful intensities of sport and this has been recognised in a number of fields and through several different projects. One example of such a project, which might be surprising, is that of football. In 2006 'One Love: The Football Art Prize' was organised at the Lowry Galleries, Salford, UK, sponsored by Umbro and launched by former England goalkeeper and sports writer David James, who is one of the few footballers to have exhibited artwork himself. The working class, male affiliations and origins of football might make it an unexpected choice of sport but football (like many sports) 'has everything – colour, movement, passion, triumph and disaster' (Barber, 2006). Barber in her review of the competition and its exhibition even goes so far as to suggest that artists might have been wasting their time painting nudes, Madonnas and flowers when they could have turned their attention to football, which does, of course have a massive global following and is 'the beautiful game' (Goldblatt, 2007).

The Lowry Gallery was well chosen for the One Love exhibition because the artist LS Lowry entered a similar competition called 'Football and the Fine Arts' in 1953, when he had already achieved a considerable reputation and won with a painting called *Going to the Match*, which is on long-term loan from the Professional Footballers' Association who bought it in 1999 for what was then the highest auction price for a modern British painting – £1.9 million. It shows supporters going to the Burnden Park, Bolton Wanderers football club's old ground, and encapsulates what many people consider the golden age of football. The head of galleries at the Lowry successfully approached Umbro for sponsorship and the competition was launched, attracting more than 800 entries from both professional and amateur artists, all male and none of whose work actually shows anyone kicking a ball around. Most are concerned with football supporters and their passion for the game. The contributions were diverse; Bryan Connor entered a witty pastiche of Gainsborough's *Mr and Mrs Andrews*, in which the Andrews are both decked in football scarves, while photographer Bob Thomas showed a close-up of a football supporter's tattoos. There was a seven-foot-high painting of a Subbuteo player by Robert White and a deeply weird painting by John Afflick that looks like a Tiepolo ceiling and shows angels floating over a football stadium (Barber, 2006). But the one that really tugs the heartstrings is by 74-year-old Gerald Cains, who actually entered the same competition as Lowry when he was 21. His painting,

Cup Fever, shows Southampton supporters arriving at Stamford Bridge to play Crystal Palace in a FA Cup semi-final in 1976 and, like Lowry's Going to the Match, conveys that sense of silent, nervous anticipation.

This example is relevant for a number of reasons. Firstly, it demonstrates the persistence of high–low art dichotomies still in play, for example, in the contrast between the high art that is implicit in the reference to Madonnas and landscapes and religious iconography which have so often been the subject of acclaimed high art and which so contrasts with sport, in this case football, as low art, which is associated with mass entertainment and the physical capital of sporting practices. As Bourdieu argued there are distinctions between the class affiliations of cultural practices of the bourgeoisie and upper classes, which have cultural capital, and the working classes who may only invest physical capital and whose activities carry less weight and importance (Bourdieu, 1984). Within sport there are distinctions, with sports like golf and polo being the purview of the affluent and football and boxing being most closely linked to the working classes (the largely white, male working class in the case of football) and to minority ethnic groups and migrant people (mostly men in the history of boxing).The high–low hierarchy remains an enduring property of much artistic discourse and informs some of the debates about the 2012 Cultural Olympiad, which was apparent in the discussion about the use of canonical figures, notably Shakespeare and the tensions between the cultural diversity of multi-ethnic Britain upon which much the London 2012 bid was based and celebration of Britain's heritage. This debate raised questions about the advisability of making the canon available and re-reading and re-versioning great work of the past for the twenty-first century and the extent to which this might inhibit diversity and new expressions of cultural value and creativity.

A second aspect of the relevance of this example of the One Love competition is that of its ordinary affects (Stewart, 2005) that are manifest in this instance in the everyday entanglements of the routine working class, largely male networks of football as represented in the art work of LS Lowry. Working-class masculinities are routinely made and re-made in the synergies between the iteration of the practices of 'going to the match' in art and in life and re-enforced through its associations with those traditional working-class sport. Art is not feminised and effete if its subject is football. Masculinity is reiterated through the association of art and football and this masculinity is strength. The version of masculinity which occupies the affective spaces between the object of art and the everyday practices of football, especially as enacted in spectatorship, is central to the ordinary affects of football. It does raise questions about who is permitted entry into these affective spaces and about the gendering of the spectator who is affected.

This example also demonstrates the interconnections between spectatorship and sport, for example, through the affects of passion and emotion which are summoned up by the enfleshed practices and the culture of football as a sport, and which extend beyond personal and individual investment. The imaginary systems of art and its technologies of representation lend themselves particularly well to these images and re-create these affects. The affect of emotion in this example is clearly central; the interconnections between art and football invoke two fields which can generate emotive responses and 'pull at the heart strings'. Passions here include the banal and the intense and offer a nexus of spectatorship, participation, place and materiality which includes the responses of sentient beings. People, affects and objects are caught up together in these assemblages, which through their inclusion of the ordinary may well offer a dynamic of egalitarian and democratic participation that divisions between high and low art deny and cannot facilitate. The example of Lowry highlights some of the issues and debates which inform using art as a technology within a diversity programme which aims to promote social inclusion and cohesion.

Art is also a mechanism for deploying the ordinary to reach the transcendent; art and sport together offer opportunities for utilising the possibilities and imaginaries for fields which take people out of the ordinary but through what is often ordinary to achieve higher states and get 'into the zone'. Aesthetics embraces the terrain of extreme passions such as fear, grief and rapture and what Terry Eagleton calls 'sensate life ... the business of affections and aversions of how the world strikes the body on its sensory surfaces, of what takes root in the gaze ... and all that arises from our most banal, biological insertion into the world' (Eagleton, 1990:13). Aesthetics is thus concerned with the ordinary as well as the vehement emotions and is primarily an engagement with material experience. This approach, through its inclusion of the ordinary, avoids both the high art–low art binary and the separation of emotion and sentience on the one hand and cognitive, rational processes on the other.

Whereas the Lowry project might have been seen to start not only with the ordinary and routine of the popular and populist intensities of football and its strong working-class fan base, the Lloyds TSB Art of Sport Project was generated in an area of privilege, being initiated by a large bank, a major sponsor of the 2012 Games and targeting its wealth management clients. It was also framed by a discursive regime of agency and choice, for example, of agentic buyers and performances, as artists or athletes as well as the assumed charitable agency and intentionality of the bank.

Banking on the Art of Sport

The Art of Sport project started by LloydsTSB bank in 2008 also presents a strategy for engaging with different dimensions of affect and by recruiting a discursive field, that of art, which has a more privileged aesthetic however far the high–low dichotomy has been challenged within the discourses of contemporary culture, to provide connections to another, generally less aesthetically highly esteemed sphere of cultural activity, whatever the rhetoric of the beautiful game and the Noble Art might suggest. The enfleshed engagements of sport render its activities less privileged in cultural hierarchies.

The Art of Sport project arose from the bank's involvement as a partner in the 2012 Games. LOCOG signed Lloyds TSB as the first national partner for the 2012 Games in a deal worth around £80 million. My discussion of the Lloyds TSB project here is based on my involvement between 2008 and 2011. I first became involved on hearing about a local event near where I live and I interviewed the curator, Ann Aldridge, in 2008, and subsequently was invited to a whole series of the exhibitions and hospitality events. Private Banking is an investment, asset management service for the bank's UK clients who currently, that is, on the basis of its private banking details in 2011, have between £250,000 and £2 million of savings and investments, or an annual income of £100,000 to £500,000 and for its Mayfair banking service £2 million and £20 million of savings and investments, or an annual income of £500,000 or more (Lloyds TSB Private Banking, 2011). Different conditions apply for international clients.

The project was described by Ann Aldridge of Lloyds TSB Private Banking, who was responsible for choosing artists for The Art of Olympic and Paralympic Sports as follows:

> Lloyds TSB is the Official Banking and Insurance Partner of the London 2012 Olympic and Paralympic Games. Lloyds TSB Private Banking's 'Art of Sport' is a cultural and sporting programme bringing together a group of established and emerging artists, working in various media, who have been selected by Lloyds TSB to take inspiration from Olympic and Paralympic sports and produce works of art which will be exhibited and made available for sale.

The artists involved include painters, sculptors and photographers, and their subjects include both Olympic medal-winners and athletes tipped to be the sports stars of the future. (Aldridge, 2009)

The project was publicised as a facility for artists to represent their country just as much as the athletes seeking gold medals (Aldridge, 2011). The Art of Sport was integrated into the hospitality programme Private Banking has always had for its clients, featuring both a sporting programme and a cultural programme, which is run throughout the whole of the United Kingdom. Sport and culture are defined as largely separate spheres within the discourses of banking hospitality, whatever the extent of their merging within the framework of governance, as in the Department of Media Culture and Sport (DCMS). This, however, has resonance with the Olympics in the organisation of the Cultural Olympiad as a parallel but separate sphere of activities operating alongside but inextricably correlated to the sporting engagements of the Olympics and Paralympics.

Ann Aldridge describes her personal commitment and interest in the project in an article on the project 'Our clients love sculpture and art. I am the internal art curator for Lloyds TSB. Four years ago I converted the LloydsTSB Private Banking offices in Mayfair, London, into a fine art gallery for two weeks and raised huge amounts of money for charity. This was the turning point of my career' (Aldridge, 2011).

Lloyds TSB stated its commitment to supporting emerging talent in the sporting and artistic sectors. The exhibition and sale of the art produced through the Art of Sport programme was designed to raise the profile of the artists and athletes involved, whilst at the same time generating much-needed funds for the Lloyds TSB Local Heroes programme, and the athletes for whom this initiative will be providing vital financial support (Aldridge 2009).

In December 2007 the Lloyds TSB sponsorship team and LOCOG approached her to suggest that the bank could tailor its artwork to sport to celebrate the London 2012 partnership. Ann had personal interest as an amateur artist and art enthusiast herself and probably even more importantly as someone who had been networking in the art world for over 25 years, she felt she could easily match the brief (Aldridge 2009). The project was generated by the bank's involvement as a partner in 2012 and the focus is London 2012. The project started with 25 artists with the aim of achieving a total number of 100 participants by 2012. The bank, however, pulled out of this project before its targets were achieved and before 2012. The project did, nonetheless, provide the

Figure 1   Ade Adepin (watercolour)

impetus for activities and events which triggered other events, notably those sponsored by BT which was the organisation which took over the presentation and promotion of the Art of Sport artists' work, including that of Jeremy Houghton (see figures 1 and 3) whose work is featured in this chapter.

The involvement of artists is paralleled by the participation of young aspiring athletes in the bank's Local Heroes programme (Local Heroes, 2011). The project for athletes provided essential equipment and training, travel and accommodation costs with 600 athletes having been assisted between 2008 and 2011, rising to an estimated 1,000 by 2012. The project was organised around web updates as well as a series of events at which artists and athletes were represented. The web pages relate the narratives of individual athletes who have been helped by the scheme in the now familiar style of personal accounts of the emergence from failure, for example, at school, to success.

For example, Josh Bolam, who was one of the 12 finalists in the LloydsTSB Art of Nurture competition, in spite of limited success at school and avowed lack of interest, succeeded in securing a place at art college (Bolam, 2011). Bolam's story is a fairly conventional narrative of finding success through self-discovery and following a particular route into further education, but it is socially located through the support he received from different agencies including Aim Higher and the LloydsTSB project. Success is also couched in terms of personal achievement and presented as a personal narrative, but it is caught up in the processes of sponsorship and the involvement of different agencies from the public and private sectors. Although there are different forces in play, the account is always one of a personal story within the discourse of social inclusion.

These biographical accounts are used for athletes and artists combining similar techniques of storying the self. Stories are told within the discourse of social inclusion as well as self-improvement. The two are interrelated, as are the specificities of sport and art. For example, in the case of sport, it is sometimes the minority sports that are implicated in the project so that the young athlete is aspiring for the success of the sport, the self and the wider community. For example, the account of Jordan Dalrymple, a 17-year-old who joined the scheme to play volleyball and benefitted from the scheme, not only in advancing his volleyball skills but also in developing personal skills and confidence framed by the language of heroic aspiration, is illustrative (Dalrymple, 2011).

The mechanisms through which the work of emerging artists and the progress of local sports heroes, who have similar aspirations, but within the field of sport rather than art, were focused upon art exhibitions staged for the artists starting with two huge events at the Edinburgh Festival during August 2008 and then at a range of different sites across the United Kingdom. Initially invited clients who wanted to purchase works of art on sale at the events were informed that 80 per cent would go to the artist and 20 per cent to a charity. A proportion of the proceeds of the sale of each piece was donated to Lloyds TSB Local Heroes, working in partnership with SportsAid (SportsAid, 2011) to provide funding for 250 emerging young sportspeople identified each year from local communities across Britain on their journey to London 2012 and beyond. In 2009, the Art of Sport engaged with 20 Local Heroes and raised over £2,000 towards supporting their journeys towards Olympic success. The benefit to athletes from Lloyds TSB's funding was largely aimed at helping with the costs of their travel, equipment and training, although they, like the artists, did also receive some public attention.

Given the focus of the events, it is likely that this publicity and actual presence at the bank's events will have been of more benefit to the artists and this is supported by my subsequent interviews with the artists, two of whose work is illustrated in this book. Each testified to the benefits of the project although Jeremy Houghton attributes more of his success to BT than to LloydsTSB. In fact, many artists who were involved with the Art of Sport went on to achieve considerably more public recognition and success.

Events, artworks, artists and athletes

The artists' work was exhibited across Britain in the offices of Lloyds TSB Private Banking and branches of Lloyds TSB. Visitors have the opportunity to buy the original art, as well as fine art reproductions. The project describes the would-be buyers as visitors, although they are invited guests and the bank's clients.

The project also provided links between artists and the athletes in a pairing scheme, the outcome of which were sport-specific works of art, although not all the art works are limited directly linked to sport in a representational sense. Thus artists and athletes met in the flesh, at events and through interpersonal connections where an artist was given the opportunity to be a spectator of the athlete's sport and use the enfleshed sporting activity to inspire their artistic work. For example, Lloyds TSB's artists were invited to be artist spectators of Local Heroes in training, such as skier Violet Miller and runner Louise Small. Jeremy Houghton (Houghton, 2011), who joined the Art of Sport in 2009 and was later selected as one of the British Telecom Olympic Artists for the London 2012 Olympics in 2011, presented a particularly successful synergy between art and sport in his fluid watercolours of the athletes in action, such as skier Louise Miller (Houghton Art of Sport, 2011). These watercolours (Oscar Winning and Ade Adepin) present examples of work which creates the movement of light and the planes of colour which generate those affects of movement in sport in the sensation that moves from the arrangement of paint to the spectator, who is in this instance the spectator of sport in art rather than sport as sport in the stadium. Sport, art, viewer and spectator Houghton whose last exhibition in London was sponsored by Lloyds International Private Banking in conjunction with Christies (Houghton, 2011) is also an example of an artist whose reputation has been enhanced considerably over this time. This example demonstrates the diverse elements in this assemblage; the artist, the materials and materiality of the technologies of artistic practice, the financial sponsorship, economic, cultural and social forces in the processes through which the artistic objects are made visible and public and the sporting practices which generate the visual representation.

The artist whose work was chosen as iconic of the Olympic Movement was Will Rochford (Rochford, 2011) whose *Olympians* (see figure 2), oil on canvas, provided a centre piece for many of the events including the one in London at Threadneedle Street. This work was included as part of Will Rochford's Olympic collection along with Paul Goodison (see figure 4), The Finishing Touches (see figure 5) and The Future (see figure 6). Rochford's large, 91.4×121.9 cm painting is explicitly representational, featuring a child on the track presenting a piece of paper to an athlete who is kneeling down to greet the child and draped in the Union Jack flag. A young black male figure on the bottom left of the canvas meets the viewer's gaze and in the bottom right corner the artist has reproduced the Five Rings of the Olympics. Unfortunately, as I discovered at one of the events it is not permissible to reproduce the rings for copyright reasons, even in promoting the Games, and the bank has not been able to use the full painting in its promotional activities (Aldridge, 2011).

Figure 2   Olympians, oil on canvas (autograph piece)

The project made meeting and speaking possible for different people and broke down some of the barriers between different fields, notably, the discursive strands of finance, art and sports. At the events, some of which were particularly prestigious, like the launch of the Winter Games at the Canadian Embassy in London and the event at the Lloyds TSB branch in Threadneedle Street next to the Bank of England in London, artists, athletes and the bank's clients were able to exchange information and situate themselves and their interests. Events were held across the United Kingdom; for example in January 2010 at the Olympic Exhibition at Terminal 5 Heathrow Airport, in December 2009 there was an Art of Wealth Exhibition in Mayfair, London in September 2008 the Olympic Exhibition at City Hall London and in April 2008 – LOCOG launch exhibition with Lloyds TSB exhibiting the Olympic Art. The contradictions of asset management, corporate finance, art objects, artists and young athletes came together in a relatively compatible, comfortable, if transient, space.

Figure 3   Oscar Winning

Figure 4   Paul Goodison, oil on canvas

The aim of the project was to recruit investors by promoting the possibilities of meeting one of their own local heroes when visiting an Art of Sport exhibition. Clients were informed that not only would they be able to enjoy the lavish hospitality of the bank at the reception and to purchase the work of new artists but also they would have the opportunity of finding out about the commitment that young athletes bring to their individual disciplines and the many challenges that they face. This was a mix of charitable discourses, functionalism (Woodward, 2008) and elements of equal opportunities, or at least the opening up of opportunity and traces of the language and practice of equality and diversity.

The greater emphasis was upon the nurturing of the athletes, as local heroes and aspiring Olympiads; as expected the athletes were young, some of them were still at school whereas some of the artists, although certainly not many, did already have an established

Figure 5 Finishing touches, oil on canvas (man painting track)

reputation. Social divisions and inequalities permeate the project just as they do the wider social worlds of art and sport and, even more so, banking. The year 2008, when the project began, was also the start of the global economic crisis, notably a banking crisis, and a time when banks were not in receipt of a very good press. There are always tensions between the different power axes which intersect in particular fields and bringing together art, sport and banking in the promotion of widening participation and providing fund raising opportunities for young athletes and artists is no exception. Some tensions are highlighted, but in particular ways. Sport is powerfully dominated by hegemonic masculinity and its networks as well as visibly racialised. Social class, gender and ethnicity operate in different but enduring inequitable ways in art and banking, although art may have a higher empirical representation of women. The artists were also more likely to be white, although so too were many of the local heroes at the events, maybe partly because of the sports that were represented, especially rowing, horse riding (e.g. McNamara, 2011) and skiing The local heroes at the events I attended were representative of a number of sports, although sports

Figure 6   The future, oil on canvas (faces)

like rowing, sailing and swimming were more prominent; boxing was not present at any event I attended, either in the art work or in the enfleshed presence of the athletes.

Boxing was a presence in the histories upon which some of the artists drew, however. For example, in the work of the sculptor Ben Dearnley (Dearnley, 2011) whose work covers a range of sports but also draws upon the heritage and ideals of Classical sculpture especially as developed in the Hellenistic period (Smith, 1991) and notably focuses upon the beautiful body. This body is male and the musculature remakes norms of enfleshed masculinity.

He described his work for the project as:

These sculpture works are forming a crucial part of my journey to find a unity of form within the material, balanced with the expression of strength and beauty of the individual athlete. It is a constant inspiration to me personally and I would like to thank everyone who has taken part in this project including my team.

As we head towards the London 2012 Games I look forward to adding more beautiful bodies to this series. I truly feel we are blessed with the good fortune to be here in this moment to witness these superb athletes achieving their dreams and I wish them all every success in their ventures. (Dearnley, 2011)

His bronze cast Adam of which he says, 'My work with Karate Grand Master champion, Matt Price has given me an exceptional body to use as reference for this limited edition bronze...The power of the torso in this compressed position gives an hint to the inner meaning with the addition on the keyhole in the left arm leading further towards what is locked inside' (Dearnley, 2011).

The torso invokes the Classical Greek statue, the Belvedere Torso in particular, although the Terme Boxer, a seated figure in contemplative pose, cited as a masterpiece of Hellenistic athletic professionalism, is also a well-known and oft-cited classical work in the genre. Whereas the Terme Boxer 'despite all his training and physique remains earth-bound' (Smith, 1991 :55) the Belvedere Torso embodies nobility and grandeur from the realm of myth (ibid.). The repertoires upon which artists, especially sculptors who work on the sporting body, have to draw upon, remain pretty firmly fixed in the annals of masculinity and male flesh. This is not to say that contemporary artists in the project do not work with women athletes, but more that the canon of the beautiful, muscular, athletic sporting body and the criteria of heroic sporting beauty is so powerfully configured around masculinity that it is difficult to think outside its constraints and to develop new possibilities and new aesthetic criteria. Maybe boxing, with all its histories of combating social exclusion and racism as well as its visceral, enfleshed conflictual capacities, can become more acceptable when translated by Classical ideals and viewed through the lens of a classical aesthetic.

Ben Dearnley's Olympic Gallery holds images of his casting sessions with a range of elite female and male athletes who demonstrate the diversity of his range, although most of the athletes are not local heroes but very well-established medal winners: Christine Ohuruogu MBE Olympic, World and Commonwealth champion Debbie Flood, Olympic 2004/08 Silver Medallist Rowing; Steve Williams OBE, Olympic 2004/08 Gold Medallist Rowing, Leander Rowing Club; Ade Adepitan MBE, Paralympics wheelchair medallist & basketball Champion., swimmer Mark Foster, 5 times Olympian, Alex O'Connell Olympic

Fencing; Louis Smith, Gymnast Olympic Bronze medallist 2008 and Lee Pearson OBE, MBE, Paralympics Dressage, outstanding 9 gold titles Leon Taylor, Olympic medallist Diving; Matt Price, UK Karate Grand Masters Champion with 13 consecutive titles.

Ben Dearnley describes his work for the Olympic Project more in terms of a celebration of elite athleticism as embodied by the flesh of elite athletes and coded within the canon of Classical art and notably the principles and ideals of classical Greek sculpture. He does not, however, explicitly attribute the Classical roots or routes of his approach: 'a return to the real in sculpture, a 21st century renaissance of truth and beauty in human form' satisfying a hunger for more skills based art and I am following the tradition of carving in pure statuary marble and casting in the classic "gun metal" bronze to create these works' (Dearnley 2011). The materials of the art object are clearly crucial to its assemblage and to the affects it generates. The project for Dearnley was

> an exploration into the world of our current top Olympic and Paralympics athletes. The desire is to create a series of sculptures which will honour their achievements and reflect their commitment and excellence within their sport. The sculptures will aim to hold a part of the key to the athletes' power zone: which I see as pivotal to them being the best in the world at what they do. Each work is a collaboration with the athlete to gain an understanding of their body's action and to capture the 'moment' in a fragmented form. They are today's 'Modern Day Heroes'. (Dearnley, 2011)

The Art of Sport project was made possible by the opportunities afforded by London 2012 and was itself generated by the coming together of different aspects of the Games, including financial opportunities and the discursive regimes of social inclusion and widening participation that are part of the Olympic Movement and the Cultural Olympiad. The project presents a means of exploring not only materiality of art and of sport but also the materialities of business and commerce as a field in which art is not only an object but a commodity; art as commodity. Commodifcation is also apparent in debates about images, including copyright and the ownership of objects, things and even the materiality of the Five Rings of the Olympics. The Movement may be about participation but not only have its regulation and organisation not always been transparent and available to all, its very symbol is private and privatised.

Social inclusion, the language of community and discourses of social cohesion and diversity, especially framed by the chances offered to aspiring athletes and young artists, frame the rhetoric of the programme, which is also consonant with contemporary understandings of art and sport as work; opportunities for young people can also be construed as work, even if the affects of the art is to reinforce the language of heroism and elite success.

The bank's involvement in such a project as the Art of Sport is largely located within the charitable discourse of trickle down and patronage; the bank's clients are entertained and have the chance to purchase work, which might be an investment as this is all original art all within the parameters of the democratic ideals of the Olympic Movement. In practice, LloydsTSB was unable to continue its commitment, largely because of decisions made about the return on its investment and primarily the pressing demands for expenditure reduction in the wake of the global crisis. The first two years of the Art of Sport were productive, offering innovative synergies between art sport and finance.

The actual art work itself is diverse and ranges across different media, content, colour and light. Histories and genealogies draw upon canon and classical ethnocentric forms of representation; to legitimise art and sport it may be necessary to comply with the criterion of aesthetic. However, the nature of the relationship between art and sport means that the project has created possibilities of movement and image that attempt to move beyond mediated representation and create the immediacy of sensation, capture some of the passion of the moment and of 'being in the zone'.

Conclusion

This chapter has extended the discussion of spectatorship that was the subject of Chapter 5 by using examples of the promotion of widening participation through sport and culture and, in particular art as an aspect of culture. Cultural practices are part of the Olympic Movement and the Olympic phenomenon, for example, as manifest in the Cultural Olympics which both present opportunities for democratisation and raise questions about the relationship between sporting practices and other cultural activities, which are sometimes underpinned by different re-workings of dichotomies of high and low, elite and populist, spectacular or routine and enfleshed or cerebral, sometimes understood as the mind–body split. One of the tensions that is most evident is the extent to which attempts at promoting social inclusion can challenge or subvert existing and enduring hierarchies, such as those of racialisation, social class, ethnicisation or sex gender.

Art has particular capacities to generate affects which include emotion, excitement and social and cultural participation. The Art of Sport project raises important issues about the possibilities of promoting equality and equal opportunities through artistic aesthetic practices and the synergies with sport. The fields of art and sport are competitive and elitist, albeit in different ways, but they can occupy shared and interstitial spaces in which people and things are brought together to create new outcomes and transformations in ways of being and ways of doing. In this chapter I have argued that cultural experience is a densely woven entanglement of substances and feelings, and that affect and materials are central to social contact and the connections and disruptions between art and sport. There are cross-modal networks which register links between perception, affect, the senses and the materialities of the social world. Both art and sport are about looking and the gaze in relation to spectatorship and the discussion in this chapter has demonstrated some of the ways in which there are synergies and points of connection between the viewer of art and the spectator of sport.

The Cultural Olympics and projects like the Art of Sport are organised around a democratisation of the gaze which recruits from a wider constituency and makes wider participation possible. This is consonant with other aspects of the processes of democratisation that are implicated in the management of the games such as LOCOG's plans to sell tickets for 2012 at reduced prices to young people and by having a lottery, which proved a strategy of limited success because of the continued dominance of corporate sales for hospitality. There are, however, other ways in which the corporate sector, for example, a major bank which sponsors the games, can facilitate a social gaze which can become more democratic. Projects such as the Cultural Olympics and within it examples like the Art of Sport are concerned with a social gaze that opens up ways of looking for viewers of art and spectators of sport.

Art raises new questions about how the gaze works and what is implicated in seeing and being seen within the field of sport as represented in art. In both the spectatorship of sport and the appreciation of art there are aspects of emotion and sentience that are elicited by the object that is perceived and how perception is shaped by that object or event. Points of contact are manifest in sensation which is the movement generated by affect and which captures the event and the emotion through light and movement, matter and flesh and the unconscious: agency is made up in the event and we are caught up in its mobilities, for example, in the spectatorship of sport and in viewing art. This experience involves revisiting the power of the gaze and of looking to encompass spectacle and display and to question the authenticity of being physically present. If art captures the intensities of sport through its arrangement of materials this appears to suggest that such intensities of expression can be experienced without being physically present and having all the senses invoked through that presence. Sport and art prioritise and privilege visual capacities which can generate forces of intensity that may not require a physical presence. Affect and the capacities of events and objects as well as people to generate affects and to be affected are constitutive of art and sport. Affect is the correspondence between action and thinking, actions and passions and between mind and body which are parallel. Thus as art concentrates on the spectator watching and the sporting event is made through enfleshed performance and sentient spectatorship, art and sport share elements of enfleshed experience which may be outside conventional structures.

The translation of sport into art forms as examples of cultural phenomena raise questions about memory. Sport with its systems of records and measurement of performance is deeply embedded in memory; remembered successes and failures and the details of scores, speeds and distances and of records broken. The example of the Lowry exhibition and the Art of Sport are both instances which open up new folds that allow correspondence between sheets of the past and layers of reality rather than the chronological narrative of a simple revelation of truths and provide pivotal moments of remembered events and key points in the history of sport. The Art of Sport re-works the past but draws heavily upon memory whether in the technologies of art as in the re-invocation of classical Greek sculpture or in the re-telling of stories and especially the heroic narratives of sport. Whilst individualised heroic narratives cannot encompass the truth of either art or sport, it is worth noting that heroes and legends are constitutive of the gendered memories of sport and one of the mechanisms whereby women are excluded. One of the silences is of narratives of women's success that are configured around heroism rather than triumph over tragedy stories of success against the odds.

Bodies and flesh are central to art and sport; the somatic and sentient enfleshed self is what perceives and is affected by the intensities of the experience. Bodies are made through the movement of forces and processes of composition of differential elements and not necessarily bounded by the organism or even the flesh, but within social inclusion and diversity projects especially those based on discourses of charity, embodied selves assume an agency that the political activism based on human rights challenges. There may be collective agency in resistance but the stress on individualism within charitable discourses of diversity is less part of political activism.

This chapter has addressed the issues of the specificities of art as a cultural practice and how art and sport are connected and has presented some evaluation of the extent to which projects that focus on art and other cultural fields have the capacities to promote social inclusion and disrupt hierarchies that are based upon the operation of enduring systems of power. There are strong traditions of the promotion of culture within the Modern Olympics which are in some ways surprising given the even longer tradition of elitism within the terrain of the arts, but, as I have argued, art has the capacities to engage with the intensities and affects of sport which are both distinctive and particularly relevant and useful. Art and culture have possibilities for creativity and expression and for opening up new challenges to traditional customs and cultures but from a discussion of what has been specifically linked to the Olympics any progress is incremental and it is unlikely that any transformations will be revolutionary given that the synergies between art and sport are always haunted by the centrality of market forces and the persistence of inequalities in the wider social terrain. They are also underpinned but the charitable discourses of promoting widening participation as compensation to those who are not only under-represented in the fields of art and sport but become configured as victims, however deserving. The discussion in this chapter demonstrates both the promise of sport and art synergies and the troubling constraints both empirically and theoretically in terms of the emphasis on emotion and sensation which can marginalise materialities of inequality. The next chapter looks at political action and disruptions and subversions that might be more radical and framed by more explicitly political challenges to traditional power bases. Political activism challenges the individualism of charitable discourses of cohesion and social inclusion and raises questions about the source of power which can also be construed as outside the liminal spaces between art and sport and spectatorship and the assemblages of light, movement, materials and flesh which make up the sporting and artistic forms. Resistance involves the identification of sources of power as well as engagement and action.

7
Contradictions, Controversies and Disruptions

Chapter 6 demonstrated how the promotion of diversity and social inclusion can take different forms and involve different stakeholders and relationships in different fields of activity, such as art and sport. Projects such as the Art of Sport remain more embedded in charitable discourses of cohesion than the more radical activism which can involve the political subversive capacities of art and locally or transnationally based activism. Resistance can be based on the discourse of human rights and a more direct language of demands for political equality.

The Olympics provide a mega event that is unsurpassed in its global reach. Its spectacles are massively visible, as was also discussed in Chapter 4. The Games offer cultural and political opportunities for which host cities and nations compete, whatever the financial costs. These global spectacles, which are now staged every two years, have the added advantage of being framed by the ideals of participation and democracy of the Olympic Movement, which provides host nations with political and social as well as economic possibilities. The nation, through the host city, is able to rebrand itself and be rebranded by staging not only a mega event with global reach, but also to be associated with a display of athletic excellence and the democratic principles of the Olympic Movement. The Olympics offer to both a very visible stage for political protest and a global set of phenomena which is underpinned by inequalities and injustices, which generate those protests, as well as opportunities for progress and democratisation. Some of the other opportunities which counter the ideals of the Olympic Movement in less positive ways, including malpractice and corruption, also instigate and inspire protest and opposition.

The expansion of the nations and sports and especially of the media coverage and concomitant sponsorship mean the Games are big business. Unfortunately, this means that, as has already been indicated, there has also been extensive opportunity for corruption and the Olympics, especially in the bidding processes, have been permeated with corruption which generates political protest. The allegations of corruption which exploded late in 1998 provoked a series of investigations which changed the regulatory practices of the Games forever. The marketing and visibility of the Olympics mean that, although there may be some unquestioned assumptions that the Olympics necessarily bring advantages to everyone involved, for athletes, spectators, local and national communities bringing economic and social benefits to the host nations, not surprisingly, the Olympic gold has become tarnished. This has increasingly been the concern of social and sports critics; some of the most effective critiques have often been mounted by journalists, for example, Andrew Jennings, who has written extensively about the Olympics (1992, 1996, 2000) and about football, as was discussed in Chapter 4, initially with Vyv Simson and more recently in his own work on the Olympics and on FIFA.

This chapter engages with questions about whether and how the Games provide opportunities for public protest and looks at how resistance at such sites might be understood through the conceptual framework of sex gender. The Olympics offer a site for political resistance (Lenskyj, 2008), as has been evident on many occasions including the focus upon human rights at Beijing in 2008 and the making of political statements. The most famous and iconic of these moments is probably the clenched fist Black Power salute of Tommie Smith and John Carlos on the medal podium in 1968 at Mexico City (Smith and Steele, 2007), although the Games have presented opportunities for the making of public political statements at a variety of sites, not the least Beijing Games in 2008 (Beijing Protests Torch, 2008, 2011, Beijing protests Tibet, 2008, 2011), which featured the disruption of the torch relay, Human rights protests around the world and especially about Chinese involvement in Tibet (SFT, 2008, 2011). The Games offer less dramatic opportunities for disruption, for example, in relation to less mainstream sports, whereby an Olympic presence can make visible a more marginal sport as well as otherwise under-represented athletes.

This chapter explores the ways in which political activism is specific to the Games, for example, through their topographies and topologies and argues that the Olympics offer particularities within sport because of their history and constitution and the enfleshed practices of sport. The relationship between the persistence of social inequalities and injustices and the ways in which these are silenced or can be made visible or voiced is complex and not as direct as some of the stories of politics and resistance which make up the history of the Modern Games might suggest. Sex gender has often been written out of this history because it has only been understood empirically, for example, in terms of the corporeal presence of women in protest movements or their concern with what are categorised as 'women's issues' such as the inclusion or exclusion of women from particular competitions and events. Sex gender also offers an intellectual and theoretical framework within which to explore the ways in which the Olympics are constitutive of and constituted by social and economic inequalities. The example of trafficking and prostitution linked to migration and mobilities presents a useful route through exploring issues of inequality and social exclusion through feminist political activism and the explanatory mechanisms of enfleshed and social sex gender. These are issues which have inspired feminist debates and protest and are much more closely linked to the diverse apparatuses through which inequalities endure than popular media coverage or much of what the literature on politics, protest and the Games might suggest.

There are specific circumstances which generate the particularities of protest and resistance at the Games. Different situations reproduce different forms of inequality and disadvantage, some of which are created by the Games themselves, and others highlight existing problems, for example, in the host city and nation. Many of these issues relate to the urban regeneration schemes which are claimed to justify capital expenditure, but which may often be more targeted at the display of the spectacle of the Olympics than on reviving communities and providing a sustainable reconstruction of housing and urban infrastructure for the people who will continue to live in the city in the future (Gold and Gold, 2007; Preuss, 2008; Poynter and Macrury, 2009).

The efforts of host cities to deal with these issues come up against different problems and challenges. The outcomes of these produce the lasting narratives of a particular Olympic Games, and determine whether the host committee's central messages reach the world in their intended form. Protest can result from unpredictable political events such as what happened in Mexico City in 1968, which might have been designed to parade the stable authoritarianism of Mexico as a nation, but this was greatly undermined by a nationwide series of student and worker protest in the months leading up to the Games, many of which were brutally suppressed. The protest in Tibet in the spring of 2008 presented a similar dilemma for the construction of a favourable narrative of the nation in Beijing (Beijing Protests, Tibet 2008, 2011).

There are also unpredictable sporting outcomes, some of which might be unwanted by the NOC. Jesse Owens, the African-American sprinter, upset the central racialised, racist messages of the 1936 Olympics by winning four gold medals. Other disruptions might not be translated as so overtly political but when the expectations of success are not fulfilled there can be tensions which have political underpinnings, especially in the power geometry of nation states which are played out in the individual competitors at the Games.

The Olympics have offered themselves to states as useful sites of political protest. Boycotts, where the message is explicitly political and allied to a public campaign, and non-attendance, as a less direct form of protest, have been seen as important diplomatic and political tools. Whatever the merits of a boycott, the hosts are always left with the problem of reconciling the universalist aspirations of the Games with the reality of empty places in their newly erected stadia.

The gigantic level of global coverage that the Olympics receive (Sugden and Tomlinson, 2002) created platforms for protest. The Palestinian kidnapping and killing of Israeli athletes at the 1972 Munich Olympics was perhaps the most dramatic example of this (Reeve, 2005). The Olympics are identified as a site that offers possibilities for terrorist attacks (Coaffee, 2009) Such spaces as those afforded by the Games present risks (Fussey et al., 2011, London 2012, 2011) which are consonant with contemporary concerns about the postmodern condition, and in particular the global city (Harvey, 1989). The Games provide a focus for tensions between nation states and global matters expressed within the discourse of human rights. Beijing 2008, in particular, attracted the most extensive guerrilla political action, as evidenced by the disastrous global flame relay of the spring of 2008, where the British, French and American legs, in particular, became the focus of political activism.

Spectacles, power and resistance

The sporting spectacle has revolutionary potential because of its visibility, but also because of how it is constituted (Harvey 1989). There has been a tendency to assume that all spectacles share the same properties and are similarly constituted; it is just a matter of scale and spectacles are necessarily large scale. Some social commentators have emphasised the repressive nature of the spectacle as the aggregation of global capital and stressed the economic dimensions of spectacle; the profit motive is a powerful motor force within the Olympics. The Games, like all global sport, generate conceptualisations of the spectator as duped and deceived, the recipient of circuses when what is needed is bread. Although the spectacle is made through the operations of global capital and to serve the interests of profit, it offers entertainment which may mask the economic and social systems which not only make the spectacle but also create and reinstate the inequalities that are routine elements in places where the spectacle is held. Guy Debord described international football on worldwide television as

> the construction and presentation of the wholly commodified game in a colourful, ritzy yet standardised society of the mediated spectacle; The SPECTACLE is capital accumulated to the point where it becomes image. (Debord, 1995:24, *capitals in original*)

Meta theories of the spectacle can obscure what is specific about each, although the manner in which the spectacular plays out in sport, led by the media, promotes 'values, products, celebrities and institutions of the media and consumer society' (Kellner, 2001). Although such approaches foreground the profit motive for staging the Games, they present an overemphasis on the singularity of economic forces that are prioritised at the expense of other social divisions such as those based on sex gender, ethnicity and race, and a top-down view of power which underestimates the myriad sites at which power and hence resistance can operate.

As was demonstrated in Chapter 5, sporting spectacles like the Games also serve the interests of the state and the politics of governance are widely imbricated in the Olympics and the sporting spectacle is not solely the prop of consumerism (Sugden and Tomlinson, 2002), although the operation of power involves the intersection of diverse forces and there are points at which it is difficult to disentangle different elements. The Olympics bring together an assemblage of different systems which also include the exhilaration, passion and excitement of sport and the specific enfleshed actualities of sport, which are never, however, entirely separate from the contingencies of the social. As has already been argued in this book, however, power involves diverse mechanisms which are both repressive and productive and creative. Sport can be intensely creative as Chapter 6 suggested in its exploration of the synergies between art and sport, but sport in general and the Olympics in particular are also enmeshed in and productive of inequities and patterns of social exclusion, which generate resistance. As Foucault argued, 'where there is power there is resistance, and yet, or rather consequently, this resistance is never in a position of exteriority in relation to power (Foucault, 1981:95).

> Power is always relational. The existence of power relations depends on a multiplicity of points of resistance: these play the role of adversary, target, support, or handle power relations. These points of resistance are present everywhere in the power network...There is a plurality of resistances, each of them a special caser: resistances that are possible, necessary, improbable; others that are spontaneous, savage, solitary, concerted rampant, or violent: still others that are quick to compromise, interested, or sacrificial; by definition, they can only exist in the field of power relations. (Foucault, 1981: 95–6)

Local protest

The Games also bring together not only different apparatuses of power, but also diverse elements of resistance which enmesh with new technologies, which provide different platforms for the expression of resistance in the twenty-first century. Internet technologies are deployed in sport not only for engagement with its directly enfleshed and regulatory practices, on and off the field of play, and the experiences of spectatorship and fandom, but also political expressions which draw in a wider constituency of oppression and disadvantage including local communities, as exemplified in local resistance to the transformations of east London prior to 2012 (Mute, 2011, We Are Bad, 2011). Local projects become global through their use of web-based technologies. For example, in the activism in east London prior to the 2012 Games, campaigns created to give voice to the feelings of local communities which have themselves been so disrupted by the re-structuring that was necessary for the Games, a sporting project which does not appeal to everyone in spite of its global reach included a series of specially commissioned posters (Mute, 2011). We Are Bad posters appeared on the blue fence that ran around the site of the London 2012 Olympic Games (We Are Bad, 2011), presenting an invective against what was perceived as the class cleansing for the urban regeneration of east London. The posters which challenge the progressive claims of the Olympic Movement and especially of LOCOG of the democratic powers of sport and in particular the enhancement of the environment in the host city of the games, occupy both material, physical space on the blue fence and on the online journal's web sites. The message that 'We Are Bad', although the transformation of the city in the interests of global capital as expressed through sport will not make us better, is delivered both virtually and locally by subverting the Olympic message and in particular the London 2012 logo.

Political activism is framed by the networks of inequality and injustice which surround the Games (Miah, 2011a, 2011b) as well as their very prominent visible global presence, which make them an attractive site at which to be seen or heard, but may take different forms; the medium of transmission and communication of the message can be virtual and actual.

Global protest

The Olympics clearly challenge any claims, such, perhaps ironically, as were made by Avery Brundage, that sport and politics don't mix. Politics permeate sport none more so than the Olympics whatever the Olympic Movement's rhetoric of amateurism and its founding fathers' claims and the dream that these spectacles of global unity might suspend conflict, imperialism and racism (Cashmore, 2005). (Nobody ever seems to have dreamed that the Games might suspend patriarchal practices, only that empirically women might be permitted to participate). After 1936 and the Berlin Games there could be no illusions about the Games and it was apparent that the cultural and political themes that adhere in any society are latent in sport and sport is always political, as has been apparent in every one of the Summer Games that followed. After the exclusion of the defeated nations, Germany, Japan and Italy, in the 1948 Olympics after World War II much of the discussion about what constitutes politics in sport has centred on boycotts. Holland, Egypt, Iraq and Spain boycotted the 1956 Games in protest against the British and French invasion of Suez. In 1964 South Africa was suspended from the Games because of its apartheid regime and expelled from the Olympic Movement in 1970, and in 1972 Rhodesia, which later became Zimbabwe, was expelled for its oppressive white regime and its Declaration of Unilateral Independence from the Commonwealth. The United States refused to attend the Moscow Games in 1980 on account of the Russian invasion of Afghanistan. Montreal in 1976 is probably the most significant boycott to date, when 25 African states boycotted the Games because of the inclusion of New Zealand, a nation whose teams had toured South Africa earlier in the year; in fact, it was the same year that South Africa was blacklisted by the Gleneagles Agreement. The legacies of colonialism have shaped much of the politics of protest and it was not until Barcelona in 1992 after the ban on South Africa had been lifted for the first post apartheid games that there were actually no boycotts; the first year since 1972.

Los Angeles in 1984 also featured a significant boycott when the Soviet Union led a boycott of 13 nations as a retaliatory protest against the United States' boycott of Moscow. Global politics and the legacy of cold war conflicts along with imperialist histories largely shaped these large-scale boycotts. In 1988 North Korea, Cuba, Ethiopia and Nicaragua boycotted South Korea which was perceived as a US collaborator.

More recently anxieties have moved on to perceived threats of terrorist attacks (Fussey et al., 2011) and in 2004 the US team in Athens refused to stay in the Olympic village and were accommodated on an ocean liner because of the US government's fear of an Al Qaeda attack.

These are boycotts played out on the global stage within a framework of the transnational and international politics of nation states. The Olympics provide a theatre in which to enact these political dramas; as massive spectacles, protest is recorded, and itself becomes dramatic. The injustices of colonialist inheritances and the inequities of the white supremacist regime of apartheid are, however, both personal and everyday; the political is personal.

Protest also takes many different forms and the big stories have been iconic moments, one of the most notable of which has been the black power salute on the medal winners' podium by Tommie Smith at John Carlos at Mexico City in 1968. Some key moments of protest take on the form of a visualised memory and this must surely be one of them. The athletes have since become folk heroes, but they paid a high price after the event; they were both sent home in disgrace, which reveals the deeply embedded racism of Brundage and the IOC at the time and how superficial its commitment to race equality actually was. As Allen Guttmann argues,

> although the members of the International Olympic Committee prided themselves, with some justice, as defenders of a multi-racial movement specifically opposed to racism...the Olympic Games were an occasion for mostly white officials to use black athletes to divert attention from the basic inequalities of American society. (Guttmann, 2002: 131)

After their protest on the podium in 1968, each athlete was subjected to vicious racist attacks, in John Carlos's case so insufferable were the invasions into his personal life that his wife subsequently committed suicide (Davidson, 2011).

Although the civil rights movement had made some progress in the United States, it was very slow progress and the Vietnam War had diverted resources and attention from the promotion of civil rights in the United States to an expensive imperialist campaign in South East Asia. It also points to the cosmetic nature of the commitment to civil rights and equality by the regulatory bodies of sport like the IOC. Although the organisation was officially and publicly committed to human rights, it seems that so dramatic and public an act, ignoring the Star Spangled Banner in favour of a black-gloved Black Power salute, was too much for Brundage and the IOC. More recently it has been pointed out that the third man on the podium at Mexico City, Australian sprinter Peter Norman, who came second in the 200 m, was wearing the badge of the Olympic Project for Human Rights (OPHR), a stateswide civil rights protest movement which Norman wore as an expression of solidarity with his fellow athletes (Davidson, 2011). The IOC was not ready for solidarity, however, and Norman's part in the protest has remained largely uncelebrated. Social inequalities can be addressed within the language and practice of equal opportunities, if not human rights, provided they are not too disruptive. For example, although Avery Brundage had expressed his antipathy to feminism and women's rights he seemed pleased at the Mexican's choice of a young woman, Enriqueta Basilio, to carry the Olympic torch into the stadium, to climb the steps and light the Olympic flame. The games are all about gestures, which could constitute their 'ordinary affects' (Stewart, 2007), but, as Guttmann notes, 'this was a political statement that Brundage approved of (because he refused to classify it as a political statement)' (Guttmann, 2002: 130).Women's presence and visibility, however, may always be political because the visible actuality of women at the Olympics in whatever capacity puts sex gender on the agenda. An analysis based on sex gender can also make evident the import of these presences. It depends on how women are presented and within what context, for example, within charitable discourses of victims and under-represented outsiders who have been able to gain access to the main stage or as elite athletes on par with male athletes, or as yet in a very unlikely category as leaders of organising bodies like the IOC.

Women elite athletes have either been tainted by accusations or insinuations of performance enhancement, as Chapter 3 demonstrated, or been situated within a more individualised narrative of resistance through overcoming personal difficulties. Eastern European and former USSR athletes have been tainted with claims of malpractice and great Olympic athletes, like heptathlete Jackie Joyner Kersee, occupy positions in the top ten women's list by virtue of their sporting achievements and personal narratives. Women athletes' heroic achievements are rarely framed in the heroic narratives of athletic masculinity. US swimmer Amy Van Dyken, who won four gold medals at Atlanta, is noted for overcoming her asthma and Natalie Coughlin, another US swimming gold medallist, is still seen as having been overshadowed by Michael Phelps. Soviet Union gymnasts like Larisa Latynina and Polina Astakhova have been accorded some status as medal winners but coverage of women is so often inflected by reference to either their looks or their personal stories or, especially in the case of the eastern bloc in the 1950s and 1960s, suggestions of inappropriate performance enhancement which detracts from their political standing in putting women into Olympic discourse.

Protest concerns the affects that actions and events have and how they are affected by their reception. It is less likely that the other protests in Mexico in 1968 will be as well remembered. Mexico City was an example of unexpected turbulence as a site of protest that the IOC had never anticipated when the city was chosen, following the first Asian Games, as a developing nation at which the IOC could celebrate its commitment to the Olympic Charter. The IOC failed to note that Mexico was the site of student unrest and protest against the entrenched bureaucratic party which was felt to have betrayed the principles of the Mexican Revolution. Thirty-five people were killed when the Mexican army moved in on the protestors which generated anxieties about whether the Games would go ahead (Guttmann, 2002).

If an event that involves protest becomes visible and even reified by the ways in which it is represented and received it may also be subject to accommodation that diminishes the impact of the protest. Richard Giulanotti has also suggested that iconic moments such as the event in Mexico City have been neutralised and commodified; 'images of the "black power" protest by two African-American sprinters at the 1968 Olympics are now found in television commercials; at the 1992 Olympics "protest politics" among the US basketball "Dream Team" consisted primarily of Nike-sponsored players covering the signs of rival merchandise companies' (Giulianotti, 2005: 56). He goes on to suggest that there is even the possibility that resistant subcultures might embrace commodification and cites the example of the Barmy army in cricket. The Barmy army of England cricket supporters may appear to transgress the rules of cricket spectatorship, although this has been achieved much more effectively by the IPL and Twenty20, but are not a commercially innocent apparently authentic subculture that is critical of the ruling bodies of the game but expresses dissent through raucous behaviour and parodic performances. This may be a relatively trivial example but it does highlight some of the ways in which protest can be accommodated and thus neutralised.

These arguments parallel some of the critiques of postfeminism (Woodward and Woodward, 2009, Gillis et al., 2007). Whilst the parodic can be transgressive, it can also subordinate some material issues of inequality and muddy the political agenda, for example, in the adoption of the discourse of empowerment which can be expressed through sexual freedoms, such as lap dancing. More recently the controversial 'slut walks', following a Toronto policeman's suggestions that young women should not 'dress like sluts' in order to ensure their personal safety and to avoid attacks of sexual violence (Slutwalk, 2011), have been hotly disputed with some arguments suggesting that they might have diverted attention from deeper sources of injustice with their emphasis upon clothing and sexuality. However, one of the main weapons that has been directed against feminist politics has been the invocation of humour which trivialises the feminist agenda; hostile, demeaning remarks are dismissed as 'only a joke' and feminists are rendered humourless and incapable of seeing the humorous side of personal encounters. The marginalisation of sexuality as not a serious political matter is a massive source of discrimination against those whose sexuality is denied or pathologised. An overemphasis upon the social construction of gender and the separation of gender from sex can lead to the compartmentalisation of issues of sex and sexuality as outside the big political issues and as only superficial dimensions of inequality. What is more pertinent about the contradictory nature of the Slut Walks is their appropriation of the sexualised image and presentation of women as a challenge to the very processes that have created this objectification. The irony of the parodic may not be as subversive as it purports or hopes to be; this is a question of tactics more than understanding, however. Sex and sexuality are not synonymous, but a conceptualisation of sex rather than gender can be attentive to enfleshed experience that is collective as well as individual and demonstrates the importance of the politics of sexuality as well as sex gender as a terrain in which there can be understanding of the ways in which power operates to reinstate inequalities. This approach, which stresses the intellectual, explanatory reach of sex, is also productive in exploring explanations of how power operates.

The dramatic protest always runs the risk of being appropriated and its message is either neutralised or distorted. Feminism and the discourses of feminism have also been neutralised in myriad ways through the language of equal opportunities and the measurements of diversity (Genz, 2007, McRobbie, 2008). Struggles that have been won have led to postfeminist claims that either feminist politics are redundant since neoliberal demands for equality have been met or, more insidiously, as in the case of the discourse of empowerment, feminist language has been appropriated or more accurately misappropriated in a pastiche of its original trajectories and critique.

Although the Olympics have been characterised by protests and boycotts, feminist critiques have not, however, been explicitly prominent in the history of protest and resistance in sport. Sport, and the IOC in this case, has a long history of being part of the white, patriarchal tradition which is particular to sporting practices and refracts the wider culture of politics and governance and unequal power relations.

The conflicts between nations which feature most prominently within the genealogies of protest may seem to be far removed from the routine inequalities that, for example, are highlighted in Helen Lenskyj's research, which is discussed in the next section on the politics of the games and the possibilities of resistance and protest, which arise from some of the routine practices of daily life in the host city and may not always occupy centre stage. Indeed, such everyday experiences are often made invisible by the machinery of the NOC and the host city.

The personal is political and the political is personal

Much of the discussion about protest at the Games has focused upon its public and visible manifestations. The public arena of the spectacle with its global reach is also where the principles are ideals of the Movement and, of course, the host city and nation are most effectively promoted. Whatever the mythological powers of the Olympic Movement and the regime of truth that has been constructed about the redemptive power of sport, the Olympics are also fraught with less elevating moments and events as the protests discussed above demonstrate, but disruptions also occupy more localised spaces. The work of Helen Lenskyj has been central to debates about the need to understand the less commendable aspects of the Games, including those that range from bribery by aspiring host cities to the taking of banned performance-enhancing drugs by athletes and the possibilities of resisting corrupt practice and challenging the deep inequalities that also permeate the Olympics. Unlike any other social commentator or analyst to date, Lenskyj's project is not only to uncover corruption but importantly to focus on making visible those whom the Olympics, like so many other institutions of the state and culture, have made invisible or marginalised and victimised.

The key issues relate to the ways in which the Olympics and their organising committees are concerned with legacy. Host cities produce a rationale for their project as regenerating and re-invigorating the city through the infrastructure that has to be put in place for the duration of the Games but will benefit future generations through a lasting legacy of vastly improved transportation, communication, employment, accommodation and leisure and community services. Recent work focuses on the transformation of the city and locates the Olympics within its topographies. For example, in the context of London 2012, *2013 and Beyond: Olympic Park Legacy in East London* uses the language of stakeholders to encompass the range of those who have an interest in the Games and includes the residents, service providers and businesses of the localities of the host city. This project focuses on the processes in and through which an Olympic Park legacy is designed, planned and shaped in consultation with the public and a range of stakeholders by examining how their work is a reflection of transforming the organisational goals set by the Olympic Park Legacy Company (OPLC) commissioning specifications and the Legacy Masterplan Framework (LMF) design team, in relation to government stakeholder requirements. Such work illustrates the tensions between the Olympic legacy and the processes of development and the resolution of conflicting interests and ambitions and the necessity to produce a final product that is, nevertheless, coherent and dynamic whilst accommodating an Olympic legacy that is always projected into the future and thus cannot be secure or certain. In the case of London 2012 this means looking at how the legacy could transform the Olympic Park from a suburban zone into an inner city hub of well-connected London activity, which is built on principles of sustainability and designed to transform the East End of London (Evans, 2011).

Lenskjy's work is based on an assessment after the staging of the Games. The display apparatuses of the Games require a vision of the host city as untainted by poverty, social problems, such as homelessness, rejection of and resistance to the Games themselves and criminality, all of which are grouped together as undesirable in the promotion of the host city. Lenskyj documented the protests of community-based groups against the onslaught of harassment, censorship and policies that arbitrarily criminalised people categorised as problems, perpetrated by corporate-styled, host city organisers of, in one case, the Sydney Olympics (Lenskyj, 2000). Lenskyj combines the skills of the academic researcher and the investigative journalist in order to interrogate the myriad ways in which the Games impact upon the spaces they occupy as well as being re-produced by those spaces. The topologies of the Olympics are most clearly manifest in the re-structuring of the host city and the ways in which sporting priorities and the concerns of sponsors outweigh those of resident communities, especially those who live in the spaces targeted for re-development.

Lenskyj's work, which drew upon a ten-year period of analysis of newspapers, reports, interviews, and participating as an advocate and an activist during the years leading up to the Sydney Games, demonstrates the complicity of the media and press in the processes through which malpractice in the organising bodies and the IOC itself has been made invisible, just as the vulnerable people whose lives are so disrupted by the bidding process and the actualities of hosting. This remains manifest in media and Internet coverage of women athletes and their extensive achievements. Internet sites of league tables of athletic performance include not only the details of performance on the track which are recorded for their male counterparts but other listings such as the top ten most attractive women Olympians (Hot Top Ten, 2011) and the top ten who posed for Playboy magazine (Playboy Top Ten, 2011)

One of the most important aspects of the silencing and marginalisation of the voices of dissent is the responsibility which the media have. Whilst the ceremonies and performance of the Olympics are transmitted worldwide to an estimated half of the world population, the media have been silent in their coverage of resistance and challenge, especially when the challenge comes from disadvantaged and marginalised people (Burstyn in Lenskyj, 2000).Lenskyj's evidence supports her argument which is based on police actions, urban sanitisation programmes, labour relations and conflicts, attacks on the homeless, race relations and the overt power of the media in marginalising the plight of the poor and disadvantaged. She makes visible the harsh realities of the most vulnerable members of communities who find themselves directly caught in the turmoil when cities bid for or host mega events, which parallels the more recent concerns of MUTE (2011) and We Are Bad (2011). She cites strong evidence that land use and environmental impact, controversial invocations of common national identity through symbols and ceremonies, security, the use of public money to secure private profit and human rights issues extant in host countries prior to and during the Games tend to polarise groups and individuals in Olympic host cities. Most effectively Lenskyj explores the complexities of relations between Australia's Aboriginal and non-Aboriginal citizens and the historical policies of white rule, the sometimes contradictory meanings engendered by participation and dissent and the ambiguous symbolism of Aboriginality positioned by Olympic ceremonies and by the success of athlete Cathy Freeman (Freeman, 2011a, 2011b, Freeman You Tube, 2011). For the generations of stolen children and their descendants, for citizens and politicians who suggested that such atrocities were exaggerated and for visitors who knew little about Australia's history, the opening ceremonies were a complicated juxtaposition of sights, sounds and hundreds of years of selectively positioned histories that could not be explicated in a matter of hours (Hargreaves, 2000).For the Sydney Games, the IOC and the NOC, politicians and Games organisers alike, Lenskyj argues, warded off efforts of resistance and protest through a strategic politics of division that effectively marginalised alternative views and actions of some Australians, including Aboriginals, the political left and specific interest groups such as the tenants who suffered from massive rent increases leading up to and during the Games. The evidence is in stark contrast to the glossy brochures and promotional materials which accompany both the bids of host cities and the regeneration and legacy plans of host cities, such as, most recently, London in 2012 (Evans, 2011).

Dissent has increasingly been expressed by those on the outside, although they may inhabit the host city and thus be inside in their relationship to the staging of the Games; they are citizens of the host city and nation. Protests were made in the run-up to London 2012 about the imbalance of ticket sales made to corporate sponsors (biz, 2011) and the failure of huge numbers to receive any tickets at all (Tickets 2012, 2011). The Games are manifestly democratic and inclusive and socially and culturally exclusive at the same time. The disruption to LOCOG and Lord Coe's apparently democratic project for ticket sales for 2012 is an example of the tensions between local and global forces which often find their expression in disenchanted local communities in host cities.

Lenskyj's evidence addresses deep issues in terms of the relationship between the Games, the spaces they occupy and disadvantaged groups of people within them as well as those who experience structural marginalisation as well, for example, through the operation of ethnicised, racialised patriarchal systems of power. Her assessment of new laws and measures aimed at cleaning up Sydney and policing 'undesirables' is particularly insightful in linking local and global forces that are spatially specific, even though she concludes that there were few recorded examples where police powers were abused and people were treated badly. Lenskyj attributes this, in part, to the efforts of community activists who fought for the rights of the disadvantaged, although it is difficult to discern the outcomes or specific effectiveness of community-based activism in Sydney. Lenskyj's evidence strongly supports her own arguments about the Olympics and the imposition of dominant forms of culture on unwilling participants and the weighted value judgements, demonstrating that *might* is not necessarily *right* and that all efforts of resistance are worth documenting, remembering, and analysing and indeed putting into discourse.

She concludes that the Olympic Games serve the interests of global capital, stating that

> What is need is the dismantling of the Olympic industry as presently constituted ... This requires the complete demystification of the Olympics through grassroots community education and organizing. The goal of this enterprise would be to demonstrate that, behind all the rhetoric, the so-called Olympic movement is simply a transnational corporation that in many instances exploits young athletes' labour and aspirations for its own aggrandizement and profit ... the educational agenda must include exposing the real nature of the Olympic legacy, which ... has meant huge deficits borne by taxpayers, the suppression of public debate and dissent, and the oppression of disadvantaged urban populations. (Lenskyj, 2000: 194–5)

Lenskyj's evidence shows that the Games mask the very inequitable socio-economic relations that persist in host cities. Prior to achieving success in the bid, the poor and disadvantaged are rendered invisible, even though benefits to host city communities are central to most bids, and having succeeded it is usually those living in poverty and on the margins whose communities are most adversely affected by the re-structuring that hosting the Games necessitates. The Olympics may be about opportunities and democratic principles but they do little to redress social deprivation and disadvantage. Whatever the rhetoric of urban regeneration and transformation and the promise of progressive new opportunities, host cities may focus more on mega event stadia than more everyday, routine enhancements to life in the city. However, whilst Lenskyj focuses on this aspect of resistance, for example, as emerging from community groups and local activists, most of what is visible and classified as the tradition of protest at the Games is seen as globalised recognisable political structures and systems and based on existing recognisable national or ethnic identifications or possibly the politics of new social movements, rather than more localised eruptions of dissent or attempts to voice protest by those denied a voice and rendered invisible by the systems and processes of the games. Protest is global/local. The lived experiences of routine disengagement and disadvantage are inseparable from the flows and networks of global capital and the cultural transformations and endurances which situate and are situated by the everyday expressions of resistance which Lenskyj identifies in her work.

Women's voices feminist protests

Although there are large numbers of women who play sport, especially the increasing numbers who participate in the Olympics and who are increasingly involved in the organisation of sport, many of which recognise women's under-representation in many fields of sport and are involved in the promotion of wider participation, women have a relatively limited presence in the most prominent spaces of global sport. Most feminist political activity takes place outside sport. The women who are most closely involved in sport are often reluctant to express their criticism. In cases of the trivialisation or marginalisation of women's sporting achievements in the public arena of the mass media, whilst critiques may be presented by feminist websites and commentators in the press, women within sport are reticent about rocking the boat (Woodward, 2011c). Similarly, women who are admitted to the regulatory bodies of sport are largely positioned within its grateful peripheries, rather than being central to decision-making or having any role in relation to the more prestigious men's game, whatever the sport. For example in cricket, the International Cricket Council (ICC) accommodates a women's section which is recognised and demarcated as such; the women's game is both separate and subordinate. At the centenary celebrations of the ICC at St Anthony's College Oxford in 2009 (ICC Centenary Conference 2009, 2011) there was a section devoted to women's cricket. I chaired a panel which included the captain Charlotte Edwards and Ebony Rainford-Brent of England's winning test team that year and former England captain Rachael Heyhoe-Flint, none of whom wanted to be anything but grateful that they had been included in the celebrations. The women wore their England team blazers and described the obstacles they had faced as individuals, especially as women, but were clearly anxious about any suggestion that the ICC had been anything but accommodating. Women know that if they are critical on the inside they may not be on the inside for very long; not that women ever really gain access to the inner networks of classed, hegemonic masculinity that still dominate the ICC. The IPL may subvert colonialist classifications of race and ethnicity and challenge the 'game of empire', but women's place in the IPL seems to be predominantly as cheer leaders, even though women's cricket is a popular sport in India and women compete in international cricket.

The gender-specific sports bodies, which mean those which organise women's sport, men's regulatory bodies are usually unmarked, do engage with what can be perceived as discrimination against women, especially in terms of full participation in competitions and access to training and support. Also, of course individual sports each have their own organisations and websites, although these are often subdivisions of the men's game which, as is especially the case in football, the men's game is the norm and the women's game is an offshoot (FA, 2011). Such organisations focus on sport and on bringing women into sport, often for reasons of health and well-being, although they may also purport to be advocates for women. For example, Women's International Sport (WSI) was formed in 1994 to present a collective voice for women and sport internationally and to ensure that sport can receive priority in the lives of women and girls (WSI, 2011). The Women and Sport Commission advises the IOC executive board on the policies to deploy when dealing with women and sport, which suggests that the commission's responsibilities are to the IOC primarily (Women and Sport Commission, 2011).Olympic Women is an organisation dedicated to women sporting pioneers, which makes visible women's contributions to sport and to tell sports women's untold stories (Olympic Women, 2011). The Women's Library archive on women and sport is in a similar tradition and includes nineteenth-century material as well as biographical collections of work on sportswomen and a range of contemporary book pamphlets and periodicals (Women's Library, 2011). Organisations like UK Sport also engage with not only opportunities in sport for women but also respond to and promote widening participation and anti-discrimination matters (UK Sport Women, 2011).

There are bodies which are more overtly political such as the Black Women in Sport Foundation which was founded in the United States in 1992 (BWSF, 2011) and Gender equity in athletics and sports which is part of the Feminist Majority Foundation (FMF, 2011).Other organisations negotiate the possibilities for women in sport in relation to particular social and cultural practices, for example, the Muslim Women's Sport Foundation which was established in the United Kingdom in 2001 provides Muslim women and girls with the opportunity to engage in structured sport training programmes, including basketball and futsal which is a variation of football 'in an environment which is sensitive to their religious values' (MWSF, 2011).

In the archive research I conducted for the British Library as part of its archive project (British Library Archive, 2011) I found that not only are women and, especially, any critical engagement with sex gender, often invisible on sport websites, on feminist websites there is a notable absence of coverage of sport and issues related to sport.

Sex work and sport

One matter that is of concern, however, is that of the movement of women to the sites of global sporting mega events, such as the Olympic Games and the men's football World Cup; the phenomenon is customarily referred to as prostitution although sometimes the news media also position the debate within the context of trafficking. Concern was expressed in the run-up to 2012 and the issue was put visibly onto feminist websites at the time of the men's football World Cup in South Africa in 2010 when issues of race, class sex gender and ethnicity were interwoven in a series of posts and blogs, for example, on the F–Word (F-Word, 2011). Feminist debates, although often contentious, avoided the polarities of the binary ethical logic of the mainstream and pointed to the impoverishment of the women working at sports sites and the need for health care and security of working women in terms of sexual health, legal protection and safety.

Much of the discussion on feminist websites and in related blogs was situated within the context of global feminism and the impact of globalisation, including issues like the differentially weighted impact of HIV/AIDS in relation to gendered inequalities and the centrality of sex gender worldwide (WHO Women's Health, 2011, UN Human Development, 2011, Woodward, 2011). HIV/AIDS disproportionately affects women and in South Africa where the men's football World Cup was held in 2010 one in five people is infected, with women three times as likely as men to be in this category (UNAids, 2011). The context to this is set out within an explicitly political framework in the language of rights rather than charity, by the World Health organisation as follows:

> Being a man or a woman has a significant impact on health, as a result of both biological and gender-related differences. The health of women and girls is of particular concern because, in many societies, they are disadvantaged by discrimination rooted in sociocultural

factors. For example, women and girls face increased vulnerability to HIV/AIDS.

Some of the sociocultural factors that prevent women and girls to benefit from quality health services and attaining the best possible level of health include:

- unequal power relationships between men and women;
- social norms that decrease education and paid employment opportunities;
- an exclusive focus on women's reproductive roles; and
- potential or actual experience of physical, sexual and emotional violence.

While poverty is an important barrier to positive health outcomes for both men and women, poverty tends to yield a higher burden on women and girls' health due to, for example, feeding practices (malnutrition). (WHO Women's Health, 2011)

The WHO definition incorporates the collective enfleshed materialities of women's lives which also demonstrates the interconnections between sex and gender which is also apparent in the experience of sexual relations which is implicated in the global HIV/AIDS crisis. UNAids claims that 70 percent of women worldwide have been forced to have unprotected sex, that women are unable to negotiate safe sex and 30 years after the onset of the HIV/AIDS epidemic health services remain intransigent to women's specific needs and requests for help (Clare, 2010). This was the context in which the UK government was asked by President Jacob Zuma of South Africa to provide 42 million condoms to cater for the half-million visitors who would travel to South Africa for the men's football World Cup to which 40,000 prostitutes were likely to go to for the month-long tournament.

The debate for feminists and critical social commentators has rehearsed some of the second-wave feminist discussions of the 1980s in relation to prostitution where there were tensions between ethical arguments about the morality of selling sex and moralistic claims that women need to be protected on the one hand and, on the other, the assertion that women working as prostitutes are doing just that, working, and have the same rights as any other workers to carry out their business. There is also the ghost of nineteenth-century patronage of fallen women and the focus on the morality of women who work as prostitutes but no discussion of the men who are their clients. Even in 2010 it was still the case that working women would have to be tested for HIV but not the anonymous men who would be their clients (Woodhouse, 2010).

There are assumptions to which feminist bloggers drew attention in relation to sex gender and sexuality and questions about who was to be protected by the condoms which are used to ensure safe sex, most likely the tourists who boost the South African economy, a source of revenue that Zuma would not want to deter by the eruption of a massive HIV/AIDS epidemic. One of the main assumptions upon which the whole debate was premised is that men attending sports events abroad will need to have sex and with little time available to them this is likely to be a financial transaction. In the stratified deposits of gendered common sense the idea that men, especially football fans, who are also assumed to be heterosexual in this myth, have to have sex and this is another service that unfortunately has to be provided. Heterosexual men's sexuality is constructed around this imperative to the extent that all other expressions of sexuality are marginalised. There is an inevitability about it, which is constitutive of the gendered discourses of sport which persist in a particular version of hegemonic masculinity (Connell, 1995, 2002). In this scenario poverty, class, race, ethnicity intersect with sex gender in particular ways to reinforce and reinstate the inequalities both within sport and in other fields of social life.

The Olympics pose a similar set of dilemmas (Livesey, 2011) and have demonstrated that prostitution and sport have a prominent recent history, being sanctioned in Athens in 2004 and in Germany for the World Cup; Beijing had a crackdown and Vancouver sex workers having campaigned for a safer working environment for the Winter Games. 'It seems that anywhere there's a gathering of athletes and sports fans there's an explosion in prostitution' (Livesey, 2011). In the case of London in 2012 there was a different constituency of women in that Eastern European countries were seen as the most likely source of the migration of women but the politics of difference and the relevance of sex gender remain central. Some of the discussion has been framed by local concerns although using the language of a globalised economy. For example, Hackney's Pre-Olympic Anti-Sex Campaign in London's east end which seemed to have been translated into a moral response by the council, albeit one that recognised the problems likely to arise for the community from the influx of sports fans, but responded by banning lap-dancing clubs, sex shops erotic cinemas and 'other sites of sexual entertainment' (Hackney 2011). The bans were, however, accompanied by more community support on the streets, reduction in violent crime and more sports funding for young people. This demonstrates some success in a local campaign, but could be more about recognition of the inevitability of the arrival of large numbers of male sports fans seeking some sexual satisfaction or entertainment and the need to contain these forces.

Feminist debates about the issue of prostitution include the context of mobilities and migration and the inequitable power relations that intersect in the ways these matters affect and most importantly are affected by sporting events like the Olympics. The forces and flows of inequitable distribution of economic and cultural resources demonstrate how sexual politics and sex gender are implicated in the disruptions and challenges that are expressed as resistance although many of the campaigns which make up resistance to the Olympics do not explicitly or directly engage with matters of sex gender. However, there are points of connection between different forms of resistance, although much of the protest that was most vociferously expressed has not focused on gender issues.

The feminist debates centring on London 2012 shifted the emphasis onto the violence and exploitation that women experience and used the term trafficking along with prostitution, which stresses the exploitative dimensions of what takes place in relation to the compulsion and force that is the motor for migration and the movement of women into the host city for the Games. Discussion is no longer framed by ethical concerns or the well-being of the women concerned and the strains on local communities of ensuring proper care for women who move into the city for the duration of the Games. Moral oppositions no longer underpin the debate as they have hitherto although the matter of agency and self-determination remains important in relation to the extent to which working in prostitution necessarily involves exploitation. Its elision with trafficking would suggest choice is seen as unlikely on the part of the women and agency is translated as power which is the purview of the traffickers and not the trafficked.

Campaigns were well informed and expressed knowledge of the UK 2010 Equality Act, also pointing out that LOCOG acknowledges its dependency on private funding which may relieve it of some of the obligations to which public-sector employers are subjected in relation to their duty of care (Livesey, 2011). Legislative frameworks can provide mechanisms through which protest can be effective and rights secured.

Local campaigns express opposition to the actual event of the Games and the extra demands the Games and all that goes with them place on local services, usually in terms of the particular deprivations of poor communities which is resonant of Lenskyj's research findings. Concerns about trafficking and prostitution are also voiced in relation to the pressure on local health, police and support services which have not been acknowledged by host cities.

What the case of feminist campaigns and debates about the issue of how sport and prostitution become entangled most fruitfully contributes is an understanding of, firstly, how different axes of power, including those of economic forces, race, ethnicity and sex gender, intersect, and, secondly, an understanding of how sex gender works within these assemblages can be productive in raising the most important underlying questions about the source of power and of inequalities that has much wider application than description of empirical sex differences.

Conclusion

This chapter has addressed the visibility and more often the invisibility of those matters which disrupt the Games, either through the silencing of protest and dissent or through a failure to acknowledge the inequalities and injustices which are generated by the very spectacles that are designed to create and publicise as an improved infrastructure in the host city that can provide an enhanced legacy of well-being for its citizens and visitors. There is some irony in the manner in which visibility and volubility play out in the staging of the games, especially in the tensions between what is reported and what is not and what is celebrated and what is denied.

The inequalities in the experience of inhabiting host cities relates directly to the topographies of the Games and the spaces the Games occupy but the history of protest at the Olympics often relates more directly to contingent global political events than to the localised injustices and exploitations suffered by those who have most investment in the legacy of the Games. One of the most enduring legacies of the Games is the persistence of a power geometry that reinstates hierarchies and unequal social and economic relations including racism and patriarchy. As Lenskjy argues, based on her work on the last two Olympics of the twentieth century, problems of poverty, racism and social exclusion have largely persisted throughout the history of the Modern Games and show no signs of being resolved through the idea of legacy unless there are massive changes in the organisation of the IOC and the management and administration of the games. There are clearly synergies between the Olympics and the contingent social worlds they occupy spatially and temporally and the staging of the Games transforms the spaces in which they are performed as well as reproduce existing tensions and ambivalences as well as inequalities and injustices.

Sport is expressive and creative and generates passion and excitement and the possibilities of transcendence and of being in harmony collectively with other enfleshed selves where mind and body are in synchrony. For women, it offers possibilities of personal pleasure and of more material, public success and the Games have provided this to a large number of women athletes. However, sport is never unaffected by nor incapable of affecting the social worlds in which it is enacted and experienced so it is hardly surprising that the Olympics as so large scale a global enterprise exaggerate both conflicts and inequalities on the one hand and the exhilaration and shared pleasures of sport on the other.

The examples of disruption and of challenges to the Game discussed in this chapter also show that change can take place, even if it is not a linear path of progression and there are powerful endurances, as, for example, of feminist responses to the issue of the inevitable congruence of increased prostitution and the mega sporting event of the Olympics. What is at one point disruptive can be accommodated and mainstream at another. The extent to which this is progress depends on the power relations that are implicated in the transformations and, most importantly, whose interests are served in these processes and how they are implemented. There remain differential weightings of the forces that are involved in the reconfiguration of systems and questions remain about the particularities of self-interest, especially in relation to sexual politics. In the field of the promotion of social inclusion and in engaging with issues of diversity there are manifest ways in which sport has generated outcomes through recognition by other regulatory bodies, especially those with a human rights agenda. The UN and WHO now take on board some of the complexities and intersections of different dimensions of social exclusion, inequality and injustice that make up sex gender difference and feminist critiques have interrupted some of the complacencies about segregating gender into a separate category or silencing or making invisible sexual politics.

What this chapter has also demonstrated is that sport is in the mix. Sport not only reflects social movements, flows and forces of inequality and social divisions, sport is constitutive of those operations of power and sport can be a site of resistance and challenge to social inequalities and injustices. In the case of the Olympics, with the movement's strong tradition of ideology and principles of democracy and participation it is not surprising that the Games have generated and been the site of protest and of disruption, as well as contradiction.

8
Conclusion: Sex Power and the Games Conclusion

This book started with a series of tensions and puzzles; firstly about the contradictions of the Olympics in negotiating the democratic principles of the Olympic Movement and the demands of elite sport in a climate of increased commercialisation and professionalisation. Secondly, there are issues of what is said and what remains unsaid, for example about unravelling the discourse of widening participation and what sort of language is it that uses sport, and the games in particular to provide equal opportunities and how can the powerful forces which are divisive and exclude some people, be explained. There is always the danger of constructing those who are targeted as outside or under represented, as victims, especially within the charitable discourses of social inclusion. Those not in the mainstream are worthy but not elite athletes. Visibility and invisibility are central to the discussion in the book as are the power axes which operate to produce opportunities and to deny them, none more so than in the case of sex gender which has been deployed to provide explanations of the processes and systems and the enfleshed engagements through which the games are constitute. The games reflect social and cultural materialities but sport is also specific and constitutive of those wider social relations and divisions. One of the particularities of sport is its enfleshed and embodied practices and encounters. Sex matters in sport; it provides the basis for the organisation of competitions, events and structures. The Olympics are more egalitarian in many ways, including participation in the sports themselves but there are diverse and multiple ways in which inequalities are perpetuated through sex gender. Sex gender is powerful constituted through the enfleshed practices of sport which travel into other social and cultural spaces.

The Olympics provide an assemblage of diverse social, political, cultural and economic systems which not only reflect the social world and the times in which the games are held, but also generate affects which impact up those social worlds. The focus of this book has been on sex gender and the operations of power, which both create opportunities and promote greater equality, and reinstate and themselves produce, inequalities.

Frameworks of power

Power works in different ways. Power can be coercive and involve force or formal enforceable constraints, such as the exclusion of women from some competitions, or it can be a whole set of everyday practices which include what becomes taken for granted and seeps into the common sense of sport and spectatorship. Power may be embedded in tradition, explicit and direct; power can be top down and involve institutional backing. Power can also operate diffusely and it may be difficult to identify where it is. In the case of gender discrimination the idea of indirect discrimination includes a whole set of discriminatory acts which together make up a culture of unequal treatment. Foucault's analysis of power has been very influential in post modernist critiques. The idea that power can work cumulatively through everyday exchanges and in micro level ways is very productive in exploring how gender works.

The focus on power as productive as well as constraining has facilitated an understanding that extends beyond the Olympic Games, yet is also specific to it. The insistence within sport on the binary logic of sex highlights wider issues that relate to sexual politics and the ways in which classificatory and regulatory systems can be repressive at some points and productive of new possibilities and opportunities at others. Because enfleshed practices and corporeality are so central to sport the games provide a means of rethinking sex in relation to gender and reconsidering the political use of sex conceptually to explore difference and inequalities more broadly. Gender and categorisation of sex gender has been used to demonstrate some of the systems through which exclusion operates, through discursive and through material regimes.

Change has been rhizomic rather than following a single or linear trajectory but examination of the plane of equality offers useful insights into the games that make up the intersections of different power axes in sport, although sport is often characterised by pivotal moments. Policies and practices change across time and space and are materially and spatially located. The Games have particular histories that can be read through the stated policies of the Olympic Movement as well as though the embodied sporting practices the Games encompass and the media and wider public

interest they generate. Because the Olympics have so explicit a set of democratic principles they offer a productive site for exploring the possibilities
of sport for promoting social inclusion as well as the impossibilities in
an increasingly commercial world in which the sports media commerce
nexus can be seen to dominate. Discursive critiques of the representations through which meanings are transmitted and re-produced do not
tell the whole story. Arguments based entirely on a critique of the operation of regulatory practices and symbolic systems cannot accommodate
the specificities of space which the Olympics present, nor how to conceptualise the engaged enfleshed action of participants and the affects of
sport, its spaces and technologies. This book has argued for a materialist
understanding of the practices of inclusion and exclusion that also permit
political activism and change, which is in a sense where the book started
with the optimism and expression of the possibilities of sport that were
highlighted in the run up to London 2012.

Systems and Processes

Another theoretical underpinning of this book has been Deleuzian
notions of assemblage which stress the primacy of processes and challenge the linear and heroic narratives of individualised protagonists
that are so commonly invoked in sport, not least the games. Chapter 2
fore grounded a post Foucauldian theoretical emphasis upon the
systems and processes through which the games are constituted and
the centrality of the governance of sport. It is clear that in order to
release the democratising potential of the Olympics, there has had to
be, and still has to be, reform of its governance. Rule making and rule
breaking are what makes up the games but the processes involved draw
upon different repertoires, many of which are specific to the Olympics,
including its heritage of the Ancient Games and the reconfiguration of
the Olympic Movement at the initial stages of the modern games. The
genealogies of the games are powerfully undemocratic and unequal in
many ways including, not only the discourse of sport which insists on
the binary logic of sex but also the iteration of inferiority and demands
for the exclusion of women's sport. This binary logic is a very uneven
and differentially weighted dichotomy. The Foucauldian approach
taken to the importance of regulatory systems in the construction and
reiteration of categories at the outset challenges the individualism of
many accounts of the history of the games as well as posing problems
for the accommodation of the corporeality of sport and the enfleshed
experience of its practices at all levels.

The Olympics can be analyzed and understood in relation to their development over the last century from a modern rehearsal and revisiting of the Ancient Games and the Olympic ideals to a highly commercialised global spectacle which is shaped by economic forces and the motor of sponsorship. Although economic forces are central to the transformations which the games have undergone they intersect with other operations of power including those of media technologies and politics in different manifestations such as racialisation, ethnicisation and the persistence of patriarchal processes. The process of commercialisation has to some extent has also enabled audiences to develop oppositional interpretations of Olympism. The Olympics have become multi-voiced and many themed, and the spectacle of the contemporary Games raises important questions about the reification of the Olympic Movement and its ideals, institutionalisation, the doctrine of individualism, the advance of market capitalism, performance, consumption as well as the consolidation of global society. Globalisation and the games are widely enmeshed and the inequalities that are spatially embedded within nations and on the transnational arena occupy both an enduring and sometimes contested terrain at the games.

Sex gender is deeply embedded in the organisation of the regulatory bodies of sport and the IOC is not only no exception, but is one of the most patriarchal of such bodies, perhaps only surpassed by FIFA. Even when offices are presented as gender neutral, it is often the case that these offices assume a male person who holds the office; gender is only marked when women occupy a position as in lady president. Women's sport is marked by such classifications and adult athletes are still called girls and women's teams are referred to as ladies' teams. Nonetheless, the Olympics in recent years are a site at which gender has been put into discourse and acknowledged the particularities of masculinity too and the experiences of men in the world can also be explored and understood in relation to other social differences with which they intersect

Not only do the Olympics create, reproduce and refract social exclusions and global inequalities, they are also the site of resistance as chapter 7 demonstrated, disruption takes diverse forms. There have been iconic moments of protest that have occupied a global stage and a high profile as well as more local protests within the communities of the host cities, among the disenfranchised and disadvantaged whose views have been least regarded in the bidding process and in the re-structuring required by the games. The games are global, local and g/local in the interconnections between the international scale of a mega event which draws in over two hundred nations and the impact upon local communities, for example in the host city and in the host nation where regional inequalities are reinforced by the concentration of resources on the host city at the expense of other parts of the nation. Resistance takes different forms, increasing enacted on line and through localised protests and expressions of dissent. Protests have focused more upon the global politics of race, ethnicity and eco-politics and the g/local politics of class than on sex gender, which may be due to the lack of direct engagement with sport, for example in feminist campaigns. As my work on the British Library archive showed, gender in sport has more often been framed by the empirical category of gender in relation to women's participation in the games although, more recently, feminist campaigns have targeted the connections between mega sporting events like the Olympics and sex work, in particular trafficking and the global exploitation of women and of sex workers is also manifest in the success of women athletes and the enormous increase in women's participation. The games offer a site at which women not only have a presence, but also they are also recognised as elite athletes and make visible the benefits of athletic engagement in what is a genuine vindication of women's rights, as argued by Mary Wollstonecraft in her famous 'Vindication of the Rights of Women.; women can never achieve recognition of their rights and any liberation without gaining access to physical activity to enable them to become robust and strong (Wollstonecraft, 2011, [1792]). The empowering capacities of sport have a long history in feminist work.

Sex gender remains a powerful presence in the twenty first century which is highlighted by the persistence of gender inequalities as well as the universal importance of gender as part of social relations. There are powerful endurances in gender differences and in dualistic classifications of gender. What the understanding of sex in gender theory and the activism that is based on such understandings of the complexity of gender categories show is that firstly, the situation is more complex than a simple binary and secondly, that sometimes, by looking at the periphery and the margins it is possible to understand more about the centre and the mainstream, which as on line activism and for example Helen Lenskyj's work on g/local inequalities demonstrates.

Within the regulatory bodies of sport, like the IOC there are distinctions between stated belief and policy on the one hand and practice on the other. Not only are there gaps between policies and the responses of governance to social change, but there are also inconsistencies and there can be a time lapse between the policies and how they are implemented. The concept of sex gender and theories which unpack sexual politics contribute a great deal to an understanding of how inequalities are played out within the field of social divisions and inequalities. Social inequalities and the marginalisation and silencing of some groups of people do not exist in discrete compartments but are interconnected and relate to each other. There are privileged systems of power, notably those which include economic systems which are more heavily weighted in the capacity to exclude people.

Feminist theories of intersectionality have pointed to the complexities of gender and directed attention to the importance of sexuality in debates about inequality. They have the advantage of encompassing masculinities and a more diverse range of gender identities than, for example second wave feminism did. However, such complex theoretical approaches run the risk of both over complicating the analysis of power and of prioritising personal life and intimacies through sexuality art the expense of deeply embedded economic and social inequalities that are located more obviously in the public arena. When underpinned by an emphasis upon discursive regimes, there is also a risk of failing to be sufficiently attentive to enfleshed actualities. There is a danger that the approach itself will become marginal if its major concerns are with the periphery and not the centre. This chapter has argued that se gender remains central to analyses of social inequality and that developments in thinking about gender can be useful and productive in exploring social and cultural change. It is necessary however to hold on to an understanding of both the detail of how sex gender is made and reproduced in everyday life and the unequal power relations that underpin gender differences.

Olympic spectacles sensation and affect

The emphasis on systems and processes through which the spectacles, politics and practices of the Olympics has demonstrated the complexity of the intersections between different power axes but it has been evident that these are both contingent upon temporal and spatial factors and that it is possible to prioritise some power relations, notably those of economic, financial and commercial elements. Global sporting events like the Olympics involve the creation and management of spectacles for consumption by massive media audiences; they are costly to stage but also provide huge potential for profit, especially given the media coverage and global stage on which they are performed. Sporting spectacles increasingly occupy these commercial spaces. The apotheosis of the cultural form of the mega event is the Olympic Games. The games can be seen as a commercial product and this is manifest in the discussion of the bidding processes and in staging the games; the Olympics can be seen to serve political and economic purposes which is a line that has been taken. However, I have argued that these intersections of power operate in relation to other elements and that there is an agency in the notion of the management of the mega event which belies its capacities to generate affects and be itself affected by the global stage it occupies. The mega event of the games offers an excellent example of a combination of elements, in which agency is swept up in the spectacle and the event itself. The games create and are created by the commercial forces and flows which constitute its spectacles. This is not to suggest that there are not responsibilities for the corruption that has also marked the history of the modern games, but to suggest that the spectacle also makes itself through the interrelationship between sporting practices, the excitement and exhilaration of enfleshed activities of competition and spectatorship and the political, cultural and commercial forces which make it possible.

I have argued that the spectacle and spectatorship involve the relationship of sensation, which challenges the more conventional cultural studies approach which claims that cultural meanings are mediated. Sensation in sport has an immediacy which, although it also carries cultural meanings, has intensities at the point of spectatorship that is also part of its appeal. There are problems with the approach however, since unmediated sensation is also made up of situated enfleshed selves who are constituted by social, political, economic and cultural relations and power forces that operate within the sport and resonate with such forces in the wider terrain of social relations.

The Cultural Olympiad and the Art of Sport project discussed in chapter 6 focuses on the possibilities of sensation and affect in exploring some of the synergies and points of connection between art and sport. These are two fields which also have a history of separation, especially within the framework of another binary, that of the high low cultural dichotomy. The Cultural Olympiad and the run up to 2012 demonstrated some of the cultural transformations that have taken place in the relationship between the two cultural discourses and the topographies of change. The phenomenon of Young British Artists has been seen to topple high art from its pedestal and art has been integrated into the practices of the promotion of social inclusion and diversity. However, tensions remain between the potential of elite success for athletes and the more democratic possibilities of engagement for young artists. The Lloyds TSB Art of Sport project is a example of such a set of activities which is also illustrative of the intersection of different axes of power, in this case the commercial and philanthropic interests of a bank which is a sponsor of the games and the cultural practices of art and of sport. The project shows how social class privilege is invoked within charitable discourses that connect art and sport. The charitable interests of the bank could be construed as part of public relations that major banks are advised to undertake following the global economic crises of 2008, but this does not undermine the argument about the intersection of different elements and discourses within the event of the Olympics.

The project also demonstrates the particularities of art and sport and the intensities of sensation in each. Both fields engage with passion and emotion as well as the disciplinary regimes through which excellence is created. Sport has more explicitly social systems of measurement whereas art directly invokes subjectivities and the subjective dimensions of emotion. It is possible to lay claim to an aesthetic personal preference for a work of art, whereas sporting success and excellence is only validated through objective systems of measurement. Sport spectatorship and viewing of artworks however, create a rhythm of sensation which occupies the space between the viewer and the object of perception through the planes of colour and the movement of light which serve to present the unity of event or the art work.

The discussion of the interconnections between sport and other cultural activities including art serves to demonstrate the possibilities for extending the scope of sport in order to embrace strategies and policies for widening participation that in part attempt to bridge the divide between sport and other activities and to cross the boundaries between the rigid boundaries of sex which are so embedded in sport through activities which are not so secured in gender specific hierarchies, for example as the hegemonic masculinity which so characterises sport. Sex gender however provides one of the endurances that militates against diversity and the opening up of opportunities.

Sex gender; enfleshed selves

Arguments about the politics of sex and the relationship between sex and gender are central to this book. Chapter 3 explored one of the dilemmas of the enfleshed actualities of sport's classificatory systems which have particular relevance to the book's discussion of sex gender and provides some redress to the overemphasis upon social systems and discursive regulatory frameworks in chapter 2. The exploration in chapter 3 was organised around the regime of truth which circulates around sex, which is constructed as a category that can be determined and ascertained beyond doubt; science might reveal the truth and position a person as either male or female. At this point regulatory practices meet flesh in a contentious entanglement in which it becomes very difficult to separate the categories of sex as biological and anatomical and gender as social and cultural. Flesh is never 'just flesh'; flesh makes things possible. Whereas bodies are bounded, the concept of flesh offers possibilities of commonality and shared connections as well as providing the material source of inequalities which can be absent from theories of intersectionality and discursive approaches to corporeality and embodiment.

The body of the athlete poses problems about conventional readings of masculinity and how far it is a feature of the body one inhabits or how far masculinity and femininity are manifestations of the presentation of the self, or, as Judith Butler argues sex as well as gender, is performative. The whole thing is socially constructed and there can be no distinctions between sex as biological and gender as socially constructed because the two are inseparable. Performance and appearance are key indicators of gender identity and sporting practice muddies the waters, because loss of body fat, muscle tone and competitive, assertive, even aggressive body practices and comportment all undermine what can be seen as feminine. Such features mean that, especially in media representations of women athletes, there may be claims that they appear masculine; masculinity and femininity are imbricated with sex and enfleshed actualities.

One of the more recent trends in understanding gender has involved examining some of the links between sexuality and gender and, indeed in the case of some thinkers of suggesting that the two are interchangeable. There are distinctions between gender and sexuality and I would argue sex can be a more useful explanatory concept especially when related to activism The recent focus on sexuality in campaigns that arise from and inform such approaches reflects as well as influences the obsessions of contemporary western societies with sex and sexuality. Sometimes the two are difficult to disentangle. Sex and sexuality are linked and activism, for example against trafficking has put sexuality on the policy agenda as well as into more popular cultural discourse.

Sex gender presents problems for those who regulate sport and categories are problematic in the reduction to anatomy, flesh muscle, body practices and even psychology that gender verification requires. The very term 'gender verification' suggests that we could get at the truth; a single truth unmediated by social, economic, cultural and political factors which make up the assemblage of the embodied self.

Women athletes have to reassure the spectator of their femininity, through comportment and appearance, even when they, through the body practices of their sport necessarily have very different bodies from their female non sporting counterparts. Men too are caught up in the same gender matrices, as is illustrated by the homophobia that haunts sport. Male athletes may feel compelled to reassure their fans-and their team mates- that they are heterosexual by the constant presence of a heterosexual, preferably conventionally attractive partner as a spectator and constant presence.

This is the context from which the debate about sex gender emerges. I have made the case for the retention of sex as a concept which incorporates the materiality of flesh and the points of connection with sexuality, rather than the, often preferred term gender. Gender has been privileged through its social constructionist underpinnings which might appear to suggest the possibilities of change and a challenge to the fixity of anatomy and biological reductionism. Flesh is plastic and technoscience can intervene in corporeality, none more so than in sport where the body is constantly transformed through body practices and technologies. Flesh and the concept of enfleshed also enables a challenge to the individualism of the body and, especially in sport the notion of the personal best exacerbated by the competitive structures of sport. There are commonalities of enfleshment and the enfleshed self is part of a community as well as an individualised unitary self who competes with others. The commonalities of enfleshment also make up some of the motivations for political action and disruption and subversion, for example to the regulatory practices of the games and the social and economic worlds that they inhabit.

The dichotomy between being female and being male is one of the most powerful and the most taken for granted in human societies none more so than in sport. It is both taken for granted in that there is limited questioning of the fixity of this binary and strongly enforced, only more and more complex strategies for determining in which category a person can be placed. As Raewyn Connell points out, if gender identity were so certain and so fixed by biology why are there so many sets of rules and enforcements socially, economically, culturally and politically across the world and throughout history to ensure that people fit into one or other of the categories (2009).

The relationship between sex and gender is more complex than approaches which suggest a clear cut distinction either between women and men or between biology and flesh on the one hand and social and cultural forces on the other claim.

Sex includes flesh, anatomy, biology and social and cultural regulatory forces and an overemphasis upon the transformative potential of gender can marginalise enfleshed actualities and underplay the affects of sporting practices and technologies on the enfleshed self as well as assuming that anatomy yields only two possibilities; intersex remains problematic in the binary separation of sex and gender. Sex and gender are interconnected related and the affects are two way; biology impacts upon cultural performances of gender and gender shapes categories of sex.

Representational systems reinstate and reinforce categories of sex gender even, maybe especially, in sport. Another advantage of a conceptualisation based on sex is that it can accommodate the enduring sexualisation of women, although in the pornification of contemporary western cultures masculinities are being similarly configured but within different trajectories and through the operation of different power systems and inequalities. Feminist critiques of the objectification and sexualisation of women's bodies have informed the wider terrain of women's obsession with weight loss and the hegemony of infantilised representations of women, for example in fashion magazines which privilege very young models who although exceptionally tall, carry very few of the characteristics of adult women in terms of breasts and fat distribution. The massive media saturation of images of exceptionally lean supermodels sets unattainable and unhealthy standards to which women may feel compelled to aspire. Third wave feminists have pointed to the exaggerated sexualisation of images of women which they describe as pornogrification or pornification, whereby women's bodies are always coded as sexual to the extent that in many cases representations of women constitute pornography even in the mainstream media where models and pop stars adopt overtly sexual poses.

Sport offers a site at which these can be challenged and the popularisation of the fit healthy athletic body can subvert the dominance of such sexualised representations which can be explained through the concept of sex and the notion of the enfleshed self, which makes material the social and cultural practices through which sexual politics play out and reproduce inequalities.

Sexed bodies exist in a world in which there are strong expectations about firstly, the existence of two sexes, secondly of what is appropriate behaviour and comportment and practice for each gender and thirdly, the impact of the social world upon the body is increasingly complex and increasingly possible, for example through the advances of technoscience.

Sexual politics plays out in sport in many of the same ways that operate in the wider social terrain but the politics of equality and difference is also made informed and materialised through sport, especially sport as enacted on the global scale of the Olympics and which also embodies the possibilities of transformation that could be configured through its democratic ideals and vast scope, temporally and spatially. Sport has been taken on board as a vehicle for effecting change in relation to sex gender through a discourse that resonates with earlier conceptualisations of healthy minds and healthy bodies, for example explicitly incorporated in UN programmes and those of the WHO. The assemblage of systems, of economics, politics and culture which make up the Olympics present particular opportunities for the promotion of social inclusion, cohesion and diversity, given the scale of the games and the principles upon which they were based, but progress has been very uneven.

In the context of sex gender progress has almost entirely been measured by the empirical inclusion of women's sports event and the number of women participating. The inclusion of more competitions for women, especially when debated in the media, as was the case with boxing prior to 2012, raises political questions, such as whether women should be permitted to engage in a sport that might incur particular risks, the morality of women competing and whether more women's events mean fewer men's can only be understood though theories of sexual politics and, I argue the retention of the category sex as well as gender. The focus upon empiricism obscures the power relations that underpin sex gender in sport and also suggest that it is only women who are gendered, thus reinstating the norms of unmarked men and marked women, as if men and masculinity were not constituted and made through being in the world.

Bodies are material and enfleshed; they are not blank sheets on which social and cultural forces inscribe gender and sex and sex gender is in the body as well as outside it. Bodies exist within social worlds that already exist but which bodies impact upon; the body and the social world interrelate and cannot be entirely separated which is another source of evidence for the links between sex and gender. The media and representational systems play a key part in the transmission of knowledge about the games and thus constitute One aspect of social worlds is how bodies and embodied selves are represented. These representations are a source of knowledge about gender and gender roles, and are themselves constitutive of gender.

In sport masculinity, especially hegemonic masculinity still dominates although in many ways it has been reconfigured. The regulatory bodies of sport as well as the enfleshed participants and spectators and the media systems through which the games are transmitted manifest patriarchal apparatuses. The regulatory bodies and the media may manifest the networks of hegemonic masculinity more forcefully than the embodied practices in the field or on the track, although it is still the case that men's competitions attract more interest than women's, with the 100 metres being a case in point; the men's sprint attracts the most interest and is on a par with the opening ceremonies as the big attraction of the games. Men too are subject to the operation of gendered constraints, however. The games remain a social world which is strongly divided by sex gender and offers a very useful site for the exploration of how gendered practices work with gender categories. Although sport operates with a particularly rigid binary gender framework, it illustrates well some of the problems of the boundaries of this gender binary. Sport as lived and made at the Olympics is also a field that shares many of the features of other aspects of popular culture and shows how social and cultural divisions are enacted including how actions that are performed themselves make masculinity of femininity, rather than simply being the affect of sex as biological category. How people live and perform in the social world of the Olympics in all its manifestations are constitutive of sex gender in a repeated interaction between enfleshed selves and social situations.

There are disruptions and challenges and even denial of any interest in the games but they remain one of –if not the greatest sports show on earth and whatever the tensions between commercialism, sponsorship, the pursuit of profit, the media domination and sporting practices they remain an amazing spectacle that draws in massive numbers of people and provide spectacular entertainment onto which aspirations and dreams are projected as well as being part of a wider social terrain of transformation and opportunities as well as the endurance and reinstatement of social inequalities.

References

AIBA (2011) (http://www.aiba.org/documents/site1/Olympics/Women's%20 Boxing'%20in%202012/women_brochure_web.pdf)

Aldridge, A. (2009) personal communication

Aldridge, A. (2011) http://www.lynnparr.co.uk/articles/ann_aldridge.pdf

Barber, L. (2006) http://www.guardian.co.uk/football/2006/nov/12/1

Barney, R.K., Wenn, S.R. and Martyn, S.G. (2002) Selling the Five Rings: The International Olympic Committee and the Rise of Olympic Commercialism, Salt Lake City, The University of Utah Press

Beijing 2008 (2011) http://www.olympic.org/beijing-2008-summer-olympics

Beijing Paralympics 2008 (2011) http://en.paralympic.beijing2008.cn/

Berger, J. (1972) Ways of Seeing, London: Penguin

Bergson, H. (1911) Creative Evolution, London: MacMillan

Blackless, M., Charuvastra, A., Derryck, A., Fausto-Sterling, A., Lauzanne, K. and Lee, E. (2000) 'How sexually dimorphic are we? Review and synthesis.' American Journal of Human Biology 12:151–166

BBC News 1948 (2011) http://www.bbc.co.uk/news/uk-12760836

BBC News Torch (2011) http://www.bbc.co.uk/news/uk-13391986

BBC News (2009) http://news.bbc.co.uk/sport1/hi/athletics/8219937.stm (last accessed, 21 March 2011)

BBC News (2007) http://news.bbc.co.uk/sport1/hi/football/7067642.stm (last accessed, 13 May 2011)

BBC (2011) 'Too Fast to be a Woman', BBC2, first broadcast 7pm 22 February 2011

Bentel (2011) http://www.paralympic.org/Media_Centre/News/General_ News/2011_03_04_d.html

Beauvoir, S. de (1989[1949]) The Second Sex, London, Vintage Books, trans. H. Parshley from Le Deuxieme Sexe, 2 Vols, Paris Gallimard

Beauvoir, S. de (2010[1949]) The Second Sex, London, Vintage Books trans. C. Borde and S. Malovany-Chevallier from Le Deuxieme Sexe, 2 Vols, Paris Gallimard

Beijing Protests Tibet, 2008 (2011) http://www.telegraph.co.uk/sport/other-sports/olympics/2510709/Beijing-Olympic-Tibet-protests-Parents-defend-arrested-Briton.html

Beijing Protests Torch, 2008 (2011) http://www.timesonline.co.uk/tol/news/world/asia/article3695050.ece

Berger, J. (1972) Ways of Seeing, London: Penguin

Beyond Sport (2011a) http://www.beyondsport.org/

Beyond Sport (2011b) http://www.beyondsport.org/the-foundation/

Biz (2011) http://www.insidethegames.biz/

Bolam, J. (2011) http://www.gazettelive.co.uk/news/campaigns-and-north-east-events/just-the-job/2011/05/11/josh-is-inspired-to-reach-lloyds-tsb-art-of-nurture-competition-finals-84229–28673107/(last accessed 25 June 2011)

Bourdieu, P. (1984) Distinction: A Social Critique of the Judgement of Taste, trans R. Nice, Cambridge MA: Harvard University Press

Braidotti, R (1994) Nomadic Subjects: Embodiment and Sexual Difference in Contemporary Feminist Theory, New York: Columbia University Press

Braidotti, R (2002) Metamorphoses: Towards a Materialist Feminist Theory of Becoming, Cambridge: Polity Press

British Library Archive (2011) http://www.webarchive.org.uk/ukwa/collection

British Library Summer Games (2011) http://www.bl.uk/sportandsociety /exploresocsci/explore.html

Brownell, S. (2008) *Beijing's Games: What the Olympics Mean to China* London: Rowman & Littlefield Publishers

Butler, J. (1993) Bodies That Matter, On the Discursive Limits of Sex, London: Routledge

Butler, J. (1990) Gender Trouble: Feminism and the Subversion of Identity, London, Routledge

Butler, J. (2009) Wise Distinctions, London |Review of Books Blog 20 November 2009, http://www.lrb.co.uk/blog/ in Merck (2010) p. 4

BWSF (2011) http://www.blackwomeninsport.org/

Calvert, J. (2002) http://observer.guardian.co.uk/osm/story/0,,626771,00. html

Cashmore, E. (2005) *Making Sense of Sports*, 5th edn, London, Routledge

Caudwell, J. (2007) 'Queering the Field? The complexities of sexuality within a lesbian-identified football team in England'. *Gender, Place & Culture: A Journal of Feminist Geography*, 14(2): 183–196

Choir (2011) http://www.bbc.co.uk/iplayer/episode/b017sv1f/The_Choir_ Military_Wives_Episode_3/

Cixous, H. (1980[1975]) 'Sorties' in Marks E. and de Courtviron, I. (eds) (1980) *New French Feminisms: An Anthology,* Amherst MA: University of Massachusetts Press

Clough, P.T. with Halley, J. (2007) (eds) *The Affective Turn: Theorizing the Social,* Durham NC: Duke University Press

Clare, A. (2010) South African Women need more than World Cup condoms, http://www.thefword.org.uk/blog/2010/03/south_african_w_1

Coaffee, J. (2009) *Terrorism, Risk and the Global City,* Aldershot, Ashgate

Coe Torch (2011) http://www.guardian.co.uk/sport/london-2012-olympics-blog/2011/may/19/olympic-torch-relay-london-2012 Last accessed May 20th 2011

Cole, C. (1998) 'Addiction, Excess and Cyborgs,' in Rail, C. (ed.) *Sport in Post-Modern Times,* New York: New York University Press, pp. 261–276

Cole, C. (2002) 'Body Studies in the Sociology of Sport' in J. Coakley and E. Dunning (eds) *Handbook of Sports Studies*, London, Sage, pp. 439–460

Connell, R.W. (1995) *Masculinities*, Cambridge: Polity

Connell, R.W. (2002) *Gender*, Cambridge: Polity

COOB (1992) http://olympic-museum.de/o-reports/report1992.htm

Cultural Olympics (2012) www.london2012.com/cultural-olympiad Last accessed 18 March 2012

Csikzentimihalyi, M. (1975) *Beyond Boredom and Anxiety: Experiencing Flow in Work and Play*, San Francisco: Jossey Bass

Cultural Olympiad (2011) http://www.bing.com/search?q=Cultural+Olympiad. &src=IE-Address

Daddario, G (1998) *Women's Sport and Spectacle: Gendered Television Coverage and the Olympic Games*. Westport Conn.: Praeger

Dalrymple, J. (2011) http://www.london2012.com/blog/contributors/jordan-dalrymple.php (last accessed, 25 June 2011)

De Coubertin, P. (2000) *Pierre de Coubertin 1863–1937: Olympism, Selected Writings*, editing director Norbert Muller, Lausanne, International Olympic Committee

Daily Mail (2009) http://www.dailymail.co.uk/news/worldnews/article-1207653/Womens-800m-gold-medal-favourite-Caster-Semenya-takes-gender-test-hours-World-Championship-race.html (last accessed 21 March 2011)

Davidson, M. (2011) *Fields of Courage: The Bravest Chapters in Sport*, London, Little Brown

Deaflympics (2011) http://www.deaflympics.com/about/

Dearnley, B. (2011) http://www.bcdsculpture.co.uk/mod1.html

Debord, G. (1995) *The Society of the Spectacle* trans. D. Nicholson-Smith, New York: Zone Books

De Coubertin (2000) *Olympism: Selected Writings*, Lausanne: International Olympic Committee

Deleuze, G. (2005) *Francis Bacon*, trans. Daniel W. Smith, London and New York: Continuum

Deleuze, G. (1994) *Difference and Repetition*, trans. P. Patton, New York: Columbia University Press

Deleuze, G. and Guttari, F. (1987) *A Thousand Plateaus: Capitalism and Schizophrenia*, trans. Brian Massumi, London: Athlone Press

Delphy, C. (1993[1992]) 'Re-thinking sex and gender', trans. D. Leonard, *Women's International Studies Forum* 16(1): 1–9

Eagleton, T. (1990) *The Ideology of the Aesthetic*, Oxford: Blackwell

Evans, G. (2011) http://www.cresc.ac.uk/our-research/current-research-themes/topologies-of-social-change/2013-and-beyond-materialising-an-olympic-legacy-in-the-east-end

F.A. (2011) http://www.thefa.com/GetIntoFootball/Players/PlayersPages/WomensAndGirls

F.A.R.E. (2011) Football Against Racism in Europe, (http://www.farenet.org/)

Fausto-Sterling, A (2000) *Sexing the Body: Gender Politics and the Construction of Sexuality*, Basic Books, Persens Books Group

Firestone, S. (1970) *The Dialectic of Sex: The Case for Feminist Revolution*, London: Jonathan Cape

Football 2012 (2011) http://www.london2012.com/games/olympic-sports/football.php

Forth, C.E. (2008) *Masculinity in the Modern West. Gender: Civilization and the Body*, Basingstoke: Palgrave Macmillan

Foucault, M. (1973a) *Madness and Civilization*, New York: Vintage Books

Foucault, M. (1973b) *The Order of Things*, New York: Vintage Books

Foucault, M. (1974) *The Archaeology of Knowledge*, London: Tavistock

Foucault, M. (1977) *Discipline and Punish*, New York: Pantheon Books

Foucault, M. (1980) *Power /Knowledge*, New York: Pantheon Books

Foucault, M. (1981) *The History of Sexuality. Volume 1: An Introduction* Trans. R. Hurley, Harmondsworth: Penguin

Foucault, M. (1982) 'The Subject and Power' in Dreyfus, H. and Rabinow, P. (eds) *Michel Foucault: Beyond Structuralism and Hermeneutics*, Chicago: University of Chicago Press

Foucault, M. (1988a) *The History of Sexuality. Volume 2: The Use of Pleasure*, New York: Vintage Books

Foucault, M. (1988b) *The History of Sexuality. Volume 3*, New York: Vintage Books

Freeman, C. (2011a) http://www.olympic.org/cathy-freeman

Freeman, C. (2011b) http://athleticssuperstars.tripod.com/cathy_freeman.htme Books

Freeman YouTube (2011) http://www.londonolympics2012.com/?atk=1304

Frosh, S. (2011) *Feelings*, Abingdon: Routledge

Fussey, P., Coaffee, J., Armstrong, G. and Hobbs, D. (2011) *Securing and Sustaining the Olympic City*, Farnham: Ashgate

F-Word (2011) http://www.thefword.org.uk/

Gammon, L. and Marshment, M. (1987) (eds) *The Female Gaze: Women as Viewers of Popular Culture*, London: Women's Press

Garcia, B. (2008) 'One Hundred Years of Cultural Programming within the Olympic Games (1912–2012): Origins, Evolution and Projections', *International Journal of Cultural Policy* 14(4): 361–376

Gender Equality Sport (2011) http://www.uksport.gov.uk/pages/equality

Genz, S. (2006) 'Third Way/ve: the politics of postfeminism', *Feminist Theory*, 7(3): 333–53

Giardina, M. (2005) *Sporting Pedagogies: Performing Culture and Identity in the Global Arena*, New York: Peter Lang

Gillis, S., Howie, R. and Munford, R. (2007) (eds) *Third Wave Feminism: A Critical Exploration*, 2nd edition, Basingstoke: Palgrave MacMillan

Giulianotti, R. (1999) *More than a Game: The Social and Historical Aspects of World Football*, Cambridge: Polity

Giulianotti, R. and Williams, J. (eds) (1994) *Game Without Frontiers: Football, Modernity, Identity*, Aldershot: Arena

Gold, J.R. and Gold, M.M. (eds) *Olympic Cities: City Agendas, Planning and the World's Games, 1896–2012*, London: Routledge

Goldblatt, D. (2007) *The Ball is Round, A Global History of Football*, Harmondsworth: Penguin

Gorton, K. (2010) *Media Audiences: Television, Meaning and Emotion*, Edinburgh: Edinburgh University Press

Gramsci, A. (1971) *Selections from the Prison Notebooks*. London, Lawrence and Wishart: International Publishers

Gregg, M. and Seigworth, G. (2010) *The Affect Theory Reader*, Durham, NC: Duke University Press

Gruneau, (1989) 'Making a spectacle: a case study in television sports production' in Wenner, L. (ed.) *Media, Sports and Society*, London, Sage, pp. 134–156

Grosz, E. (1994) *Volatile Bodies: Towards a Corporeal Feminism*, Bloomington, IN: Indiana University Press

Gruneau, R. (1989) 'Making a Spectacle: a case study in television sports production' in Wenner, L (ed.) *Media, Sports and Society*, London: Sage

Guardian, 2008 (2011) http://www.guardian.co.uk/sport/2008/jul/28/olympic-games2008.china1

Guilianotti, R. (1999) *Football: A Sociology of the Global Game*, Cambridge: Polity Press

Guttmann, A. (1984) *The Games must Go on: Avery Brundage and the Olympic Movement*, New York: Columbia University Press

Guttmann, A. (1991) *Women's Sports : A History*, New York: Columbia University Press

Guttmann, A. (2002) *The Olympics: A History of the Modern Games*, 2nd edition Chicago: University of Illinois Press

Guttmann, A. (2005) *Sport in the First Five Millennia*, Amherst and Boston: University of Massachusetts Press

Hampton, J. (2009) *The Austerity Olympics: When the Games Came to London in 1948*, London: Aurum Press

Haraway, D. (1985) 'A manifesto for cyborgs: science, technology and socialist feminism in the 1980s', *Socialist Review*, 80: 65–107

Haraway, D. (1991) *Simians , Cyborgs and Women: The Re-invention of Nature*, London: Free Association Books

Haraway, D. (2003) *The Companion Species Manifesto: Dogs, People and Significant Otherness*, Chicago, University of Chicago Press

Hargreaves, J. (2007) *Heroines of Sport: The Politics of Difference and Identity*, London: Routledge

Hargreaves, J. (1994) *Sporting Females: Critical Issues in the History and Sociology of Women's Sport*, London: Routledge

Harvey, D. (1989) *The Conditions of Postmodernity: An enquiry into the Origins of Cultural Change*, Oxford: Basil Blackwell

Hill, C. (1996) *Olympic Politics*, Manchester: Manchester University Press

Holy Trinity (2011) http://www.goal.com/en-gb/news/2914/champions-league/2011/05/28/2508131/the-new-holy-trinity-barcelonas-ballon-dor-trio-of-xavi

Horne, J. (2007) 'The four knowns of sports mega events', *Leisure Studies Journal*, 26(1): January: 81–96

Hot Ten (2011) http://uk.askmen.com/top_10/celebrity/top-10-hot-2008-olympians.html

Houghton, J. (2011) http://www.iwantahoughton.com/

Houghton Art of Sport, (2011) http://www.theartofsport.co.uk/exhibitions.asp

Houlihan, B. (2008) (ed.) *Sport and Society*, 2nd edition, London: Sage

Howson, A. (2005) *Embodying Gender*, London: Sage

Hughson, J. (2009) 'The Global Triumph of Sport', *Sport in Society* 12(1): 134–140

IAAF Gender Verification (2006) http://www.iaaf.org/mm/document/imported/36983.pdf

ICC Centenary Conference, 2009 (2011) http://news.bbc.co.uk/sport1/hi/cricket/counties/8172918.stm

ICC Sport in Society (2011) http://www.tandf.co.uk/journals/sportinsociety/

Inglis, D. (2008) 'Cultural *agonistes*: Social Differentiation, Cultural Policy and Cultural Olympiads', *International Journal of Cultural Policy* 14(4): 463–477

IOC Women (2011) http://www.olympic.org/content/The-IOC/Commissions/Women-and-Sport/

IOC Women and Sport (2011) http://www.olympic.org/en/content/the-ioc/commissions/women-and-sport/

IPC (2011) http://www.paralympic.org/IPC/

Irigaray, L. (1991) 'This sex which is not one' in Whitford, M (ed.) *The Irigaray Reader*, Oxford: Basil Blackwell

Irigaray, L. (1984) *Speculum of the Other Woman*, trans. Gillian Gill, Ithaca, NY: Cornell University Press

Kaplan, E.A. (1992) *Motherhood and Representation: The Mother in Popular Culture and Melodrama*, Cambridge: Polity Press

Kick it Out (2011) http://www.kickitout.org/

Jacobs, B. (2004) *The Dick Kerr's Ladies*, London: Robinson Publishing

Jennings, A. (1992) The Lords of the Rings, Power, Money & Drugs in the Modern Olympics,

Jennings, A. (1996) *The New Lords of the Rings: Olympic Corruption and How to Buy Gold Medals*, New York, Pocket Books

Jennings, A. (2000) *The Great Olympic Swindle*, London: Pocket Books

Juvenal (1967) *The Sixteen Satires*, trans. Peter Green, Harmondsworth: Penguin

Kesler, S.J. (1998) *Lessons from the Intersexed*, New Brunswick: Rutgers University Press

Kessel, A. (2011) 'When I won the world title, I was never happier' in Observer Sport, 12th June 2011, pp. 10–11

Kimmel, M. 'The bigotry of the binary: the Case of Caster Semenya 2009', http://www.huffingtonpost.com/michael-kimmel/the-bigotry-of-the-binary_b_267572.html last accessed 21 March 2011)

Lee, M. (2006) *The Race for the London Olympics*, London: Virgin Books

Lenskyj, H.J. (2000) *Inside the Olympic Industry: Power, Politics and Activism*, Albany: State University of New York Press

Lenskyj, H.J. (2002) *The Best Olympics Ever? Social Impacts of Sydney 2000*, Albany: State University of New York Press

Lenskyj, H.J. (2008) *Olympic Industry Resistance: Challenging Olympic Power and Propaganda*. SUNY Series on Sport, Culture and Social Relations, Albany: State University of New York Press

Lefkowitz, M.R. and Fant, M.B. (2005) *Women's Life in Greece and Rome*, London, Duckworth

Levy, A. (2006) *Female Chauvinist Pigs: Women and the Rise of Raunch Culture*, New York: Free Press

Livesey, L. (2009) http://www.thefword.org.uk/blog/2009/01/the_olympics_an

Ljungqvist, A. Martnez- Patio, M.J., Martnez-Vidal, A., Zagalaz, L., Daz, P., Covadonga, M. (2006) 'The history and current policies on gender testing in elite athletes', *International Journal of Sport Medicine Journal*, 7(3): 225–230

Lloyd, M (2007) *Judith Butler*, Cambridge: Polity

Lloyds TSB Private Banking (2011) http://www.lloydstsb.com/private_banking/private_banking.asp (last accessed 11 June 2011)

Local Heroes, (2011) http://www.lloydstsblondon2012.co.uk/en/In-your-community/

LOCOG (2011) http://www.london2012.com/about-us/the-people-delivering-the-games/the-london-organising-committee/

London 2012 (2011) *London 2012: Olympic and Paralympic safety and security strategy.* [London: COI on behalf of the Home Office], 2011. British Library Lending collections shelfmark: m11/.13744

Los Angeles Times (2009) http://articles.latimes.com/2009/aug/26/world/fg-africa-runner26 (last accessed 21 March 2011)

Markula, P. (2009) *Olympic Women and the Media: International Perspectives*, London: Palgrave

Marqusee, M. (2005) *Redemption Song, Muhammad Ali and the Spirit of the Sixties*, London, Verso

Massumi, B. (2002) *A Shock to Thought, London: Expression After Deleuze and Guattari* London and New York: Routledge

Massumi, B. (1995) 'The Autonomy of Affect', *Cultural Critique*, Autumn 1995 No 31: 83–109

Matteo, S. (1986) 'The effect of sex and gender-schematic processing on sport participation'. *Sex Roles*, 15: 417–432

McGeoch, R. and Korporaal, G. (1994) *Bid: How Australia won the 2000 Games*, Port Melbourne: Vic. William Heinemann Australia

McNamara, J. (2011) http://www.janemcnamara.co.uk/5.html

McRobbie, A. (2008) *The Aftermath of Feminism: Gender, Culture and Social Change*, London: Sage

McRobbie, A. (1994) *Postmodernism and Popular Culture*, London: Routledge

Merck, M. (2010) 'The Question of Caster Semenya', *Radical Philosophy* 160 March/April pp. 2–8

Miah, A. (2011a) http://www.culturalolympics.org.uk/editors-2/andy-miah/

Miah, A. (2011b) *A Digital Olympics: Cybersport, Social Gaming and Citizen Media*, Cambridge MA: MIT

Miller, T., Lawrence, G., MacKay, J. and Rowe, D. (2001) *Globalization and Sport*, London: Sage

Morgan, N. and Pritchard, A. (1998) *Tourism, Promotion and Power: Creating Images, Creating Identities*, Chichester: John Wiley

Mulvey, L. (1975) 'Visual pleasure and narrative cinema', *Screen*, 16(3): 6–18

Mulvey, L. (1989) *Visual and Other Pleasures*, Bloomington, IN: Indiana University Press

MUTE (2011) http://www.metamute.org/en/We-AreBad-Posters

MWSF (2011) http://www.mwsf.org.uk/the_foundation.html

Oakley, A. (1972) *Sex, Gender and Society*, London: Maurice Temple Smith

Oates, J.C. (1987) *On Boxing*, London: Bloomsbury

Olympic Charter (2010) http://www.olympic.org/Documents/Olympic%20Charter/Charter_en_2010.pdf

Olympic Movement (2011) http://www.olympic.org/content/The-IOC/Governance/Introductionold/

Olympic Women (2011) http://www.olympic.org/women-sport-commission

Paralympics (2011) http://www.paralympic.org/Paralympic_Games/

Pausanias, *Guide to Greece* Vol 2 Southern Greece trans. Peter Levi, Harmondsworth: Penguin

Pfister, G.(2001) *Breaking Bounds: Alice Profé Radical and Emancipationist, in freeing the Female Body: Inspirational Icons* edited by J. A Mangan and Fan Hong, London: Frank Cass, pp. 98–118

Playboy Top Ten (2011) http://www.toptenz.net/top-10-beautiful-athletes-who-posed-for-playboy.php

Popper, K. (2002[1959]) *The Logic of Scientific Discovery*, London: Routledge

Poynter, G. and MacRury, I. (2009) (eds) *Olympic Cities: 2012 and the Re-shaping of London*, Farnham: Ashgate

Preuss, H. (2004) *The Economics of Staging the Olympics: A Comparison of the Games, 1972–2008*, Cheltenham: Edward Elgar

Preuss, H. (2008) *The Economics of Staging the Olympics*, Cheltenham: Edward Elgar Press

Price, M. and Shildrick, J. (1999) *Feminist Theory and the Body*, Edinburgh: Edinburgh University Press

Queen's Speech (2010) http://www.cbc.ca/world/story/2010/12/25/queen-xmas-speech.html

Reeve, S. (2005). *One day in September: the story of the 1972 Munich Olympics massacre and Israeli revenge operation 'Wrath of God'*, London: Faber

Rinehart, R. (2005) 'Babes and Boards: Opportunities in New Millennium Sport?' *Journal of Sport and Social Issues*, 29(3): 232–255

Rinehart, R. and Sydnor, S. (2010) 'Alternative Sport and affect: Non Representational Theory Examined'. *Sport in Society*, 13(7): 1268–1291

Rinehart, R. and Sydnor, S. (2003) (eds) *To the Extreme: Alternative Sports, Inside and Out*, Albany: State University of New York Press

Riordan, J. and Cantelon, H. (2003) 'The Soviet Union and Eastern Europe' in James Riordan and Arnd Kruger (eds) *European Cultures in Sport: Examining the Nations and Regions*, Great Britain: Intellect Books, pp. 89–102

Roche, M. (2006) 'Mega-events and modernity revisited: globalization and then case of the Olympics', *Sociological Review*, 54(2): 25–40

Roche, M. (2000) *Mega-events and Modernity: Olympics and Expos in the Growth of Global Culture*, London: Routledge

Rogge, J. (2011) http://www.olympic.org/Documents/Reports/EN/en_report_1341.pdf

Ronay, B. (2011) http://www.guardian.co.uk/sport/blog/2011/mar/24/olympics-2012-football-englandfootballteam (last accessed 13 May 2011)

Rowbotham, S. (1974) *Hidden from History: 300 years of Women's Oppression and the Fight against it*, London: Pluto Press

Royalty (2010) transcript http://www.royal.gov.uk/ImagesandBroadcasts/TheQueensChristmasBroadcasts/ChristmasBroadcasts/ChristmasBroadcast2010.aspx

Sammons, J. T. (1988) *Beyond the Ring: The Role of Boxing in American Society*, Urbana and Chicago: University of Illinois Press

Sandomir, R. (1996) 'Atlanta: Day 1; Samaranch has only praise for the Games', New York Times, 20 July

Sandford, S. (2011) 'Sex: A Transdisciplinary Concept', *Radical Philosophy*, 165(Jan/Feb): 23–30

Scambler, G. (2005) *Sport and Society: History, Power and Culture*, Maidenhead: Open University Press

Schweinbenz, A.N. and Cronk, A .(2010) 'Femininity Control at the Olympic Games', *Thirdspace: a Journal of feminist Theory and Culture*, 9(2) "Gender Sport and the Olympics, http://www.thirdspace.ca/journal/article/viewArticle/schweinbenzcronk/329 (last accessed, 19 March 2011)

SFT, 2008 (2011) http://www.studentsforafreetibet.org/article.php?id=1471

Slutwalk, (2011) http://www.bbc.co.uk/news/world-us-canada-13320785

Simson, V. and Jennings A. (1992) *Dishonored Games: Corruption, Money and Greed at the Olympics*, New York: SPI Books

Sky   (2011)   http://news.sky.com/skynews/Home/UK-News/Fifa-Impropriety-Lord-Triesman-Gives-Evidence-To-Commons-Culture-Media-And-Sport-Committee/Article/201105215989077

Smith, R.R.R. (1991) *Hellenistic Sculpture*, London: Thames and Hudson

Smith, T. and Steele, D. (2007) *Silent Gesture: The Autobiography of Tommie Smith*, Philadelphia: Temple University Press

Special Olympics (2011) http://www.specialolympics.org/

Sobchack, V. (2004) *Carnal Thoughts: Embodiment and Moving Image Culture*, Berkeley CA: University of California Press

Spivey, N. (2004) *The Ancient Olympics*, Oxford: Oxford University Press

SportsAid (2011) http://www.sportsaid.org.uk/

Stanton, R. (2000) *The Forgotten Olympic Art Competitions the Story of the Olympic Art Competitions of the 20th Century*. Victoria, B.C.: Trafford

Stewart, K, (2007) *Ordinary Affects*, Durham, NC: Duke University Press

Strauss   Kahn,   (2011)   http://www.google.com/hostednews/afp/article/ALeqM5jTOwlxE0V7oAjnige1NjHhOoCGEA?docId=CNG.ccc3b0204b5da8e7c-ce5b8854b144bdf.c31

Stead, D. (2008) 'Sport and the Media' in Houlihan, B (ed.) *Sport and Society*, (2nd edition) London: Sage, pp. 328–47

Sun,   (2011)   http://www.thesun.co.uk/sol/homepage/news/3599179/Imogen-Thomas-believed-that-Ryan-Giggs-wanted-to-MARRY-her.html

Super leagues, (2011) http://www.thefa.com/Leagues/SuperLeague

Sugden, J. (1996) *Boxing and Society: An International Analysis*, Manchester University Press

Sugden, J. and Tomlinson, A. (2002) (eds) *Power Games: A Critical Sociology of Sport*, London: Routledge

Sugden, J. and Tomlinson, A. (2011) (eds) *Watching the Olympics: Politics Power and Representation*, London: Routledge

Taylor, Y. (2010) (ed.) *Classed Intersections, Spaces, Selves, Knowledge*, Farnham: Ashgate Publishing

Taylor, Y., Hines, S. and Casey, M.E. (2011) (eds) *Theorizing Intersectionality and Sexuality*, Basingstoke: Palgrave Macmillan

Tickets 2012 (2011) http://www.bbc.co.uk/news/uk-england-london-12181583

Timmers, M. (2008) *A Century of Olympic Posters*. London: V&A Publishing

Torch Route 1948 (2011) http://www.la84foundation.org/6oic/OfficialReports/1948/OR1948.pdf#page=296

Tomlinson, A. (1996) 'Olympic spectacle: opening ceremonies and some paradoxes of globalization', *Media Culture and Society*, 18: 583–602

Tomlinson, A. (2011) 'Lording it: London and the getting of the Games' in Alan Tomlinson and John Sugden (eds) *Watching the Olympics*, Routledge, London

Top Ten (2011) http://www.toptenz.net/the-top-10-female-olympians.php (last accessed 5 December 2011)

Ueberroth, P. with Levin, R. and Quinn, A. (1985) *Made in America: His Own Story*, New York, NY: William Morrow

UK Forum, (2011) http://forums.whyweprotest.net/threads/uk-superinjunction-ryan-giggs-imogen-thomas.79573/

UK Sport, Leadership (2011) http://www.uksport.gov.uk/pages/women-and-leadership-development-programme/

UK Sport Women (2011) http://www.uksport.gov.uk/pages/women/

UN Aids (2011) http://www.unaids.org/en/dataanalysis/

UN HABITAT (2011) http://www.unhabitat.org/categories.asp?catid=1
UN   Human   Development   (2011)   http://hdr.undp.org/en/reports/global
/hdr2011/
Wagg, S. (2004) *British Football and Social Exclusion*, London: Routledge
Wall Street Journal (2011) http://blogs.wsj.com/corruption-currents/2011/05/27
/high-tide-from-a-blatter-probe-to-fleeing-a-ban/
Wamsley, K.B. and Pfister, G. (2005) 'Olympic Men and Women. The Politics of
Gender in the Modern Games' in Kevin Young and Kevin B. Wamsley (eds)
*Global Olympic Historical and Social Studies of the Modern Games Research in the
Sociology of Sport*, Vol 3, New York, NY: Elsevier, pp. 103–125
Ward, S.V. (2007) 'Promoting the Olympic City' in Gold, J.R. and Gold, M.M.
(eds) *Olympic Cities: City Agendas, Planning and the World's Games, 1896–2012*,
London: Routledge
We Are Bad (2011) http://www.00wearebad00.blogspot.com/
Wheaton, B. (2004) *Understanding Lifestyle Sport: Consumption, Identity and
Difference*, London: Routledge
WHO Women's Health (2011) http://www.who.int/topics/womens_health/en/
Wollstonecraft, M. (2001[1792]) http://www.bartleby.com/144/5.html
Women Boxing, (2011) http://www.womenboxing.com/
Women's Library (2011) http://www.londonmet.ac.uk/thewomenslibrary/
Woodhouse L (2009) 'Calls to legalise prostitution during World Cup in South
Africa', F-Word Blog, 12 October 2009
Woodward, K. (2011a) *Planet Sport*, London: Routledge
Woodward, K. (2011b) *Gender A Short Guide*, Bristol: Policy Press
Woodward, K. (2011c) http://humankinetics.wordpress.com/2011/02/10/whos-
really-offside/
Woodward, K. and Woodward, S. (2009) *Why Feminism Matters: Lost and Found*,
Basingstoke: Palgrave Macmillan
Woodward, K. (2009a) *Embodied Sporting Practices: Regulating Regulatory Bodies*,
Basingstoke: Palgrave Macmillan
Woodward, K. (2009b) 'Bodies on the Margins: regulating bodies, regulatory
bodies', *Leisure Studies*, 28(2) April 2009: 143–157
Woodward, K. (2008)'Hanging Out and Hanging About: insider and outsider
research in the sport of boxing', *Ethnography*, Special Edition, No 10, 4/5 July
2008
Woodward, K. (2007a) 'New Footballing Identities?' *Cultural Studies* Special
Edition, 4/5, pp. 758–778
Woodward, K. (1997) 'Motherhood; identities, meanings and myths' in
K. Woodward (ed.) *Identity and Difference*, London, Sage, pp. 239–98
Woodward, K. (2006) *Boxing, Identity and Masculinity: The 'I' of the Tiger*, London:
Routledge
Woodward, K. (2008) *Introduction to the Social Sciences: The Big Issues*, (2nd
edition) London: Routledge
Woodward, K. (1997) 'Motherhood, Identities Meanings and Myths' in
K. Woodward (ed.) *Identity and Difference*, London, Sage, pp. 239–98
WSFF (2011) http://www.wsff.org.uk/who-we-are
WSI (2011) http://www.sportsbiz.bz/womensportinternational/
Young, I.M. (2005) *Female Body Experiences: Throwing like a Girl and Other Essays
on feminist Philosophy and Social Theory*, Oxford: Oxford University Press

Index